PENGUIN BOOKS

FROM HARDTACK TO HOME FRIES

Barbara Haber has had a distinguished career as Curator of Books at the Schlesinger Library at Harvard University's Radcliffe Institute for Advanced Studies. Haber is a popular speaker and writer on culinary history and has been profiled in *Newsweek*, *The New York Times*, *Bon Appétit*, and other prominent publications. For her contributions to food and cooking, she was elected to the James Beard Foundation's Who's Who in American Food and Beverages, and given the prestigious M.F.K. Fisher Award by Les Dames d'Escoffier. She lives in Winchester, Massachusetts.

Praise for *From Hardtack to Home Fries*

"What a pleasure to have an illustrated peep into American history through the treasures of the Schlesinger Library's culinary collection. Barbara Haber, the library's distinguished culinary curator, gives us here a short tour through some fascinating insights that we would probably never have known about were it not for the cookbooks involved.

"Why was the F.D. Rooseveltian food so notably bad, for instance? What about celebrity diets, Dr. Kellogg and his vegetarian and health legacy, and food reformists in general? There is the miserable life of the Irish immigrants and the veritable slave labor they performed. We see rare aspects of black history through its cooking, Jewish life through Jewish cooking. History becomes more meaningful when we can relate it to life, and food is indeed life."
—Julia Child

"An intriguing rendezvous between food and history . . . Barbara Haber is one of the few who understands the subtleties of the relationship of food to history. This collection of stories is fascinating. Even the bibliography is fascinating."
—Mark Kurlansky

"There's nothing like a good book to make your commute fly by, and Barbara Haber's *From Hardtack to Home Fries*, was so fascinating I actually found myself yearning for subway delays. The curator of books at Radcliffe's Schlesinger Library at Harvard University, Haber uses food as a prism through which to view America: A White House cook so bland that guests were warned to eat before attending state dinners, POWs who fantasized about elaborate feasts, and an iron-willed nurse who used Jewish chicken soup to cure the wounds of the Civil War all appear in these pages. Basing her research on old diaries and cookbooks, Haber makes a case for the primacy of food as a cultural influence that reaches far beyond the table."
　　　　　　—Kemp Minifie, *Gourmet*

"To anyone who has ever wondered whether food is anything more than the familiar tastes of home and memorable meals spent with friends and family, I can only say, READ THIS BOOK. I was moved, amused, uplifted, entertained, and instructed by Barbara Haber's fascinating look at American history through stories of the uses (and misuses) of food. Food is indeed a window on the culture and Barbara Haber's intriguing observations open an original way to understand women's roles in the public sphere. It is a rare pleasure to find a book as riveting and illuminating as this one."
　　　　　　—Carol Field, author of *In Nonna's Kitchen: Recipes and Traditions from Italy's Grandmothers*

BARBARA HABER

FROM
Hardtack
TO
Home Fries

*An
Uncommon
History of
American Cooks
and Meals*

Penguin Books

PENGUIN BOOKS

Published by the Penguin Group

Penguin Putnam Inc., 375 Hudson Street, New York, New York 10014, U.S.A.

Penguin Books Ltd, 80 Strand, London WC2R 0RL, England

Penguin Books Australia Ltd, 250 Camberwell Road,
Camberwell, Victoria 3124, Australia

Penguin Books Canada Ltd, 10 Alcorn Avenue, Toronto, Ontario, Canada M4V 3B2

Penguin Books India (P) Ltd, 11 Community Centre,
Panchsheel Park, New Delhi – 110 017, India

Penguin Books (N.Z.) Ltd, Cnr Rosedale and Airborne Roads,
Albany, Auckland, New Zealand

Penguin Books (South Africa) (Pty) Ltd, 24 Sturdee Avenue,
Rosebank, Johannesburg 2196, South Africa

Penguin Books Ltd, Registered Offices:
Harmondsworth, Middlesex, England

First published in the United States of America by The Free Press,
a division of Simon & Schuster, Inc. 2002
Published in Penguin Books 2003

10   9   8   7   6   5   4   3   2   1

THE LIBRARY OF CONGRESS HAS CATALOGED THE HARDCOVER EDITION AS FOLLOWS:
Haber, Barbara.
From hardtack to home fries : an uncommon history
of American cooks and meals / Barbara Haber.
p.   cm.
ISBN 0-684-84217-3 (hc.)
ISBN 0 14 20.0297 6 (pbk.)
Includes bibliographical references and index.
1. Diet—United States—History.   2. Cookery—United States—History.
3. Food habits—United States—History.   I. Title.
TX360.U6 H33 2002
394.1'0973—dc21   2001058482

Printed in the United States of America
Designed by Karolina Harris

ACKNOWLEDGMENTS

Herb Haber, my husband, is the first person to thank in the long line of people and institutions that have helped this project come to be. For years he has listened to me talk about food as something more than what's for dinner, although he is just as willing to engage in that discussion as in any conversation about what food means. Once this book was under way, he read drafts and offered vital help in shaping the manuscript.

Other major support for this project has come from my institution, the Radcliffe Institute for Advanced Study at Harvard University. I am deeply grateful to Linda Wilson, the last president of what was then Radcliffe College, who awarded me a Professional Development Leave in 1999, giving me the gift of time to conduct research when this book was in an early phase. The following year I was the recipient of a grant given by the Extended Professional Development Opportunity Review Committee of the Harvard University Library, which allowed me another summer away from my usual professional responsibilities to work on the book. I want to thank Professor Sidney Verba, Carl H. Pforzheimer University Professor and Director of the University Library, and Dr. Barbara Graham, Associate Director of the University Library for Administration and Programs, for their help in establishing this opportunity.

I am indebted to many people at the Schlesinger Library: Mary Dunn, former director, for her encouragement and help; Jane Knowles, current acting director, for her support; Mary Harrington, associate curator of books, for filling in for me during my leaves so that new books could be ordered; reference librarians Ellen Shea and Sarah Hutcheon, for all sorts of help, including interlibrary loans; Marie-Helene Gold and Jaclyn Blume for retrieving photographs; Susan von Salis and Joanne Donovan for technological assistance; all of the manuscript department for their impeccable skills in organizing and caring for our remarkable collections; and the administrative staff of the library for making things run smoothly.

My debt to librarians and archivists extends to those connected with many other libraries at Harvard University, not only to those currently there but also to past generations of professionals responsible for building such great research collections. It is impossible to overestimate the importance of those resources or the luxury of readily finding just about every book I ever needed.

I am grateful to Les Dames d'Escoffier, who in 1998 made me the recipient of their M.F.K. Fisher award and to Heida Thurlow, president of Chantal Cookware Corp., for the financial support she provided on that occasion. The James Beard Foundation also exhibited interest in my work in 1997 by honoring me with one of their Who's Who in Food and Beverage in America awards.

The most difficult task for me in acknowledging my appreciation to others is to identify everyone who has helped or influenced me. The temptation is to thank every author of every book I have read and everyone I know, for that is the scope of the intellectual debt I feel. Certain people, however, do spring to mind. Barbara Wheaton and Joyce Toomre, dear friends and colleagues, have taught me so much, especially when we worked together creating a landmark exhibition on food that was installed at Harvard's Widener Library. Dunn Gifford and his organization, Oldways Preservation and Exchange Trust, provided me with numerous opportunities to speak at professional meetings, where I first tested some of the ideas that appear in this book. My thanks also to The Oxford Symposium, an annual forum on food history, and especially to Theodore Zeldin, who gave me words of encouragement when I needed to hear them. Members of The Culinary Historians of Boston, a treasure house of experts, have also helped me, most recently, nutritionists Joe Carlin and Ruth Palumbo, who gave me valuable information for this book. In searching for photographs, I ran into generous people who extended themselves. Captain Barbara Wilson sent me the image of the World War II poster I needed; naval historian Jan Herman gave me a spare copy of a photograph I had been unsuccessfully searching for of nurses in the Philippines; and a former colleague, Kathy Marquis, who now works at the Bentley Historical Library at the University of Michigan, found needed photographs from their John Harvey Kellogg collection.

Others I have found important include Sidney Mintz, whose work has influenced me, as it has so many others; Laura Shapiro, author of the groundbreaking *Perfection Salad,* the first book to connect modern women's history with the history of food; and Arlene Avakian, whose anthology *Through the Kitchen Window* links the study of food to women's studies.

My agent, Sandra Dijkstra, has been a great booster from the start, always full of energy and ideas. Bruce Nichols, my editor, has been a crucial player in this project, initially by expressing his enthusiasm for my topic, and then by putting his considerable talents to work helping me shape the book.

B.H.

For Herb

CONTENTS

INTRODUCTION
Follow the Food

Writing about food as a way to understand American history has not been a stretch for me. I was prepared for the task by my academic training and experience (more about that in a moment) but perhaps even more by a lifelong interest in and curiosity about food and the meaning it has for people beyond satisfying hunger.

Take the time I went on an elementary-school field trip to a U.S. naval vessel when I was a child growing up along the Great Lakes. The ship was probably a destroyer—I have a vague recollection of big guns lining the deck, and of hordes of white-uniformed sailors scurrying around and looking busy—but the only part of the tour that I remember clearly was a visit to the ship's galley, where tray upon tray of pigs in blankets (hot dogs wrapped in a biscuit dough) were being prepared by the ship's cooks. I was intrigued with the size of those trays, three feet square at least, and the alarming size of the ovens, which summoned up impressions of the one owned by the witch in Hansel and Gretel. I wondered how many men these cooks were expected to feed and how many pigs in blankets each of them would be allowed to eat. I was full of questions, but my classmates were in a hurry to get back to the big guns and busy sailors, so we were hustled along and I never found out what I really wanted to know about the ship and the U.S. Navy.

Years later, in the midst of the student protest movement in the early 1970s, I slipped into a building on the Harvard campus that had been taken over by a group of young women demanding that the university supply low-income housing and a women's center for the women of Boston. Along with other sympathizers, I heard the demands of the protesters and read their position papers, but what I remember most about the meeting was an enormous vat of brown rice fortified with raisins and chopped almonds that I saw in the kitchen, giving me the impression that the students were preparing for a long siege. As I look back on the incident, that big pot of brown rice seems to me to conjure up the spirit of the times. Cheap, sustaining, and unpretentious, it was the food of choice for the counterculture of the late sixties and the seventies, a symbol of protest against the establishment and of a commitment to the poor and disenfranchised.

This preoccupation with food and what it means to people has persisted and sometimes gotten me into trouble. Not long ago I was at a dinner party when another guest who was chatting about grocery shopping confided that she had to remember to buy the snacks her husband liked to have in his study. The husband—within earshot—was a full professor of physics at a major university and a rather formal gentleman. I was suddenly overcome with curiosity about what this man munched on while working behind closed doors on his complex equations. So I asked him and got a curt answer: candy bars and peanuts. A less persistent person might have left it at that, but I had to know precisely what brands he liked and the sizes of his bars and jars. So I probed and was satisfied to learn that he liked plain half-pound milk-chocolate Hershey bars, not the miniatures or the kind with the crunch. I could also easily relate to his preference for Planters roasted peanuts lightly salted instead of those awful ones that are dipped in sugar as well as salt. In just a few moments, I had learned some pleasant and endearing things about this former stranger, and believed that we had broken the ice. Imagine my surprise, then, when the professor's wife told me later that he had thought my questions nosy, and was deeply embarrassed by my line of inquiry. He might not have been so offended had we found that we shared a passion for Bach or the Boston Red Sox, but I learned too late that snacks can be too intimate a subject for some people to talk about comfortably.

My private inclination to use food as a way of sizing up people and public events caught up with my professional life when I became Curator of Books at the Schlesinger Library at Harvard University's Radcliffe Institute for Advanced Studies. Here I have been responsible for developing the library's comprehensive collection of books and other printed materials on the history of women in America—a collection that from the first has included cookbooks and books on the history of food.

Founded in 1943, this social history research library has a distinguished manuscript collection that includes the papers of such notable American women as Betty Friedan, as well as the records of the National Organization for Women and other organizational papers that document women's collective activities. At the same time, the Schlesinger Library has collected the records of women who were not well known, including labor organizers, activists for women's health, and ordinary homemakers. It was for this reason that cookbooks became part of our collection, and that the Schlesinger Library holdings now include 16,000 cookbooks, as well as the papers of such noted food writers as Julia Child and M.F.K. Fisher.

Cookbooks were recognized by the library as having essential connections to women's history well before women's history was recognized as a respected field of academic study. The field took off at the end of the 1960s, when academic women who had been activists in the civil rights, antiwar, and women's rights movements came to realize that women in general had been excluded from the historical record. By way of setting the record straight, the resources of the library were called upon by faculty members, students, and independent researchers from all parts of the country and abroad who came to research and write about women's history. The cookbook collection, however, was generally ignored during this period as evidence of the past preoccupations of American women. Instead, women's studies specialists were more immediately intent on bringing visibility to the public activities of women and downplaying their kitchen duties, which seemed to symbolize women's subordination and oppression by the patriarchy.

This would change when women's history came of age and its subject matter became more inclusive. Historians of women had always been sensitive to the fact that women are not a monolithic group but range in age, income level, race, and ethnicity. In the last several years, however, studies in women's history have appeared that demonstrate how customs surrounding food and food itself reveal important distinctions among women and their connections to the communities in which they live. At the same time, for scholars in traditional fields such as literature, psychology, sociology, and anthropology, the study of food is beginning to become an academic growth industry.

In some ways, these scholars are late to the scene. Well before food became a legitimate and exciting area of investigation in colleges and universities, groups of nonacademic culinary historians were laboring in the vineyard of food history. In fact, it was these groups especially, which had been using the library's cookbook collections for years, that nurtured my inclination to see food as a way of understanding not only individual and group behavior but whole civilizations and major world events.

In particular, I found like-minded researchers among the Culinary Historians of Boston, an organization that has met for years at the Schlesinger Library and served as a model for similar groups that have formed around the country. These groups contributed to my sense that the study of food could be broad in its scope rather than narrowly elitist and antiquarian. The venerable Oxford Symposium, held annually at the university for worldwide historians of food, and the Oldways Preservation and Exchange Trust, advocating traditional approaches to diet and nutrition, also provided occasions for me to test out my ideas about the place of food in history, literature, and popular culture. Most of all, they have vindicated my natural inclination to focus on food and to use that focus as a way to illuminate some of the major events of American history.

Food was my way of discovering unforeseen but revealing aspects of otherwise well-documented events. So, for example, the importance of food in defining life came home to me in diaries written by Americans who were herded into Japanese prison camps in the Philippines after the bombing of Pearl Harbor and had to reconstruct their lives around whatever food they could find to eat. Later, looking at cookbooks written by African Americans, I was struck by how, when virtually every other vestige of a people's heritage has been viciously removed, food remains to preserve their identity and connect them with one another and their homeland.

My approach in this uncommon history has been to follow the food in published and unpublished memoirs, diaries, and oral histories that came out of some of the most defining moments of our country's past. So, for example, a manuscript collection from the Schlesinger Library allowed me to document the life of a famous Viennese restaurant in Harvard Square that gave welcome work to World War II refugees. Cookbooks have been especially valuable as primary sources and sometimes even more reliable than traditional scholarly evidence. In one instance, a cookbook written by FDR's housekeeper proved more revealing than her memoir of her Washington years, its dull recipes proof that White House guests had been justified in complaining about the food.

Cookbooks, which I consider to be a vastly underutilized resource, have been relied upon throughout this book. As historic artifacts they bring to life the American past through accounts of what foods were available, how they were prepared, and the meanings people gave to them. Finally, individual recipes are also included to allow the reader to connect directly with the figures in this book and what they cooked and served and ate—or longed to eat when the food they loved was no longer available.

ONE

Feeding the Great Hunger

The Irish Famine and America

The first object I beheld at the foot of a hill at sunset, when I had gained the road, was an old woman with a sack of potatoes on her back, suspended by a rope across her forehead. The whiteness of her hair, the deep wrinkles of her face, the sadness of her countenance, and her feebleness under her burden, so affected me, that never had the miseries of Ireland stood before me in so broad an outline as now.

ASENATH NICHOLSON, *Ireland's Welcome to the Stranger*

In 1844, on the eve of the Irish famine, a middle-aged widow from New York City sailed to Ireland as a self-appointed Protestant missionary to live with the Irish Catholic poor and offer them free Bibles—not to convert them but to try to make them better citizens *before* they came to America as immigrants. Asenath Hatch Nicholson must have cut a comical figure as she trekked alone across the Irish landscape dressed in a velvet bonnet, polka coat (named for the then current dance craze), and India rubber shoes, with a bearskin muff, bags of English and Irish New Testaments, and other belongings that she constantly misplaced or irretrievably lost. Yet this genuine American original believed firmly in her reasons for coming to Ireland: "To learn the true condition of the poor Irish at home, and ascertain why so many moneyless, half-clad illiterate emigrants are daily landed on our shores." That was the answer she gave when first asked by Irish landowners about her mission, and later too when she defended her purpose to a Protestant woman she met on the island of Omey: "I told her plainly I came to Ireland because I had the *right* to come; that they were daily sending loads of beggared and abused emigrants to us, and I had come to see how and what they could become at home; and she understood me when I said, 'I have seen and am satisfied.'"

What Nicholson saw was the poverty and oppression that influenced the character of Irish immigrants she had helped years before in New York's Five Points district, a slum section of the city that had been ravaged by a cholera epidemic in 1832. How Nicholson came to love the Irish is a remarkable story that illustrates the way in which nineteenth-century New England reformers combined devotion to Protestant Christianity with such progressive causes as abolition, temperance, and dietary reform. Named prophetically after the wife of the Biblical Joseph in Genesis who distributed food during the Egyptian famine, Asenath Hatch was born in 1792 into a hardworking, straight-talking rural Vermont family committed to Congregationalist values of individual freedom, independent thought, and religious tolerance. "He hung no Quakers, nor put any men in a corner of the church because they had a colored skin," Nicholson boasted of her father, Michael Hatch. "He rebuked sin in high places with fearlessness, and forgave all personal injuries before forgiveness was asked." In particular, her father was sympathetic to the people who would become her special care, telling his daughter that "the Irish are a suffering people; when they come to your doors never drive them empty away." Her mother likewise "remembered the poor and entertained strangers, hated oppression, scorned a mean act and dealt justly by all." These models of acceptance and compassion would inspire Nicholson as she became, in turn, a teacher, a crusader for temperance and vegetarianism, a Bible-bearing missionary among the Irish, and, most memorably, a relief worker and witness to the famine. Thanks to Maureen Murphy, whose new edition of Nicholson's *Annals of the Famine in Ireland* came out in 1998, the incomparable Asenath Nicholson is receiving renewed attention.

Asenath Hatch began teaching at the age of sixteen in her hometown of Chelsea, Vermont, and sometime later fell prey to a pattern of digestive, nervous, and circulatory ailments that she would attribute to poor eating habits and lack of proper rest and exercise. On the advice of a physician who recommended a geographical cure, she moved to New York, where she opened her own school and met and married Norman Nicholson, a merchant with whom she would open a Temperance Boarding House in 1832. This was the first of a number of such establishments the Nicholsons operated for more than a decade under the principles of pioneer diet reformer Sylvester Graham, to whom Asenath Nicholson attributed her recovery. *Nature's Own Book,* first published in 1833, contains her vegetarian recipes and tributes to Graham. Even after her husband's death in 1841, the Nicholsons' boardinghouses continued to provide a haven for those who believed in Graham's regimen of cold baths, fresh air, and sexual restraint combined with natural foods and proper rest and exercise.

Living at the Nicholson boardinghouses or in the same neighborhood were well-known New York antislavery advocates and moral and religious reformers of every progressive stripe. These included temperance leaders like William Goodell, and Lewis and Arthur Tappan, brothers whose fortunes from the silk trade also benefited numerous evangelical and abolitionist causes, as well as Horace Greeley, who would become editor of the influential *Tribune,* a liberal New York newspaper. At the Temperance House too were members of the American Anti-Slavery Society, who may have introduced Asenath Nicholson to the abolitionist William Lloyd Garrison, and through him to the Irish Society of Friends.

It was through this group, in turn, that Nicholson, widowed and childless in 1844, traveled to Ireland to try to make future immigrants more sympathetic to her passionate causes. Nicholson's *Ireland's Welcome to the Stranger*, published in 1847, describes the country's thatch-roofed stone cabins where, along with farm and domestic animals, the typical Irish rural family gathered on the dirt floor around the turf fire in the hearth as a massive cast-iron pot boiled the twenty or more pounds of potatoes required for a meal. These single-room dwellings rarely held more in the way of furniture than a few stools and a bed, under which the potatoes were commonly stored, usually a large prolific variety the cottagers called lumpers. They were the floury sort, what the Irish prefer to this day instead of varieties that are waxy. The potatoes were sometimes scraped but more often scrubbed clean and placed in the pot and cooked until tender. They were then poured into a wicker basket called a skib over a hole in the floor, where the water and any peels or leftovers would be left for the pigs. The family meanwhile would gather on stools around the skib to eat the potatoes and drink fresh buttermilk, a meal that packed a good nutritional wallop. The milk was taken in sips from a common mug while the potatoes were eaten by hand, with no knife, fork, or plate. Salt, though highly taxed and expensive, was usually available for seasoning or "kitchening" the potatoes, and when times were good, the meal would be accompanied by a boiled egg and some bacon or salt fish, if only for the man of the house or a visiting guest.

Nicholson felt at home and comfortable in these rural cabins where she shared food with rustic Irish families and was not at all offended by the presence of the pigs that shared their quarters.

I had always heard the Irish were celebrated for giving the pig an eminent berth in their cabins, and was a little disappointed to find that though it was really so, yet there was some nicety of arrange-

ment in all this; for in two cabins I found a pig in a corner snugly
cribbed, with a lattice-work around him, a bed of clean straw under
him, and a pot of food standing near the door of his house, to which
he might go out at his option. . . . The family pigs snored snugly in
their cribs, and, in all justice, I must say that these pigs were well
disciplined, for when one of them awoke and attempted to thrust
his nose into a vessel not belonging to him, he was called a dirty pig,
and commanded to go to his own kettle, which he did as tamely as a
child or dog would have done.

This cheerful acceptance of the dining habits of Irish poor,
which others regarded as brutish and degrading, can be found
throughout Nicholson's account of pre-famine Ireland, beginning
with her early visit to a Dublin poorhouse that accommodated
close to two thousand people of all ages:

> The dinner hour was near; three pounds and a half of potatoes were
> poured from a net upon the table for each individual; fingers sup-
> plied the place of knives and forks, and the dexterity of a company
> of urchins, in divesting the potato of its coat, and dabbing it into the
> salt upon the table, caused me imprudently to say, "I am happy, my
> lads, to see you so pleasantly employed."

Here as elsewhere in Ireland, Nicholson would find much to
praise in the simple potato diet of the Irish poor, which she was
pleased to see supplemented at the poorhouse with other vegetarian food, such as porridge, which the Irish still call stirabout:
"Twice a week soup is given, and stirabout and buttermilk in the
morning; the aged and invalids have bread and tea when required." Later, in provincial Clonmel, Nicholson would again endorse the nutritional value of the potato, attributing the strength
and stamina of Irish workers to their common source of nourishment: "Hard as is the fate of the labouring man, I think he is
greatly indebted to the potato for his flow of spirits and health of
body."

As a Grahamite, Nicholson strongly disapproved of much that

traditionally eased the life of the Irish working class, especially alcohol, tea, and tobacco. Only rarely, however, did she attempt to
impose her restrictive notions about food and drink on the Irish
poor. Her heaviest complaint about tobacco use, which seemed to
her to cut across all classes in Ireland, was that it denied the
homeless admission to where they could find food and shelter:
"Thousands are now strolling the streets in hunger, when they
might be made comfortable in a poorhouse, because the inmates
are forbidden to use this nasty weed." As for drinking, Nicholson
mostly left temperance to Irish priests like the legendary Father
Matthew, whom she deeply admired for getting many thousands
to take the pledge and, later, for his heroic efforts in helping the
hungry during the famine.

In contrast to this kind and hospitable priest and the Irish
Catholic poor in general, most of the well-born Protestant women
Nicholson met in Ireland were rude and openly hostile to her efforts and beliefs. Not only did they defend their right to drink wine
and eat meat but they also viewed the American visitor with the
deepest suspicion for her lack of class-consciousness. More than
anything else, however, it was Nicholson's frankly expressed feeling that the Catholic poor in Ireland were victims of social and
economic oppression that earned her the enmity of Irish Protestant landowners, one of whom angrily declared that Catholics
were not oppressed by anything but their "nasty religion." Against
such claims, Nicholson remonstrated that it was not Catholics but
members of her own faith in Ireland who were abusing and ex-
ploiting their laborers and servants as badly as were slaveholders
in the American South. She also faulted her co-religionists for
showing her little or no hospitality when she needed food and
lodging. "I make a practice of going among all the poor without
distinction," she told the wife of a Protestant clergyman, "but am
sorry to say that 'my own' often reject me, and I should more than
once have been without a shelter, if the Catholics had not received
me, when the Protestants would not."

Nicholson's sense of the downtrodden state of the Irish poor was confirmed most vividly when she returned to Dublin near the end of her first tour of Ireland and observed the Mendicity, a workhouse for beggars and their children that contrasted unfavorably with the poorhouse she earlier visited in the city.

> Paupers assemble here in the morning, and stay till six at night, and get two meals for picking oakum. The breakfast is stirabout; the dinner, potatoes and some kind of herbage pounded together, well peppered, put into barrels, shovelled out into black tins, and set out upon the floor—there were no tables. Here they sit upon the dirty boards, and eat, some with spoons and some with their fingers. It was a most disgusting sight.

Because of her criticism of the kind of political economy that could create such degrading conditions, Nicholson was accused in the *Achill Herald* of June 1845 of being an unwomanly troublemaker, if not a subversive foreign agent.

> This stranger is evidently a person of some talent and education; and although the singular course which she pursues is utterly at variance with the modesty and retiredness to which the Bible gives a prominent place in its delineation of a virtuous female, she professes to have no ordinary regard for that holy book. It appears to us that the principal object of this woman's mission is to create a spirit of discontent among the lower orders and to dispose them to regard their superiors as so many unfeeling oppressors. There is nothing either in her conduct or conversation to justify the supposition of insanity, and we strongly suspect that she is the emissary of some democratic and revolutionary society.

There is some truth in the *Achill Herald*'s account. From Nicholson's very American point of view, what needed change in Ireland was not more enlightened and compassionate management by the landed gentry but overall land reform to give the Irish poor the self-sufficiency they needed to achieve self-respect and self-fulfillment. Nicholson wished for reform of this kind not only for the sake of the Irish in their own country but also for those who were coming to America so that they might join the abolitionist cause and fight the same kind of oppression they had suffered in Ireland. Near the end of *Ireland's Welcome to the Stranger*, she admits it as a painful fact that after years of virtual enslavement in their native land, the Irish immigrants she met in New York seemed as indifferent to the plight of slaves in the South as their rulers had been to them in Ireland: "It must be told of the Irish in America that too many strengthen the hands of the avaricious oppressor, and help him to bind the chains tighter about the poor black man."

Not until she experienced the caste-ridden country that was Ireland in the mid-nineteenth century did Nicholson realize that moral reform could only come when a whole society became more just and equitable. But these considerations became moot in the wake of the Great Hunger, when reform of any kind took a back seat to saving lives.

What drove so much of Ireland's underclass to America and other countries can hardly be understood without recalling the lamentable causes and effects of the Irish famine itself. Before the famine, Ireland, with 8.5 million inhabitants, was described as the most densely populated country in Europe. By the end of the decade that circumscribed the Great Hunger, 1846–1855, between an eighth and a ninth of the country's population, anywhere from 1.1 to 1.5 million people, died from starvation and diseases related to malnutrition caused by successive failures of the country's potato crop. (The worst effects of the famine were seen in the winter of 1847, known as "Black '47," when hundreds of thousands succumbed to hunger as well as scurvy, dysentery, typhus, and cholera, and still others suffered blindness from vitamin B deficiency.) The death toll, according to Nobel laureate Amartya Sen, represented the greatest proportion of people killed by a famine in any nation in the world. Then too, within the famine decade, over two million more of the Irish left their country and settled elsewhere—the vast majority in England and the United States—with the result that modern Ireland is the only country in Europe with a population that is smaller today than it was in the early 1840s.

Blame for this massive human devastation and displacement has been put not only on the blight that destroyed the staple food of the Irish poor but on the laissez-faire policies of the English government, which had already reduced much of Catholic Ireland to unredeemable poverty. Both before and after the famine, the vast majority of Irish Catholics were indigent tenant farmers, ill-paid laborers and domestic servants, and homeless beggars and charity cases. The famine flourished in part because of the indifference of absentee landlords who profited from the rents of tenant farmer families and then evicted them when they could no longer pay, leaving many who did not die of hunger and disease to perish from exposure.

As for the blight itself, no one knows for certain where the fungus-like infestation came from that rotted most of Ireland's supply of potatoes. Nor, for that matter, has anyone definitively determined who it was who first brought the potato from the New World to Ireland, where it flourished, though many believed it was imported in the late sixteenth century by Sir Walter Raleigh. There is no doubt, however, that over several generations the potato did became the mainstay of the Irish poor. Large families lived almost exclusively on this cheap and plentiful food. "Three hundred and sixty-five days a year we have the potato," a young Irish workman was heard to say before the famine began in earnest. "The blackguard of a Raleigh who brought 'em here entailed a curse upon the labourer that has broke his heart."

In rural Ireland, before the evictions began, poor families could rent an acre or less of land, spend a total of about three months cultivating enough potatoes to live on for the year, and pay most or all of their annual rent by selling one or more pigs they raised during the same period. (To help pay rent and other expenses, tenants typically sublet part of their land to other families or members of their own, took in a boarder or two, or took whatever paid work they could find nearby.) The political and economic climate of Ireland in the mid-nineteenth century made it practically impossible for Irish tenant farmers to break this cycle of bare subsistence or to abate their dependence on the potato as a single easily grown source of sustenance. Only the famine and the resultant expulsion of thousands of families from their rough cabins and small patches of land could threaten this near-feudal way of life.

Nicholson was aware of earlier failures of the potato crop, but neither she nor anyone else in Ireland was prepared for the blight that started in 1845 and grew worse in 1846, when continuous rain caused the plant disease to spread widely and turn almost every healthy and abundant field into a decaying and putrid mess. Even potatoes that looked fine when first harvested would rot within a few weeks, creating a stench that caused some to believe that the wrath of God had been visited upon the people. By early 1847 the famine was in full force, and Nicholson could be found in Dublin distributing bread and cooking meals made mostly of imported American cornmeal, known as Indian meal or, as the Irish derisively called it, the "yaller Indin." She continued this work, traveling to the most severely devastated parts of Ireland until the summer of the following year, when she optimistically believed that the worst of the famine was over.

Though she often found it hard to come by enough food and money to support her efforts, Nicholson was no stranger to the job of putting together nourishing and enjoyable vegetarian meals for large groups of people on a limited budget. She had done so on a daily basis at the boardinghouses she managed in the early 1840s, creating simple starch-based dishes within the rules laid down by Sylvester Graham. Her cooking skills served her well as she prepared free meals for the poor with whatever food she could buy with her own limited funds or find supplied by the government and charitable agencies. Nicholson herself was happy to live on little more than bread and cocoa as she made her daily rounds delivering meals to famine victims who were too weak to come to any of the soup kitchens that had been set up throughout Ireland by the government.

What soon became clear to Nicholson was the absence of cooking skills in middle-class women who were called upon to prepare meals for the starving. Foods that were unfamiliar to these feckless cooks—mainly rice and cornmeal—were so violently boiled that they became unfit for human consumption, which exasperated and infuriated Nicholson.

> When the famine had actually *come,* and all the country was aghast, when supplies from all parts were poured in—what was done with these supplies? Why the *best* that these inefficient housekeepers *could* do. The rice and Indian meal, both of which are *excellent* articles of food, were cooked in such a manner that, in most cases, they were actually unhealthy, and in *all* cases unpalatable. So unused were they to the use of that common article, rice, that they steeped it the night before, then poured the water off, without rubbing, and for three and four hours they boiled, stirred, and simmered this, till it became a watery jelly, disgusting to the eye and unsavoury to the taste, for they never salted it; besides unwholesome for the stomachs of those who had always used a dry potato for food.

When the poor complained that rice cooked in this fashion made them sick, they were called ungrateful and warned that they would not get any more. Others were given uncooked rice, which most of them could not prepare for lack of fuel, and often tried to eat raw if they had the teeth to do it. In fact, Nicholson believed that it was healthier and tastier to chew uncooked rice than to eat it in the unsavory way it was commonly cooked. Even worse in Nicholson's judgment was the way that Indian meal was served to the poor. Either it was cooked in so little water that it became quite dry and crumbled away, or it was made into such a thick stirabout that it could not be stirred or cooked in any way that made it edible. "The 'stirabout' then became a 'standabout,'" Nicholson observed, "and the effect of eating this was all but favourable to those who had seldom taken farinaceous food." As an American vegetarian, Nicholson was not only familiar with these two staple foods but had learned how to cook rice and Indian meal so that they were palatable as well as nourishing. She knew about polenta, crediting Italians for their ways of making cornmeal delectable. She also knew that rice pudding was a comforting food of almost universal appeal, but was quick to admit that the sugar, butter, and spices required to enhance that dish were scarce in famine-stricken Ireland. Nicholson nevertheless expected that those responsible for cooking cornmeal and rice in this time of crisis would at least learn to do it simply and well. Her recipe for rice, written in the 1830s, when open-hearth cooking was routine, exhibits her knowledge of how the ingredient ought to be treated and how it should taste.

Nicholson's respect for rice was unusual for a mid-nineteenth-century American living in the North, where it was not a popular food. It was, however, an extremely important food in the American South, particularly South Carolina, where, according to food historian Karen Hess, it had been introduced by African slaves who knew how to grow and cook it. As a vegetarian, Asenath Nicholson had realized the importance of a food that was nourishing and filling as well as cheap and easily transported. She understood that it could play an essential role during the famine if only people could learn to cook it.

STEAMED RICE

From Asenath Nicholson's Nature's Own Book

Wash your rice well, rubbing it through three or four waters, put it into boiling water, with salt, let it boil *twelve minutes only;* then drain off the water, uncover the vessel, place it before the fire, minding to turn it about often, till the moisture has all evaporated. The rice will then be whole, dry, and tender, with the additional benefit of being much better for the stomach, than when reduced to a pulp in water.

Horror stories abound in Nicholson's account of the Great Hunger, including her tale of a widow who was arrested for picking potatoes from her landlord's plowed field and then discovered to be cooking a dog in the same pot as the potatoes to feed herself and her famished children. The arresting magistrate presented the evidence (pot, potatoes, and dog) to an astonished but compassionate judge who refused to sentence the woman but instead give her three pounds and told her to return when that was gone.

In Nicholson's *Annals of the Famine in Ireland* (1851), this story of human desperation serves as a prelude to Nicholson's stirring peroration on the progress of the famine and the unjust social and economic circumstances that caused it to flourish. The passage deserves to be quoted at length, for the rhetoric and righteous indignation are pure Asenath Nicholson.

The work of death now commenced; the volcano, over which I felt that Ireland was walking had burst, though its appearance was wholly different from anything I had ever conceived. A famine was always in Ireland in a certain degree, and so common were beggars, and so many were always but just struggling for life, that not until thousands were reduced to the like condition of the woman last mentioned did those who had never begged make their wants known. They picked over and picked out their blackened potatoes, and even ate the decayed ones, till many were made sick, before the real state of the country was known; and when it fell, it fell like an avalanche, sweeping at once the entire land. No parish need be anxious for neighboring ones—each had enough under his own eye and at his own door to drain all resources and keep alive his sympathy. It was some months before the rich really believed that the poor were not making false pretenses; for at such a distance had they ever kept themselves from the "lower order," who were all "dirty and lazy," that many of them had never realized that four millions of people were subsisting entirely on the potato, and that another million ate them six days out of seven entirely; they did not realize that these "lazy ones" had worked six or eight months in the year for eight pence and ten pence, but more for sixpence, and even three-pence in the southern parts, and the other four months had been "idle" because "no man had hired them." They did not realize that the disgusting rags with which these "lazy" ones disgraced their very gates, and shocked all decency were rags which they had contributed to provide; and such were often heard to say that his judgment was what they might expect, as a reward of their "religion and idleness." But the wave rolled on; the slain were multiplied; the dead by the way-side, and the more revolting sights of families found in the darkest corner of a cabin in one putrid mass, where, in many cases, the cabin was tumbled down upon them to give them a burial, was somewhat convincing, even to those who had doubted much from the beginning.

The famine is given human form in Nicholson's near clinical account of the first starving person she saw in Ireland and in her description of the stages of emaciation and dementia by which "the walking skeleton is reduced to a state of inanity—he sees you not, he heeds you not, neither does he beg." The victim in this case was typical of Irish laborers who for years had been used to consuming an estimated seventy potatoes a day, along with oatmeal stirabout and buttermilk when it was available. During the famine, Nicholson found, these men were reduced to two meager meals a day supplied to laborers on public works: "This man was fed on Indian meal, gruel, buttermilk or new milk and bread in the morning; stirabout, buttermilk and bread at four." Worse still, workmen like this one had to wait a week for their pay, by which time many of them died from a combination of exhaustion and starvation, while others were carried back to their cabins, half-dead, "with the spade in their hands."

Profiteering, hoarding, and bureaucratic bungling prevented much food that was available from being distributed in time, in sufficient amounts, and in a form that would actually help the hungry and not harm them. In one case that Nicholson describes, Indian meal was sent by the government in barrels where it became moldy and unfit for use, but was nevertheless consumed by some of the desperate poor, who died as a result. Nor was the faulty preparation of rice and cornmeal the only instance of ignorance and incompetence in matters of food and cooking. Nicholson found pathetic the misbegotten attempts to substitute turnips and black bread for the blighted potato.

Turnips in particular were initially regarded as a godsend during the famine, especially since they were easy to grow and resistant to rot and could be eaten cooked or raw. Here again, however, few could afford the fuel it took to cook the turnips, and those who could afford the fuel usually used only enough to cook the tops, which were the hardest part to eat raw. It also took many more turnips than potatoes to satisfy the cravings of the hungry, so that after a few weeks the stomachs of those who ate nothing but these watery vegetables became swollen and hard, the children's especially. Many died who relied solely on this nutritionally deficient food or de-

Bridget O'Donnel and Children;
Illustrated London News,
Dec. 22, 1849.

Tenant families evicted from their cabins were often depicted in the press as scantily clad women and children.

voured any other edible form of plant life they could scrape from the soil. "Like cattle," Nicholson declared, "these poor creatures seemed to be driven from one herb and root to another, using nettles, turnip tops, chickweed in their turn, and dying at last on these miserable substitutes."

Sometimes as fatal as turnips, and always more unappetizing, was the bread being distributed in County Mayo by government relief officers. "It was sour, black and of the consistency of liver," Nicholson reported of the first loaf she saw, the standard reward for a hard day's work by local laborers who usually walked three to five miles to claim it. Even worse was the black bread she later saw being given out to a large crowd of waiting schoolgirls. To Nicholson the loaf looked like a piece of turf.

It came, was cut in slices, and having been baked that morning the effluvia was fresh, and though standing at the extremity of a long room, with the door open, the nausea became so offensive that after taking a slice for a pattern, and having ascertained from the teacher that this was the daily bread which she had been cutting for weeks, I hastened home with the prize, placed the bread upon paper where good air could reach it; the disagreeable smell gradually subsided, but the bread retained all its appearance for weeks, never becoming sour, but small spots of greenish color like mould here and there dotted upon it. These spots were not abundant: the remainder appeared precisely like turf-mould, and was judged to be so.

The memory of the Irish famine would never cease to haunt Nicholson. Following her return to America, she continued to write about the Great Hunger until her death from typhoid fever in Jersey City, New Jersey, in 1855. By that year, in New York City, where Nicholson's mission had begun, the number of Irish immigrants had swelled to 176,000, about 28 percent of the city's total population, with many more to come from their homeland. In America the problem of the Irish was not starvation—for those who escaped the famine, this country must have seemed a horn of plenty—but overcoming the distrust of native-born Americans and finding work.

Unlike Italians and Jews, who typically came to America as families, many of the Irish newcomers were young single women, and as many as half of them became domestic servants in the years that followed the exodus from the Irish famine. The work was appealing to country people, who preferred living in private homes to finding housing in unfamiliar cities or working in factories or on isolated farms. With jobs as cooks or housemaids or nursemaids in American homes, where almost all of their expenses were taken care of, young Irish women could buy luxuries unavailable in Ireland and still afford to send money to the members of their families who had remained behind. This allowed their brothers and sisters to come to America in a sequence that has been dubbed "chain migration." Once here most Irish women remained in domestic service until they married, when they typically quit to take care of their own households and children. If their families needed more money, they took in lodgers or did laundry and sewing at home. This pattern of first finding domestic work and later managing their own families would persist for most female Irish immigrants until well into the twentieth century.

Irish immigrants had an advantage over other newcomers in that they spoke English, but they were nevertheless often hired only as a last resort by anti-Catholic Americans. Stories circulated that reinforced stereotypes of Irish men as unreliable drunkards and brawlers and young Irish women as ignorant rustics who were ludicrously unused to urban life and modern homes. Typical jokes had Irish housemaids named Bridget and Biddy answering the door by yelling through the keyhole or descending stairs backwards because they were more accustomed to climbing down ladders. Among those who complained most bitterly about the quality of Irish domestic help was Mrs. Henry Ward Beecher, a famously exacting housekeeper, wife of the renowned nineteenth-century minister. She tyrannized legions of immigrant women, for in her view "not one in a hundred" young Irish women could ever be trained to be "neat, energetic, faithful and truthtelling."

In contrast, a more fair-minded assessment of Irish servants and their situation came from Mrs. Beecher's sister-in-law,

UCR/California Museum of Photography, Keystone-Mast Collection.
University of California, Riverside

***Arriving immigrants were checked for obvious signs of
infection and sometimes put into quarantine when thought
to be contagious.***

Catherine Beecher, in *The Housekeeper's Manual* (1873), an influential guide to domestic science she wrote with her sister, Harriet
Beecher Stowe:

> The complaints made of Irish girls are numerous and loud; the fail-
> ings of the green Erin, alas! are but too open and manifest; yet, in
> arrest of judgment, let us move this consideration: let us imagine
> our own daughters between the ages of sixteen and twenty-four, un-
> taught and inexperienced in domestic affairs as they commonly

are, shipped to a foreign shore to seek service in families. It may be questioned whether, as a whole, they would do much better. The girls that fill our families and do our house-work are often the age of our own daughters, standing for themselves, without mothers to guide them, in a foreign country, not only bravely supporting themselves, but sending home in every ship remittances to impoverished friends left behind. If our daughters did as much for us, should we not be proud of their energy and heroism?

In spite of prevailing prejudices, Irish immigrant women usually had little trouble securing positions as domestic servants, because Americans born in this country were reluctant to take such jobs, which looked to them like slavery. Household help was especially in demand by the time the Irish arrived in force in the United States. By the middle of the nineteenth century, as many as 30 percent of American households had live-in domestics.

Many of the newcomers and those who sought to employ them were served by "intelligence offices," employment agencies that supplied clients with reliable household help—men and women who would cook and serve food, clean houses, and look after children and the personal needs of their employers. Intelligence offices served a clear need during a time when clients were always complaining about "the servant problem" and stealing good domestics from one another by offering them hiring bonuses and better pay and working conditions. Unfortunately, many agencies were operated by fly-by-night exploiters who collected fees from both servants and employers and frequently cheated both. Runners from such disreputable places were known to snap up immigrant women as soon as they came off the boats at Ellis Island and sometimes send them to "sporting houses" to serve as prostitutes. In contrast, New York's more established intelligence offices would require references from prospective employees and take pains to know their patrons' needs and desires to ensure compatible placements.

Such an intelligence office was the one owned by Lida Seely, an honest job broker in New York who started her business in 1886 and maintained it until her death in 1928 at the age of seventy-four. Seely not only found jobs for immigrants seeking domestic employment but also published a cookbook that laid out the rights and responsibilities of servants as well as those who employ them. The book, *Mrs. Seely's Cook Book, A Manual of French and American Cookery with Chapters on Domestic Servants, Their Rights and Duties and Many Other Details of Household Management*, serves today as an invaluable artifact, capturing what domestic life was like in the prosperous homes of New Yorkers during the second half of the nineteenth century.

Only in an age like Seely's, when virtually every household task was done by hand, could one picture a job like that of the Second Laundress who "is to rise not later than six-thirty, make the laundry fire and put the laundry in order. She washes and irons all the plain clothes, and sometimes when the fine wash is very large she assists the head laundress in ironing." But it is in Seely's description of the family food handlers—the cooks and kitchen and scullery maids especially—and in the recipes that constitute the bulk of Seely's cookbook that we get the most vivid sense of how hard domestic servants worked, and for how long.

> The cook rises and is downstairs at six o'clock, and opens the door for the furnace or useful man. She makes her fire and cleans her range, and cooks and serves at seven o'clock the servants' breakfast. After this breakfast, she cooks the breakfast for the family, which is usually at eight o'clock. While the family is at breakfast she washes up her kitchen dishes and saucepans, and tidies up her kitchen. Later she puts on a clean white apron, and goes to her mistress's room for orders for the day. The servants have their lunch at twelve o'clock, the family at one. The family dinner is at seven or eight, and the servants have theirs afterward.
>
> The cook has every other Sunday from three o'clock until ten-thirty, the laundress cooking the dinner. She has also one evening in

the week after she cooks and serves her dinner, the laundress washing up for her. The cook takes care of her own kitchen, ice-boxes, closets, windows and cellar stairs.

The kitchen maid had a few light cooking responsibilities, like putting the breakfast oatmeal over the fire, grinding the coffee, and preparing vegetables for the servants' dinner, but otherwise she spent most of their time assisting the cook and mopping up afterward.

She washes pots and pans and tidies up the kitchen, and before going to bed sees to the fastening up of all windows and doors on kitchen floor. She cleans out refrigerators one day, china closet another day, pot closet another day. She takes care of the lower floor, scrubbing kitchen, basement and stairs. Where only one housemaid is kept, she is expected to attend the servant's bedrooms, back halls and staircase.

She generally washes all the kitchen towels, roller towels, and servants' table linen, and answers the basement bell.

Similar tasks were performed by the scullery maid, who was lowest on the kitchen worker totem pole:

She washes dishes, prepares vegetables, washes towels, helps keep the kitchen clean, cleans refrigerators, etc., and kindles fire in the morning where there is no watchman.

Seely wisely recommended that employers allow servants an hour to themselves during the day to replenish the energy they needed for their duties. For the same reason, she also advises that decent food be made available for the staff: "Don't allow the cook to stint the table of the servants. They should be well fed. It pays to drop into the kitchen at meal time and see if their meals are properly cooked and served."

In this 1902 drawing by Charles Gibson, a maid mocks the airs of her mistress to the merriment of other servants and a visiting policeman.

Kitchen staff needed strength and stamina to prepare daily meals that involved not only peeling and chopping vegetables, but also skinning and cleaning eels, wild rabbits, and other game. Possibly the nastiest and most difficult job Mrs. Seely's cookbook describes is preparing stewed terrapin, a mud turtle dish that was much in demand a hundred years ago but now has all but disappeared from the American table. The fact is not surprising when one sees from Mrs. Seely's recipe what it took just to ready the dish for cooking.

STEWED TERRAPIN
From Mrs. Seely's Cookbook

Select live female terrapins, cover them with boiling water, and cook for ten minutes. Remove them from the fire, and when sufficiently cool, scrape the skin and pull out the toe nails. Then cover them with fresh boiling water. Let them boil until they are tender. When cool, break open the shell, remove the meat, liver, and eggs. Be careful not to break the gall sac which is embedded in the liver. Save all the juice that comes from the terrapin while opening it. To each terrapin have one half-pound of butter, one half-pint of cream, salt and pepper to taste. Roll the butter thoroughly in flour, put it in a saucepan with the cream, terrapin, eggs, liver cut in small pieces, and the terrapin juice. Boil steadily for five minutes. Rub the yolks of four hard-boiled eggs with enough Madeira wine to make a paste. Stir this with the terrapin; scald it, but do not let it boil. Serve in chafing dish or individual covered dishes. If necessary, add more Madeira wine.

Even today's most adventurous cooks might hesitate before serving a dish so rich in butter, cream, eggs, and liver.

Dishes like terrapin were typically part of what Mrs. Seely referred to as a "simple menu" for six. This menu was an eight-course dinner that began with oysters or clams, went on to soup, and then to fish, poultry, and meat, each with a sauce, an array of side dishes, and finally fruit, dessert, and cheese. Small wonder that Seely's cookbook insisted that two servants were necessary at table, one to serve hot food while the other followed with the appropriate sauce. But if those who waited on table had to be alert and deft, cooks and kitchen staff needed fortitude as well. Stoves of the day were fueled with wood or coal and had no automatic regulators, requiring cooks to stick their hands in ovens to judge their temperature. (Here, too, Mrs. Seely offered a helpful solution that called for pans of hot and cold water to be kept at the ready—the cold water to be placed in the oven to bring down the temperature when necessary, the hot water to serve as a protective bath for pans of food that might otherwise burn in the oven or on top of the range.) In the absence of blenders and food processors, ingredients for soups or forcemeat fillings had first to be minced, then pounded in a mortar and pushed through a sieve.

Difficult lives in domestic service were typical of the newly arrived, but the Irish were upwardly mobile and eager to reap the rewards of their hard work. By 1900, almost a third of Irish-American families had realized the dream of owning their own home. At the same time, most immigrant women who had worked as cooks and maids made certain that their daughters as well as their sons received an education. The result was that the first American-born women of Irish background were more likely to wind up as secretaries, stenographers, schoolteachers, and nurses than as domestic servants and factory workers. Many other first-generation Irish-American women entered religious orders, where they contributed to the quality of American life through their work in social services and in Catholic hospitals and schools.

To an extraordinary degree, Irish-American women also made a lasting mark on the American labor movement, beginning with the redoubtable Mary Harris Jones, better known as Mother Jones. Left alone in the wake of an 1867 epidemic of yellow fever that claimed the lives of her husband and four children, she devoted herself to the cause of the United Mine Workers, helping striking miners and leading marches against strikebreakers by miners' wives who brandished brooms and mops. By the turn of the century, other Irish-American women had joined their male counterparts as American labor leaders. Mary Kenny O'Sullivan became the first woman organizer for the American Federation of Labor; Leonora O'Reilly founded the New York chapter of the Women's Trade Union League; Elizabeth Gurley Flynn was a leader of the radical Industrial Workers of the World. Other Irish-American women—such as Flannery O'Connor, Mary McCarthy,

Maureen Howard, and Mary Gordon—became major contributors to American letters. And more generally, in cities like Boston, New York, and Chicago, Americans of Irish descent achieved political dominance that would last for decades and lead to wider power on the state and national level. For most Irish Americans, this progress in achievement and acceptance would culminate in the 1960 election of John F. Kennedy as the first Irish Catholic President of the United States.

The success of the Irish in America has created the misconception that practically all today's Irish Americans are descendants of poor Catholics who came to this country to escape the potato famine and make their fortune in the New World. In fact, records show that smaller but significant waves of Irish immigrants arrived before and after the Great Hunger, nor were all of them Catholic or impoverished cottagers. A related misconception, fostered by the famine itself and complaints about the limited cooking skills of Irish kitchen servants, is that the Irish never knew how to cook anything but the potato, and that not well. The truth is that there has long been a distinctive Irish cuisine, and that some of the best Irish cookbooks of the last century describe varied and delicious country dishes that predate the famine and have continued to be cooked in rural Irish kitchens.

In *The Cookin' Woman* (1949), Florence Irwin, a cooking teacher from Belfast, toured the north of Ireland gathering recipes that had been passed down orally by generations of women for such homey dishes as meat dumplings, fried bacon and mushrooms, and wholemeal scones. More recently, Myrtle Allen, chef/owner of Ballymaloe House, a world-famous County Cork resort celebrated for its homegrown food, and her daughter-in-law, Darina Allen, who operates a nearby cooking school, have researched and written about traditional Irish food. Their cookbooks, including Darina's *The Complete Book of Irish Country Cooking* (1996), offer recipes for seasonal dishes using local fish, game, and vegetables, and for such Irish specialties as brown bread, farmhouse cheeses, and homemade sausages.

The one old-time dish that is raved about by every modern-day writer on Irish food is champ, described by all as the most popular and delicious potato dish in the Irish repertoire. It is also an authentic recipe, a sensual reminder of the power of food to make connections between one generation and another and between a new homeland and the one left behind.

The appeal of Irish country cooking has been registering with Americans, who have been flocking lately to Irish pubs as much for the food as for the music and the drinking. This spotlight on the cooking is new, for until recently, most people thought of Irish pub food as a choice between dried-out sandwiches and pickled eggs. Instead, we are finding platters of smoked salmon or trout, savory pies made with eggs and bacon or other smoked meats, fresh salads, and pork steaks and beef tips braised in Guinness stout and served with mushrooms in a bowl shaped from bread. That last dish is an imaginative twist on a simple stew, much like the bistro food, usually based on French or Italian traditions, now being offered in neighborhood restaurants nationwide. Irish bakeries are also springing up, for they too can fall back on a rich tradition of such products as soda breads, or loaves made with whole wheat or oats. Apple pies and cakes, shortbread, and gingerbread are also strong favorites. Unpretentious, hearty, and comforting, Irish food is taking its place as a source of satisfaction for all food lovers.

CHAMP WITH ONIONS

Adapted from Darina Allen's The Complete Book of Irish Country Cooking

6 to 8 unpeeled baking
    potatoes such as Russet or
    Yukon Gold
1 bunch scallions—bulbs
    and green tops

1½ cups milk
1 large onion, sliced
8 tablespoons butter
Salt and pepper

(continued on page 33)

Scrub potatoes and boil them in their jackets. Finely chop the scallions. Cover them with cold milk and bring slowly to a boil. Simmer for about 3 to 4 minutes, then turn off the heat and leave to infuse. In the meantime saute the onion in 2 tablespoons of the butter until browned. Peel and mash the freshly boiled potatoes and, while they are hot, mix with the boiling milk and scallions. Beat in 3 tablespoons of the butter and season with salt and pepper.

Pile the potatoes into individual bowls, make a well in the center of each mound, and place in it a knob of the remaining butter. Sprinkle onions over the top and serve. Diners should fork up potatoes and onions, then dip into butter before eating.

SERVES 4

TWO

Pretty Much of a Muchness

*Civil War Nurses and
Diet Kitchens*

The very idea of that kitchen was savory in the wards, for out of it came, at the right moment, arrow-root, hot, and of the pleasantest consistence; rice puddings, neither hard on the one hand nor clammy on the other; cool lemonade for the feverish; cans full of hot tea for the weary, and good coffee for the faint. When the sinking sufferer was lying with closed eyes, too feeble to make moan or sign, the hospital spoon was put between his lips, with the mouthful of strong broth or hot wine, which rallied him till the watchful nurse came round again. The meat from that kitchen was tenderer than any other, the beef tea was more savory. One thing that came out of it was the lesson on the saving of good cookery.

HARRIET MARTINEAU on Florence Nightingale's
Crimean War hospital kitchen

Florence Nightingale is not usually remembered for her cooking, but during the Civil War, newspaper accounts of how she fed the sick and wounded were inspiring models for so-called diet kitchens set up in military hospitals by Confederate and Union nurses. Most of these women came from middle- and upper-class families and served as middle managers, making sure that diets designed by the surgeons in charge were properly prepared by others. Sometimes those who actually prepared the meals were convalescing soldiers or lower-class white women, more often slaves in the South and free African Americans (called contrabands) in the North. Of course, cooking was not the nurses' only duty. They were responsible for writing letters for battlefield victims, standing vigil while soldiers waited to die, and sending notices of their death to loved ones—jobs judged fitting for females. But for most nurses in the North and South their greatest challenge—and their greatest source of self-fulfillment—came from finding ways to prepare nourishing food for wounded soldiers. This work, sometimes performed in defiance of male hospital authorities, saved far more lives than primitive Civil War surgery.

Like the Crimean War, when Florence Nightingale won worldwide fame, the Civil War made nursing a respectable profession. But in both the North and the South, women who wished to serve in military hospitals met resistance and criticism from those who feared they would suffer from denaturing contact with rude soldiers and the horrors of war. Many of the women who did become full-time hospital workers during the war were widows and spinsters somewhat less subject to patriarchal pressure to remain in "women's true sphere." This pressure was especially strong in the Confederacy, where well-born women were dogged by their culture to retain their traditional identity as genteel ladies, committed to ideals of delicacy, modesty, and refinement.

It took a rare breed of Southern women to serve in military hospitals, yet where they did, the mortality rate dropped from 10 to 5 percent, a statistic that encouraged the Confederate Congress in 1862 to legislate paid positions for female hospital matrons and nurses and put them in charge of food, laundry, and medicine. More often than not, however, genteel women of the

South preferred to help fallen soldiers at a distance, by partic-
ipating in fundraising events or campaigns to collect and transport food, clothing, medicine, and personal necessities. As Drew
Gilpin Faust observed in her study of Confederate women, *Mothers of Invention* (1996), "in spite of the variety of opportunities
for hospital work and the sometimes all but irresistible demands
for their labor, most elite women served intermittently or not
at all."

Among elite Southern women who served only intermittently
in Confederate hospitals the best known is Mary Boykin Chesnut,
whose diaries were compiled under the title *Mary Chesnut's Civil
War* in an edition by C. Vann Woodward that won a Pulitzer Prize
in 1982. Chesnut's diaries offer the most intimate and detailed picture of what life was like during and immediately after the war, as
observed by a literate woman of great charm and intelligence who
had married into a wealthy and influential family. The scion of
rich South Carolina planters, Chesnut's husband held high government posts in the Confederacy. He brought his wife to Richmond, the seat of the Southern government, where the couple
enjoyed close relationships with the leadership of the South, including President Jefferson Davis and his wife. Chesnut's writings
reveal the full range of responses from women of her class to the
cause of caring for fallen Confederate soldiers, from those who
avoided hospital service altogether to casual volunteers like Chesnut herself to women like Sally Tomkins and Louisa McCord, who
financed and ran their own hospitals.

On August 5, 1861, Chesnut reported the first of her many visits
to "Miss Sally Tompkins' hospital." With a survival rate of almost
95 percent, this old Richmond house became one of the most successful military hospitals in the South. Sally Louisa Tompkins was
even commissioned a captain of cavalry by Jefferson Davis, becoming the only woman in the Confederacy to ever hold military
rank. Chesnut's contributions to the hospital consisted principally
of buying and delivering food, but she was strongly affected by
what she saw there. On one visit, she brought a carriageload of

peaches and grapes, then returned to the market for more when the supply gave out and she saw how wistful the men were who had not gotten their share. "Those eyes sunk in cavernous depths haunted me as they followed me from bed to bed."

Worse sights awaited Chesnut at other hospitals she visited in the same area. "I can never again shut out the view of the sights I saw of human misery," she wrote after stopping at a converted tobacco house where every hospital activity was crowded into a large narrow room. "Long rows of ill men on cots. Ill of typhoid fever, of every human ailment—dinner tables, eating, drinking, wounds being dressed—all horrors, to be taken in at one glance."

Library of Congress

Maimed Union soldiers and others in front of an office of the U.S. Christian Commission.

At another Richmond hospital where she went to help a boy from home, Chesnut was equally appalled by the spectacle of disorder and death: "Horrors upon horrors again—want of organization. Long rows of them dead, dying. Awful smells, awful sights." As she was arranging to hire a male nurse for the boy, Chesnut fainted dead away and had to be lifted, "a limp rag," to her waiting carriage.

Chesnut's privileged life stands out in bold relief when we compare the plain food served at local Richmond hospitals with the elegant and abundant fare that she and her circle enjoyed at innumerable breakfasts, luncheons, dinner parties, weddings, and other social receptions. Until almost the end of the war, Chesnut's diaries report that she and her husband routinely dined with their well-off friends on fine food and wine sent every month from the family plantation. They seem never to have been short of beef, poultry, hams, eggs, butter, rice, potatoes, pickles, and fresh vegetables and fruits, not to mention imported delicacies like pâté de fois gras and truffles. The couple's wartime Christmases included plum puddings, mince pies, and other traditional holiday dishes served on damask with fine china, glassware, and silver. And later in the conflict, when supply routes were cut off to all but the most intrepid blockade runners, the Chesnuts could afford the exorbitant prices being charged for scarce staples. (In June 1864, Mary Chesnut reported spending $800 for two pounds of tea, forty pounds of coffee, and 60 pounds of sugar.) Even near the end of the war, which would leave her husband and his family in debt, Mary Chesnut enjoyed what seemed to her perfect fare for hot August nights in 1864—ices, cake, and melons, accompanied by a wide choice of refreshing alcoholic beverages.

In contrast to the opulent meals described in Chesnut's diaries, *The Confederate Receipt Book* (1863) records the privations suffered by most civilians and soldiers. Culled from Southern newspapers and other sources, this unique collection offers ways to prepare everyday dishes with substitute ingredients and alternative cooking methods. A telling example is the book's recommendation that readers short on salt adopt techniques used by Native Americans to preserve meat and fish by drying them with fire, smoke, or sunlight, or all three methods at once. A recipe for ersatz coffee uses acorns that are parched, shelled, and roasted with a little bacon fat before being brewed in the usual way. In the absence of wheat flour, rice flour recipes are offered for breads similar to those made with corn flour—griddle cakes rather than puffy, yeast-risen loaves. Perhaps the most surprising recipe in the collection is for "apple pie without the apples," made from crackers that are soaked in tartaric acid, then sweetened with sugar and flavored with butter, cinnamon, and nutmeg. (An almost identical recipe called "mock apple pie" made with Ritz crackers routinely turns up in modern cookbooks.)

MOCK APPLE PIE

1¾ cups water

2 cups sugar

2 teaspoons cream of tartar

2 tablespoons lemon juice

1 grated lemon zest

Pastry for two-crust 9-inch
   pie plate

1¾ cups Ritz crackers,
   coarsely broken

2 tablespoons butter

½ teaspoon cinnamon

Preheat the oven to 425°F. In a saucepan, heat water, sugar, and cream of tartar to a boil and simmer for 15 minutes. Add the lemon juice and zest; let cool. Line pie plate with pastry. Place broken crackers in crust. Pour cooled syrup over crackers. Dot with butter; sprinkle with cinnamon. Roll out top crust; place over pie, crimp, and with fork make holes for steam. Bake for 30 to 35 minutes.

The shortages in the South that occasioned this cookbook were described by a deeply committed Confederate nurse, Kate Cumming, a Scots-born woman whose family had settled comfortably in the prosperous cotton port of Mobile, Alabama. In the spring of 1861, when talk of war began, Cumming was single and in her mid-twenties. Her mother and two married sisters had left for England. Loyal to the cause of the South, Kate remained behind with her father, brother, and brothers-in-law, one of whom roundly opposed her stated intention to go the front, declaring that "nursing soldiers is no work for a refined lady." Kate Cumming believed otherwise, and cited the example of Florence Nightingale: "I knew that what one woman had done another could." Her first nursing assignment had her helping victims of the battle of Shiloh, and she served for the full course of the war in a number of hospitals throughout the deep South.

Preparing and distributing food would become Cumming's most important responsibility, in which she demonstrated a great capacity for enterprise and innovation under the most difficult circumstances. At her first hospital post in Corinth, Mississippi, she found patients being handled roughly by male nurses who were regular soldiers assigned on a rotating basis to hospital duty. Worse still was the spectacle of the massive numbers of amputations that took place in all Civil War hospitals. About 30,000 men on each side of the conflict suffered surgical loss of limbs, a procedure that became so commonplace as to require special operating rooms of the kind Cumming passed on her way to her kitchen in Corinth. "The passage to the kitchen leads directly past the amputating room below stairs," she recalled, "and many a time I have seen the blood running in streams from it."

Of the kitchen itself, where she took her own meals with other nurses and surgeons, Cumming remarked that "it is not the cleanest place in the world," though she adapted quickly and with good humor. "Hunger is a good antidote for even dirt," she observed: "I am aware that few will think so except those who have tried it." In short order, however, Cumming and other nurses were able to transform the kitchen with help from the women of Natchez, who sent food, wine, and dinnerware to serve meals properly. "We have dishes to feed the men, which is a great improvement. The food is much better cooked. We have negroes for cooks, a good baker, a nice dining room, and eat like civilized people." Cumming was also able to compensate ingeniously for shortages, as when she found a substitute for milk, which frequently became scarce in the South but was always wanted for certain illnesses.

> We have a quantity of arrow root, and I was told that it was useless to prepare it as the men would not touch it. I thought that I would try them, and now use gallons of it daily. I make it quite thin, and sometimes beat up a few eggs and stir in while hot; then season with preserves of any kind—those that are a little acid are the best— and let stand until it becomes cold. This makes a pleasant and nourishing drink; it is good in quite a number of diseases; will ease a cough; and is especially beneficial in cases of pneumonia. With good wine, instead of the preserves, it is also excellent; I have not one man to refuse it, but I do not tell them of what it is made.

Cumming would effect similar turnarounds at each of the hospitals at which she served, including her next assignment to Okolona, Mississippi, where she was initially dismayed to find that patients were given just one meal a day that consisted of "badly-made soup, and as badly-made bread." Here, as at her first post, hospital conditions reflected the fact that the Confederacy, as badly as the North, had failed to mobilize for war until it was inescapably clear that the conflict was going to last longer than anyone imagined and create an appalling number of casualties. In Chattanooga, Cumming found a better organized hospital but one where mounting casualties placed great demands on a few volunteer nurses, forcing them to work almost round the clock. In March 1863, she described the nurses' daily routine, which included preparing certain "delicacies," the only hands-on cooking job performed by members of her class:

Mrs. Williamson and I live like Sisters of Charity; we get up in the morning about 4 o'clock, and breakfast by candle-light, which meal consists of real coffee without milk, but sugar, hash and bread; we eat in our room. Unless we get up early, we find it impossible to get through our duties. Mrs. Williamson prepares toddies and egg-nogs; I see that the delicacies for the sick are properly prepared. After the duties of the day are over, we then write letters for the men, telling their relations they are here, or informing them of their decease; other times mending some little articles for them. Mrs. Williamson is up many a night till 12 o'clock, working for her "dear boys," as she calls them.

At Chattanooga, Cumming had the help of white male cooks, re-covering soldiers she believed were serving the Confederacy as much as men still in the field. She only criticized the lack of vari-ety in the standard daily menu.

The great trouble about hospitals is the sameness of the diet, in the morning we have batter-cakes made of the mush left from the previous meal, rice and stale bread, (I do not mean what the men leave, as nothing is used which has been in the wards,) hash made out of the soup-meat, toast, mush, milk, tea, coffee, and beefsteak. Our batter-cakes never have eggs in them; they have a little flour and soda, and are very nice. For dinner, we have beef and chicken soup, potatoes, rice, dried fruit, and for dessert a *luxurious* baked pudding, made of the same materials as the batter-cakes, with mo-lasses for sweetening, with the addition of spices.

Special diets prescribed for sick patients with digestive problems consisted of lighter foods such as chicken, beef tea, arrowroot, sago, boiled milk thickened with flour, regular milk and butter-milk, tea, and toast "or whatever we could get the patient to eat." Supper for such sufferers consisted of dried fruit, toast, tea, and coffee.

Like Chesnut, Cumming observed that these staples were abundant early in the war but became increasingly scarce and expensive when the Union cut off supplies and blockade runners started charging "famine prices" for coffee, tea, sugar, and flour. Coffee became particularly hard to come by in the South, causing a level of consternation that struck Cumming as humorously excessive.

> I have noticed that some who did not touch it before the war, talk as gravely about its loss as if their very existence depended upon it, and indeed they are quite melancholy about it. It is amusing to see how seriously it is discussed. I said jestingly that I do believe it will yet be the means of subjugating us.

It never occurred to Cumming that complaints about the lack of coffee—or about poor coffee substitutes made of acorns or yams—were as good a way as any for soldiers and civilians to give vent to the larger frustrations they were suffering on account of the war.

And the suffering was great. Chimborazo Hospital, in Richmond, was reputed to be the largest military hospital in the world, caring for as many as 76,000 patients during the course of the war. Phoebe Yates Levy Pember, a distinguished Jewish Confederate who served for a time as the matron of the hospital, recalled the challenges of dealing with so many who were so sick. With no preparation in cooking for the well or ill, Pember was suddenly required to produce meals for the sickest of some 600 patients using a small, rusty stove that was only fit for a family of six. At a loss at first as to what she would serve, Pember tapped into her Jewish heritage and came up with an ancestral remedy: "My mind could hardly grope through the darkness that clouded it, as to what were my special duties, but one mental spectrum always presented itself—*chicken soup*."

> Having vaguely heard of requisitions, I then and there made my first, in very unofficial style. A polite request sent through "Jim" (a small black boy) to the steward for a pair of chickens. They came in-

An African-American army cook at work at City Point, Virginia.

stantly ready dressed for cooking. Jim picked up some shavings, kindled up the stove, begged, borrowed or stole (either act being lawful to his mind), a large iron pot from the big kitchen. For the first time I cut up with averted eyes a raw bird, and the Rubicon was passed.

Only later did Pember discover that the Confederate Congress had licensed her to be more of a supervisor than a housekeeper and cook. As a result she would be able to appoint an assistant matron, three or four cooks and bakers, and a couple of kitchen workers to perform the tasks she had tried to handle alone. Yet her first attempt at making chicken soup had proved to be unexpectedly empowering, helping her realize in herself an atavistic gift for cooking.

> Nature may not have intended me for a Florence Nightingale, but a kitchen proved my worth. Frying pans, griddles, stew-pans and coffeepots soon became my household gods. The niches must have been prepared years previously, invisible to the naked eye but still there.

Not everyone took joy in Pember's newly discovered sense of vocation, however. Though she believed that her chicken soup was "undeniably a success, from the perfume it exhaled," the first patient she served it to refused to eat it, partly because he found the soup unfamiliar, but mostly because Pember had garnished the soup with parsley. " 'My mammy's soup was not like that,' the patient whined. 'But I might worry a little down if it war'n't for them weeds a-floatin round.' "

The patients' rejection taught Pember a lesson in the vagaries of human taste. The homesick soldiers yearned for familiar cooking, prepared just as it had been by Mom. As often as she would try to recreate dishes injured soldiers requested, sometimes following recipes they supplied, Pember got the same woeful response that it did not look or taste like what "Mammy" made. "Many would not eat unless furnished with food to which they had become accustomed at home," Pember remembered, "and as unreasoning as brutes resisted nutriment and thus became weaker day after day." Only buttermilk and sweet milk were universally craved. When milk of any kind became critically scarce, Pember had to scold a Kentuckian who kept pleading for a cupful. "Why man!" she told him. "The very babies of the Confederacy have given up drinking milk, and here are you, six feet two, crying for it."

A Southern Woman's Story contains Pember's full account of hospital life at Chimborazo throughout the conflict. In the first year of the war, food was relatively plentiful and individual desires could often be satisfied if surgeons approved. But the surgeons often did not approve.

The doctors insisted that patients stick to prescribed dishes even when the men refused them or actually threw up their food. "The habit so common among physicians when dealing with uneducated people, of insisting on particular kinds of diet, irrespective of the patient's tastes, was a peculiar grievance that no complaint during four years ever remedied," said Pember. The effect of the doctors' obstinacy was that seventy out of a hundred patients at Chimborazo stopped taking nourishment altogether. As she saw it, some men fasted because they were weak and discouraged by sickness and defeat, others because they sought sympathy or release on furlough, but most because they could not stomach the tasteless convalescent food they were served. "Men who had never been sick, or swallowed those starchy, flavorless compounds young surgeons are so fond of prescribing, repudiated them entirely, in spite of my skill in making them palatable."

The other enduring problem Pember experienced was the hospital's supply of medical whiskey, the control of which the Confederate Congress had legally ceded to the ward matrons. Not surprisingly, the chief surgeon volunteered to relieve Pember of this unladylike burden. But she stubbornly refused to give up the key to the liquor locker. The result was that she fought unending battles not only with the medical staff but with other male hospital workers as well, who connived to rob patients of their liquor allotments or steal locked-up supplies of whiskey. Only at the very end of the war, when federal troops confiscated the hospital stores at Chimborazo, did Pember's whiskey wars abate, but not before she was forced to pull a gun on a crew of "hospital rats" who sought to keep a thirty-gallon barrel of whiskey from falling into the hands of the Yankees.

Pember's recollections of her work on behalf of Chimborazo's "diet kitchens" reveal the charm and humor that made her a favorite among patients, enlightened surgeons, and members of her own set, whose social gatherings she often graced on evenings in Richmond when she was off duty. Her most memorable and deeply affecting stories describe her attendance upon dying young soldiers. On one occasion she was called to the side of a mortally wounded boy who kept calling for a friend named Perry. Pember took pains to find the friend and bring him to the hospital, where the wounded boy was just awakening from a troubled sleep. " 'Perry,' he cried, 'Perry,' and not another word but with one last effort he threw himself onto his friend's arms, the radiant eyes closed, but the smile still remained—he was dead."

In another sad instance, Pember attended a wounded boy named Fisher who remained heroically cheerful through months of pain. All of the nursing staff grew to love him. When he suddenly began to bleed, Pember put her finger over the wound and kept it there to stop the flow, even after the surgeon arrived and told her that a sliver of bone had severed an artery so that nothing could save the youngster. "The hardest trial of my duty was laid upon me; the necessity of telling a man in the prime of life, and fullness of strength that there was no hope for him." Even when the soldier was told of his plight and gave Pember permission to release her finger from the wound, she could not bring herself to do so, knowing that as soon as she did he would bleed to death. Only when she fainted was the tragic dilemma resolved.

Wrenching as they were, these experiences convinced Pember that wartime hospital service did not inevitably cause a woman to "lose a certain amount of delicacy and reticence" but instead could elevate her spiritually, to the extent that she steadfastly gave herself over selflessly to the needs of stricken solders. "If the ordeal does not chasten and purify her nature, if the contemplation of suffering and endurance does not make her wise and better, and if the daily fire through which she passes does not draw from her nature the sweet fragrance of benevolence, charity and love,—then, indeed a hospital has been no fit place for her."

The call to serve sick and wounded soldiers was heard as loudly by women of the North as by their Southern counterparts. Among those who made contributions that would outlive the war were

Dorothea Dix, who became the Union's first Superintendent of Women Nurses; Clara Barton, the founder of the American Red Cross; and doctors Elizabeth and Emily Blackwell, pioneer women physicians who formed the Women's Central Relief Committee to train nurses for battlefield hospital service. Less well known were an estimated 6,000 Union nurses.

At the outset of the war, the Union faced the same problems as did the South in supplying appropriate and sufficient food, clothing, and medicine to soldiers in the field. Like their Confederate counterparts, many Northern women were caught up in the general war euphoria and engaged in a patriotic frenzy of sewing items and collecting food that often proved useless. Undergarments made for Union soldiers proved ludicrously inadequate, based as they were on patterns that idealized the male anatomy. Improperly canned, preserved, and potted foods later had to be thrown out when they were found decaying and fermenting in Union baggage cars. Nor was Union officialdom any better prepared. When the war began, the U.S. Army Medical Department was headed by an eighty-year-old veteran of the War of 1812 who for years had hired unqualified civilian doctors and stinted on camp sanitation, decent food, and pure water. As a direct result of these conditions, thousands of federal soldiers would die unnecessarily during the war, more from infection and disease than battlefield wounds.

The initiative for establishing a network of clean, well-equipped military hospitals and encampments came from fifty prominent Northern women who met in New York City in April 1861 and formed the Women's Central Association of Relief for the Sick and Wounded of the Army. The members' earlier work on behalf of abolition, temperance, and women's rights gave them the organizational and political skills they needed to push for the formation of the more broadly empowered United States Sanitary Commission. Formed to acquire and distribute food, medical supplies, and other resources required by Northern field hospitals, this remarkable organization overcame resistance from the corrupt and incompetent Medical Department and would account for the far lower rate of mortality among Union soldiers than in the Confederacy, where no comparable body had been established. In support of the Sanitary Commission, women from all parts of the North raised over $5 million ($75 million in today's money) by staging Sanitary Fairs, huge regional events that featured public exhibitions of livestock and machinery as well as arts-and-crafts shows and bake sales.

The Sanitary Commission recruited women to serve as hospital nurses under the austere supervision of Dorothea Dix. Her advertisements stated, "No woman under thirty years need apply to serve in government hospitals. All nurses are required to be very plain-looking women. Their dresses must be brown or black, with no bows, no curls, no jewelry, and no hoopskirts." These strict qualifications were Dix's way of heading off the kind of frivolous young women who she knew would alienate doctors and compromise good hospital order. However, her attempts to screen candidates did not prevent troublesome women from turning up. Some women who proclaimed themselves to be nurses were food faddists who believed that soldiers would overpower the enemy if only they would eat enough jelly, pickled cucumbers, or other empowering foods. Others swarmed into the hospitals to look after their own relatives. Yet most Northern nurses served with as much courage and dedication as their sisters in the South.

Of Northern women who left detailed accounts of their hospital experiences, the best known is Louisa May Alcott, the author of *Little Women* (1869), who spent barely more than a month as a volunteer nurse at the Union Hotel Hospital in Georgetown in the winter of 1862 and afterward wrote a fictionalized account of her brief service in *Hospital Sketches* (1863). Like Cumming, Alcott arrived at the scene of an early Civil War bloodbath, the battle of Fredericksburg, and she too complained about the general disorder of her hospital, a converted tavern that she nicknamed "the Hurly-Burly Hotel." With no prior training, she was called upon to wash wounded soldiers and then join other women nurses and attendants in serving great trays of bread, meat, soup, and coffee. For herself, Alcott preferred crackers, cheese, and apples she purchased from a local market rather than submit to the hospital's stale and unvarying diet. Alcott recalled:

> The three meals were "pretty much of a muchness," and consisted of beef, evidently put down for the men of '76; pork, just in from the street; army bread, composed of saw-dust and aleratus; butter, salt as if churned by Lot's wife; stewed blackberries, so much like preserved cockroaches, that only those devoid of imagination could partake thereof with relish; coffee, mild and muddy; tea, three dried huckleberry leaves to a quart of water—flavored with lime—also animated and unconscious of any approach to clearness. Variety being the spice of life, a small pinch of the article would have been appreciated by the hungry, hard-working sisterhood, one of whom, though accustomed to plain fare, soon found herself reduced to bread and water; having an inborn repugnance to the fat of the land and the salt of the earth.

Alcott was spared dispensing this diet when she contracted typhoid and was taken home to Concord, Massachusetts, by her father. She was later treated with the mercury compound calomel, which left her chronically ill for the rest of her life—a steep price to pay for a few weeks of hospital duty.

Neither in Northern hospitals nor in the field was the fare much better than that served at Alcott's "Hurly-Burly Hotel." Union soldiers were typically issued more meat than their enemies but often complained that their usual daily ration of a pound and four ounces of salt beef had a disagreeable yellow-green color and odd flavor. Much of the tainted or inferior food that reached the military resulted from bureaucratic bungling and corrupt suppliers, but on good days Northern troops could expect over a pound of fresh beef and almost a pound and a half of soft bread, cornmeal, or hardtack, the latter a ubiquitous cracker that could also be found among Confederate army rations. Made of plain flour and water, hardtack was similar in shape and design to a modern saltine cracker, but larger and thicker and a lot harder, especially when stale (as it almost invariably was). Hardtack was commonly crumbled into coffee or soup or soaked in water and then fried in pork fat until brown. But regardless of preparation, so notoriously hard was the cracker that it was the constant subject of derisive songs and jokes, like the one about the Kansas soldier who found something soft in his hardtack—a ten-penny nail. In Northern camps and hospitals, milk toast was made of hardtack soaked in condensed milk, a product that became widely available to federal troops when the Union appropriated the entire output of Gail Borden's condensed milk plant in Connecticut.

Perhaps the best account of how food was apportioned and served in Union hospitals appears in *Hospital Days*, by Jane Stuart Woolsey, who with her older sister Georgeanna established a model nursing system at the Union hospital in Alexandria, Virginia, in the fall of 1863. In a chapter devoted to the elaborate mechanisms set up to prepare and distribute food, Jane Woolsey described the care with which Surgeon in Charge David Page Smith spelled out her responsibilities as superintendent:

> She was required to know in what quantity and quality of raw material was furnished by the commisary steward; to see that this was properly cooked, properly distributed from the diet kitchen, received in good order from the wards, carefully divided there; that each patient got, without lawful leakage, the exact articles ordered for him by the ward medical officer; in short, she was expected to follow the food from the commissary store down the sick man's throat.
>
> To these duties the Superintendent added in her own mind, among others, that of learning whether the permitted articles were cooked according to the taste and fancy of the individual, knowing well that A prefers salt and B sugar in the same kind of porridge, and disliking from her soul the tall-men-powders-short-men-pills system she has observed elsewhere.

Elsewhere, as the Woolsey sisters had seen for themselves, doctors in the North were as obstinate as their Confederate counterparts in insisting upon patients' eating whatever was routinely prescribed to them, whether or not it proved palatable or beneficial. At Alexandria, a range of diets were developed for particular illnesses such as inflammation of the stomach, chronic diarrhea, and typhoid fever, but care was taken to alternate diets for each complaint for the sake of variety. The need for this kind of variance was demonstrated by a soldier who was served chicken stewed in rice so often as a result of a mistake in changing the diet order that he grew to hate the sight and smell of the meal. Jane Woolsey reported that "weeks afterward when the same dish was brought for his next neighbor, he seized the moment when his comrade's back was turned, crawled from his bed and threw the whole mess, dish and all, out of the window."

Woolsey also noted the wisdom of the surgeon in charge in allowing for the inclusion of tempting "home dishes" prepared to patients' desires and "unlimited quantities of food and stimulants" for badly wounded soldiers. These innovations aside, however, the diets prescribed for patients at Alexandria illustrate the misguidedness of much nineteenth-century medicine and nutritional science, as when fatty, hard-to-digest foods like hotcakes, cheese, and molasses candy were prescribed for a soldier with inflammation of the stomach. Two other meals detailed by Jane Woolsey also contained dishes that would be of little use as cures.

PRIVATE J. (CHRONIC DIARRHEA.)

BREAKFAST	DINNER	SUPPER
Coffee	Roast Beef	Oyster Soup
Steak	Fish	Raw Cabbage
Eggs	Radishes	Cheese
Bread	Boiled Cabbage	Bread
Butter	Bread	Butter
Milk-punch	Tea	Coffee

PRIVATE K. (TYPHOID FEVER.)

BREAKFAST	DINNER	SUPPER
Mutton Chops	Beefsteak	Milk
Potatoes	Potatoes	Tea
Bread	Tea	Arrowroot
Coffee	Coffee	Cake
Doughnuts	Butter	Butter
Butter	Plum Pudding	Pudding

In assigning these meals, Dr. Smith was not much different from other physicians of his time (or today, for that matter) in assuming the sufficiency of a few standard diets for the sick. "The Surgeon in Charge held that a roast beef and pudding diet, an eggs and milk diet, a vegetable diet for men with scurvy, a milk-porridge diet, a beef-tea diet, and a gruel diet, would cover the majority of cases," Jane Woolsey reported. What speaks much better for Dr. Smith and the Woolseys is the pioneer system they evolved to itemize the responsibilities of everyone involved with food—nurses, doctors, kitchen workers, and even vendors. As described in *Hospital Days*, their elaborate system of written treatment orders and sign-offs by nurses is clearly a forerunner of modern hospital practices.

At Alexandria, convalescents included not only Americans mostly from New England and the West (what we now call the Midwest) but a number of antislavery supporters from Germany, Italy, France, and Switzerland, as well as some African Americans and Native American Chippewas and a few Confederate prisoners. Woolsey records the special efforts by the nurses to make this diverse patient body feel more at home. Flowers were found for mortally sick soldiers, including carnations for a sergeant who "died with one clutched in his thin fingers" and lilacs for a New England boy who Woolsey knew would enjoy this reminder of home. ("The lilacs outlived him," the nurse recalled.) For a Frenchman who wanted nothing more than "two drops of red wine, *du vin de mon pays,*" Woolsey obtained a small daily ration of Burgundy that inspired her patient to break into a patriotic French song about drinking wine and dying for one's country. "The *deux gouttes de vin rouge* seemed to brighten the whole ward," she wrote.

The most memorable and certainly most independent of the Union nurses to serve in the war was Mary Ann Bickerdyke. A widow with two young sons, she had been living in Galesburg, Illinois, in the spring of 1861 when she first heard about the appalling field conditions that were causing soldiers downstate to die of typhoid and dysentery. Bickerdyke saw for herself that disease rather than weaponry was the biggest scourge of the war. Indeed, it has been estimated that three out of five Union troops who died in the war succumbed to disease, and on the Confederate side, two out of three. On both sides, measles, chickenpox, typhoid, and dysentery were epidemic, along with wound infections and dehydrating diarrhea from intestinal disorders, all brought about by unspeakably bad sanitary conditions in military encampments and hospitals. In 1861, for example, a federal inspector found Union camps "littered with refuse, food, and other rubbish, sometimes in an offensive state of decomposition; slops deposited in pits within the camp limits." Conditions were not much better in the hospitals Bickerdyke visited when she volunteered to travel south to Cairo, Illinois, to oversee the distribution of money raised to help sick and injured boys from her hometown.

In what was to be her typical approach to the many crises she met during the war, Bickerdyke rolled up her sleeves and got to work, doing whatever she felt necessary and ignoring any command but that of her own conscience. Mother Bickerdyke, as she was called, was one of the few volunteer nurses who defied Union officers by serving in field hospitals and open-air medical tents erected close to battlefields instead of staying well behind the lines. These outdoor infirmaries turned out to be more hygienic than the dirty and badly ventilated old buildings the Union commonly converted into hospitals, but they were so poorly staffed that Bickerdyke would personally take over cooking, cleaning, laundering, and bedside care of casualties—everything short of hands-on doctoring.

Most of the stories about Mother Bickerdyke survive through the writings of Mary Livermore, a Boston-bred woman who had been a leader in the Sanitary Commission and a strong supporter of the Illinois widow as she did battle with male authority. Bickerdyke liked to brag that her husband would have lasted twenty years longer if he had not tried to resist her will, and she proved just as indomitable with Union officers and doctors when they stood on ceremony or were derelict in their duty to "her boys." One target of her wrath was a tippling ward surgeon who was late in making his rounds, holding up the serving of meals and administration of medicines. "You miserable, drunken, heartless scalawag!" Mother Bickerdyke is said to have screamed at the doctor. "What do you mean by leaving these fainting, suffering men to go until noon with nothing to eat, and no attention?" With that, she threw him out of the hospital and made charges against him that led to his dismissal. Later, when the infuriated surgeon brought countercharges directly to General Sherman, who knew and admired the work of Mary Ann Bickerdyke, Sherman is reported to have told the disgraced doctor, "I can't help you. She has more power than I—she outranks me." Bickerdyke herself made a similar claim during the battle of Shiloh when another surgeon disputed her right to act as a one-woman diet kitchen dispensing hot soup, tea, crackers, whiskey, and water to wounded men in the field. "I have received my authority from the Lord God Almighty," she told the doctor. "Have you anything that ranks higher than that?"

Bickerdyke's wrath knew no bounds when it came to dealing with those who stole food. At Cairo, she found out who was stealing food by mixing a tartar emetic with some stewed peaches she left in plain sight. Not long after, she was greeted with the sound of retching and groaning from guilty cooks, waiters, stewards, and wardmasters. She warned them that if they kept on stealing food

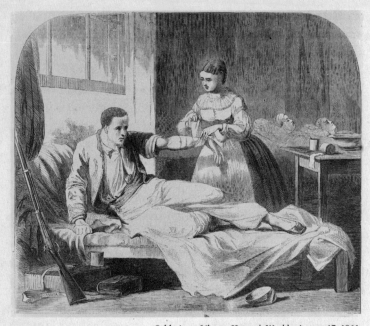

Schlesinger Library; Harper's Weekly, *August 17, 1861.*

A volunteer nurse tending a wounded Union soldier in Washington, D.C.

meant for soldiers, they might eat something seasoned with rats-bane. Equally extreme were the lengths to which Bickerdyke went to find nourishing eatables for her wounded soldiers in enemy territory. On one memorable occasion, after searching Tennessee farms in vain for enough fresh milk and eggs, she took off for St. Louis by way of Memphis and returned at the head of a procession of more than a hundred cows and a thousand chickens. "These are loyal cows and hens," she told the Tennessee farmers, "none of your miserable trash that give chalk and water for milk, and lay foul-smelling eggs." Bickerdyke's animals became a new breed of camp followers, supplying troops with wholesome products wherever they traveled in the South.

Her resourceful approach to providing food was also evident in dishes she invented when supplies were limited. Her favorite postoperative offering was "panado," a mush made up of whiskey, hot water, and brown sugar into which she crumbled hardtack. Bickerdyke took pardonable pride in the way she was able to prepare delicious food from an all but empty larder. "When I get home, boys," she told her satisfied patients, "I shall publish a starvation cook-book, containing receipts for making delicious dishes out of nothing."

Bickerdyke never fulfilled her promise, but another Union nurse did. This was Annie Wittenmyer, a well-to-do Iowa widow who compiled *A Collection of Recipes for the Use of Special Diet Kitchens in Military Hospitals* (1864) for the U.S. Christian Commission, a group whose work complemented the Sanitary Commission by training nurses to oversee hospital cooking under the direction of surgeons in charge. After the war, she became the first president of the Women's Christian Temperance Union and later lobbied Congress for a home and pensions for former Union nurses. "It is the verdict of history that this system of special-diet kitchens saved thousands of lives," Wittenmyer declared: "During the last eighteen months of the war, over two million rations were issued monthly from this long line of special-diet kitchens, established, many of them, almost under the guns."

Initially distributed to a hundred "gentlewomen" recruited to supervise diet kitchens, Wittenmyer's cookbook holds no surprises for anyone the least bit acquainted with sickroom cookery. There are light broths and soups, many puddings, rice dishes, egg dishes, and the standard milk punch. Much of the dietary wisdom passed on by Wittenmyer was gleaned from Florence Nightingale's *Notes on Nursing,* including the author's endorsement of the nutritive power of milk over beef extract, and her stress on allowing the patient to determine his own nutritional needs. "The patient's stomach must be its own chemist," Nightingale wisely noted.

Wittenmyer also relied on the work of Mrs. Winslow, a contemporary cookbook writer who published an almanac cookbook in pamphlet form each year throughout the 1860s. The recipes were for standard nineteenth-century fare such as scalloped oysters, milk puddings and sauces, ginger snaps, and gingerbread. But not all of Wittenmyer's ideas and recipes are derivative. She understood the place of appetite in determining how standard dishes like rice and beef hash should be cooked. "Many soldiers have lived on rice so long prepared so badly that the taste of rice is disgusting to them," she observed, "and although a healthy article of food for the sick, and best suited to many patients, it is rejected by them with loathing unless the taste is disguised in some way." Her own common sense shows through in her advice against such false economies as cooking wormy fruit: "Sometimes, persons, from considerations of economy, or fear of censure, do not separate the flawy, worm-eaten fruit from the good," she warns, "and, after adding sugar and spices, have to throw the whole away, because they cannot be eaten." In the same spirit, she saves the reputation of beef hash by warning, "Hash should never be made of dry, stale, or gristly meat. The common habit of using meat unfit to be eaten, and old boiled potatoes, in making hash, has created a just prejudice against it." Always practical, she offers a recipe for chicken soup thickened with the ever-present hardtack.

ANNIE WITTENMYER'S CHICKEN SOUP

From A Collection of Recipes for the Use of Special
Diet Kitchens in Military Hospitals *(1864)*

1 large stewing fowl, jointed   ⅔ cup cream or milk
1 gallon cold water   Salt and pepper
6 pulverized hardtack crackers

Skin the chicken. Cover with the water and cook until done (approximately 1 to 2 hours, depending on the toughness of the chicken). Skim off all fat. Add crackers and cream or milk. Season with salt and pepper.

After the war and for years to come, the proper feeding of hospitalized patients remained a sketchy affair left largely to the initiatives of individual women. Sarah Tyson Rorer, a cooking teacher and cookbook author from Philadelphia, is credited with being the country's first dietitian, largely because in 1879 she taught a course on diet for the sick at the Woman's Medical College when no one else could be found to do so. In the 1880s she established a cooking school, where she soon added a special diet kitchen at the request of local doctors. They would send in prescriptions and in return receive well-cooked food they deemed appropriate for special diseases. Soon Mrs. Rorer was invited by the Medical School of the University of Pennsylvania to lecture to fourth-year medical students. Women who attended her cooking school would go on to specialize in dietetics, working in hospitals around the country.

Similarly in Boston, after the Boston Cooking School was established, successive teachers, including Fannie Merritt Farmer, taught invalid cookery and offered a course for doctors. Carrie Dearborn, an instructor in physiology at the school, described the school's philosophy in an 1894 article written for the *New England Kitchen Magazine:* "Trifles assume tremendous proportions when one is ailing, and as much attention should be given to the serving of foods as to the administration of medicines." This was the same message delivered by women who had cared for patients during the Civil War. In 1903, the Boston Cooking School became connected with Simmons College, where courses in feeding the sick were taught along with other courses in the home economics curriculum.

The home economics field had been established by Ellen Swallow Richards, who had helped set up the nation's first school lunch program in Boston in 1894 and was soon consulting with hospitals about institutional diet. As women were trained, they became interested in the fledgling field of dietetics and taught other women to work with patients who required special foods, giving close attention to such diseases as diabetes and nephritis that could be helped with proper diet therapy. By 1910, knowledge of calories helped systematize thinking, and demonstrations of 100-calorie portions of various foods became part of classroom teaching.

By 1917, when the United States was again involved in war, the American Red Cross trained and provided dietitians to serve in base hospitals, and the American Dietetic Association was founded that same year. At the time of the armistice in November 1918, there were 356 dietitians in the service. Today there are 70,000 members of the association, an indication of how the field has grown. Those who work in hospitals either work directly with patients as diet therapists or work as administrators who plan appropriate meals for the sick and oversee their preparation. By now the field has become highly specialized, with practitioners focusing on therapies for specific problems—for example, diabetes, cardiovascular and renal diseases, and obesity. More changes affecting the profession are now afoot. Less diet therapy is taking place in hospitals because patient stays have become so abbreviated. Also, instead of hiring registered dietitians, many hospitals are using outside corporations that use computers to plan menus and then deliver the food. And now that nutrition is of growing importance and health plans are starting to cover costs for diet therapies, doctors are setting up lucrative practices to deal with nutrition-related ailments. Ironically, the success of this field, fought for by generations of concerned women, beginning with the Civil War, may lead to its being taken out of their hands.

They Dieted for Our Sins

America's Food Reformers

The plump cheeks of Elizabeth Cady Stanton, a leading intellectual and prominent reformer for abolition and suffrage, attested to the fact that she enjoyed a square meal at the end of the day. More evidence of Stanton's hearty appetite can be found in her memory of her first meeting in 1840 with Angelina and Theodore Weld, well-known fellow reformers who lived on a farm in New Jersey in a house she described as cheerless, "destitute of all tasteful, womanly touches." Tired from her journey, Stanton longed for hot tea or coffee, and possibly a beefsteak with the usual trimmings. As she woefully recalled, "They came not." Instead she was served cold oatmeal and apples, with only water to drink.

How did this famous abolitionist couple become partisans of such a pinched and meager form of vegetarianism? In fact their stringent regimen had become as much a part of the life of mid-nineteenth-century American reformers as would the brown rice diet of the counterculture movement of the 1960s. The Welds' religious background did not forbid them from serving meat or other more flavorful eatables. Rather, their austere diet was part of a doctrine set down by food reformer Sylvester Graham (1794–1851), whose health principles appealed to many mid-nineteenth-century Americans. While other health reformers were flourishing at this time, Graham's focus on food set him apart.

Known now only for the brown cracker that bears his name, Graham was the forerunner of a long line of crusaders, crackpots, and enterprising capitalists who have shaped the food habits of all Americans. The popularity of his Spartan diet came in part because for most Americans in the early nineteenth century it seemed easier to fix oneself than so much else in the country that needed change. Slavery was still a social norm. Women throughout the United States were not allowed to vote or own property, and were expected to wear cage-like corsets and long skirts that could easily catch fire near open hearths. Children were considered the property of their parents. Medical practice of the day was primitive. Spittoons for chewing tobacco attested to the general indifference to public sanitation. And the typical American diet was not much better, consisting largely of corn, pork, molasses, puddings and pies, and potatoes cooked in lard, with plenty of whiskey to wash it all down.

To Graham and his immediate successors, no cause was more urgent than vegetarianism and the overall improvement of American diets. Starting in his day, comprehensive nutritional plans of the most radical kind were pushed by evangelical religious leaders, then health food experimenters and commercial entrepreneurs, and eventually by trained scientists and specialists in home economics, nutrition, and modern weight control. Early advocates for changing America's eating habits were at least as outspoken and militant as other reformers of their times who were intent on curing major social and political ills. Indeed, the proliferation of modern-day diet gurus, stridently telling us what constitutes good nutrition and a healthy way of life, had its historical root in the Age of Jackson, when middle-class Americans first started looking to self-proclaimed experts to explain what they should and should not eat and drink to enjoy long and robust lives.

Sylvester Graham, a Connecticut-born clergyman, was the prototype for America's early food reformers, and his preaching and writings had a major impact on subsequent diet authorities. As the linchpin of his campaign, which emphasized vegetarianism, temperance, and sexual abstinence, Graham seized upon the sorry state of commercial bread that had begun to enter the New England marketplace after the 1830s. Advances in technology had made possible new milling techniques that produced quick-baking wheat bread that was light, thin-crusted, and often adulterated with additives like sulfate of zinc, sulfate of copper, chalk, and alum. In reaction, Graham crusaded for a return to home-baked brown bread made of wheat flour that included bran.

For Graham, the departure from bread made "within the precincts of our own thresholds" represented not only a breakdown in nutritional quality but a loss of the primal connection between mother and child. In an otherwise dry little book entitled *Treatise on Bread and Bread-Making*, Graham rhapsodized on a mythical American past:

> Who that can look back 30 or 40 years to those blessed days of New England's prosperity and happiness, when our good mothers used to make the family bread, but can well remember how long and how patiently those excellent matrons stood over their bread troughs, kneading and molding their dough? And who with such recollections cannot also well remember the delicious bread that those mothers used invariably to set before them: There was a natural sweetness and richness in it which made it always desireable; and which we cannot now vividly recollect, without feeling a strong desire to partake of such bread as our mothers used to make for us in the days of our childhood.

Graham was shrewd in making bread a fundamental part of his philosophy. Throughout much of European and American history,

bread was not only "the staff of life," a mainstay of human sustenance, but a focal point for the center of social and political conflict. Governments established regulations about its purity and
citizens rioted when prices rose. But Graham's fantasy of an ideal
childhood is a marked contrast to the bleak reality of his experiences as a lonely and essentially motherless child. Graham was
the youngest of seventeen children when his seventy-two-year-old
father died and left his mother to care not only for her own but
several of the ten children from her late husband's first marriage.
If she did find time to bake bread for this brood, it did not keep her
from becoming mentally deranged. She was sent away, and the
young Sylvester Graham spent the rest of his youth passed from
one relative to another. No wonder he later longed for a stable
household where a loving mother made old-fashioned coarse,
crusty bread for her family.

Graham's work as a preacher and temperance leader helped
him become an articulate missionary for his special brand of food
reform. He found Biblical evidence that God did not intend for the
bran to be separated from the wheat in the making of bread, giving him license to attach moral superiority to home-baked bread.
His support for vegetarian diets was similarly supported by the
Bible, but he later came close to anticipating Darwinian theory
when he concluded that humans were physiologically comparable
to orangutans and should therefore eat the same natural food.

More often, Graham's quasi-scientific notions about diet re-
sembled the medieval doctrine of the humors, in which it was assumed that different balances of bodily fluids (blood, phlegm, and
black and yellow bile) determined human temperaments and that
these in turn could be aggravated or assuaged by certain foods.
Graham likewise believed that an improper diet aroused the
body's organs in ways that were harmful to overall health. He
feared that meat and hot, spicy foods, as well as too much food, inevitably created an excess of digestive activity, causing sexual
arousal that could only sap vitality and well-being. "All kinds of
stimulating and heating substances; high-seasoned food; rich

dishes; the free use of flesh; and even the excess of aliment; all, more or less—and some to a very great degree—increase the concupiscent excitability and sensibility of the genital organs."

For Graham, nocturnal emissions, masturbation, and marital sex beyond procreative activity weakened and damaged the body by overstimulation. To avoid these practices he prescribed not only his signature grain-based diet but also cold showers, hard mattresses, fresh air, and exercise. Paralysis, senility, blindness, and genital afflictions were some of the diseases he catalogued as caused by masturbation, though in Graham's time they mostly resulted from syphilis and gonorrhea. He likewise devised long, frightening lists of ills that would befall young people who engaged in "lascivious day-dreams" and "amorous reveries," and married couples who indulged in "sexual excess." Husbands and wives who copulated more than once a month could expect such afflictions as:

> Languor, lassitude, muscular relaxation, general debility and heaviness, depression of spirits, loss of appetite, indigestion, faintness and sinking at the pit of the stomach, increased susceptibilities of the skin and lungs to all the atmospheric changes, feebleness of circulation, chilliness, head-ache, melancholy, hypochondria, hysterics, feebleness of all the sense, impaired vision, loss of sight, weakness of the lungs, nervous cough, pulmonary consumption, disorders of the liver and kidneys, urinary difficulties, disorders of the genital organs, weakness of the brain, loss of memory, epilepsy, insanity, apoplexy—and extreme feebleness and early death of offspring.

Graham was not the first to issue puritanical warnings against self-abuse, impure thoughts, and sexual excess in marriage. His emphasis fell less on the moral sinfulness of unrestrained sexuality, however, than on the catastrophic harm it could do to the body.

Graham's philosophy had a place for the carrot as well as the stick. The best way to curb sexual appetite and enjoy a long, healthy life was to live "entirely on the products of the vegetable kingdom and pure water." Nocturnal emissions, for example, could be cured by sticking to the cereals he recommended.

> Farinaceous food, properly prepared, is incomparably the best ali-
> ment for such a sufferer; and good bread, made of coarsely-ground,
> unbolted wheat, or rye-meal, and hominy, made of cracked wheat,
> or rye, or Indian corn, are among the very best articles of diet that
> such a person can use.

To be avoided were all condiments and spices such as pepper, ginger, mustard, cinnamon, and horseradish, which he considered "all highly exciting and exhausting." Dairy products—including milk, eggs, and butter—were not altogether forbidden but were supposed to be used only sparingly and carefully. Cheese was permitted if it was mild and not aged. Coffee, tea, alcohol, and tobacco were considered poisons, as were drugs offered by physicians and other medical practitioners. "All medicine, as such, is itself an evil," Graham insisted, at a time when all medical licensing laws were rescinded or unenforced and any quack could call himself a doctor.

Graham was not alone in denouncing orthodox medicine of his day. "With few exceptions," Oliver Wendell Holmes would memorably remark, "if the whole materia medica, as now used, could sink to the bottom of the sea, it would be all the better for mankind, and all the worse for the fishes." Nor was Graham the only health reformer offering drug-free alternatives to contemporary medical practice. It was during this period that other now popular forms of nontraditional medicine took root: the homeopathy of Samuel Hahnemann (1755–1843), which favored herbal remedies for disease; the botanic medicine of Samuel Thompson (1769–1843), which looked to folk medicine and steam-heat treatments; and hydropathy with mineral or spring water applications, a treatment first popularized as a cure-all by a Silesian peasant named Vincenz Preissnitz (1799–1851). Mesmerism and phrenology were also offered as cures for a variety of mental and physical illnesses.

For a time, Graham achieved unique popularity as an evangelical diet reformer. He attracted thousands of followers, who attended his lectures and adhered to his dietetic plan, known as the Graham System. In Boston and New York, Graham temperance boardinghouses for men sprang up, offering meals based on his program. His *Lectures on the Science of Human Life*, published in 1839, became a leading text on health reform. At the same time, he had many detractors who ridiculed or remonstrated against his reforms. A few years before, his followers had to defend him from a mob of Boston bakers and butchers who violently disapproved of his warnings about the inferiority of commercial white bread and the perilous effects of eating meat. By the late 1840s, moreover, Graham's pronouncements on diet had begun to fall on deaf, or at least fewer ears, and his recommendations became more and more subject to derision. Ralph Waldo Emerson disparaged Graham as the "poet of bran and pumpkins," and a month before his death, his hometown newspaper ridiculed him as "the philosopher of sawdust pudding." In the end, the regimen he advocated did little to help his own health, which was never very good and rapidly declined. By the time he was forty-five he had retired to rural Massachusetts to recover from a lifetime of suffering from chronic nervous collapse. His wife, who rejected his strict diet, tried to get him to eat more fully and joyfully, but for the most part he stuck to his abstemious menu and died in 1851 at fifty-seven, a broken and disappointed man.

Graham would have been aggrieved to know that his name would be attached to sugary crackers used for s'mores, where they are topped with melted chocolate and marshmallows, or crushed with butter and sugar and used as a platform for assorted cream pies. He used to condemn such indulgences as "among the most pernicious articles of human aliment." He would be happier to see his name on bags of the course-ground wheat flour that is still used nowadays to make the kind of bread he considered both wholesome and holy.

Graham's teachings particularly struck a chord with Ellen Harmon White (1827–1915), who outdid the New England preacher by becoming, at the age of eighteen, the cofounder and visionary prophet of the Seventh Day Adventist Church, a worldwide religion that institutionalized vegetarianism and other Grahamite health initiatives.

As with Graham, early years of illness had an important effect on Ellen White. Born Ellen Harmon in Maine, she was not more than ten when she was struck in the face by a heavy stone thrown by an older girl and became so debilitated that she was unable to

---

A MODIFIED GRAHAM BREAD

1 package yeast
  (not fast-acting)
¼ cup lukewarm water
2 teaspoons brown sugar
2 teaspoons salt
2 tablespoons butter

⅓ cup molasses
1 cup evaporated milk,
  scalded
1 cup boiling water
4 cups whole-wheat flour
1 to 2 cups white flour

In a small bowl, mix the yeast with the water. Add the brown sugar. In a large bowl, combine the salt, butter, molasses, milk, and boiling water. Stir well. Let cool to room temperature and add the yeast mixture. Add the whole-wheat flour and just enough of the white flour so that dough is not sticky and can be kneaded. Knead for 7 minutes. Let rise until doubled (2 hours). Knead 1 minute. Cut in half, shape into loaves, and place in buttered 9-inch pans. Let rise until doubled (1½ hours). Bake at 400°F for 20 minutes. Lower oven to 350°F and bake 35 minutes longer. Brush surface with butter and turn out on a wire rack to cool.

continue with formal schooling. Sickness also plagued her adult life. She and her husband, James White, a cofounder of the church, experienced chronic illnesses and lost two of their four sons to disease.

Despite such setbacks Ellen White served for more than seventy years as an author, speaker, and administrator of the Seventh Day Adventist Church, where she was—and still is—believed to have enjoyed God's special guidance as a spiritual leader. The Adventists evolved from the teachings of William Miller, a Baptist preacher and former army captain in the War of 1812 who foretold that Jesus would return to earth on October 22, 1844. When the date came and went without event, it was ever after referred to as "the Great Disappointment" by Miller's followers, many of whom left the Millerite movement in disillusion. A small group, however, struggled on and established the Seventh Day Adventist Church, convinced that Miller's prophecy meant that Christ on that date had started to prepare Heaven for the Second Coming and the Day of Judgment, and that these events would occur when the preparation was complete. In 1845, the eighteen-year-old Ellen White and her husband James adopted this interpretation of the New Testament. The couple added other readings of the Bible, including the Millerite Joseph Bates's scriptural justification for celebrating the Sabbath on the last day of the week instead of the first, a rite that was thought to encourage Christ's return.

In addition to religious reforms, Ellen White advocated essentially the same diet that had already been vigorously promoted by Sylvester Graham and other reformers, including strict vegetarianism and the avoidance of alcohol, tobacco, coffee, and tea, as well as medical drugs of any kind. Fresh air, sunshine, exercise, and lots of water were also borrowed from Graham. And like Graham, White advocated doing away with restrictive clothing, going so far as to endorse the loose-fitting reform dress made popular by Amelia Bloomer, which featured comparatively short skirts with pants.

White justified vegetarianism for Adventists on both religious and psychological grounds: "God gave our parents the food He designed the race should eat. It was contrary to His plan to have the life of any creature taken." Years later she would put Genesis aside and point to the harm it seemed to her meat eating does to those who slaughter animals and witness the killing. "Think of the cruelty meat-eating involves," she wrote, "and its effect on those who inflict and those who behold it. How it destroys the tenderness with which we should regard those creatures of God."

In 1866 White established the Western Health Reform Institute as a retreat for sick and suffering Adventists. Her model for the Institute was a Danville, New York, sanitarium started by James Caleb Jackson, another food reformer, who combined Graham's diet with hydropathy, the then highly popular "water cure" that was achieved by drenching residents in icy cold water via showers, tubs, soaks, and wet packs. Adventist history has it that Ellen White visited Danville on the advice of an angel, and that there she had a vision telling her to duplicate Jackson's facility in Battle Creek, Michigan, the new home of the Adventist Church. Her own treatment center advertised familiar strategies for improving health:

> In the treatment of the sick at this Institution, no drugs whatever will be administered, but such means employed as NATURE can best use in her recuperative work, such as Water, Air, Light, Heat, Food, Sleep, Rest, Recreation, etc. Our tables will be furnished with a strictly healthful diet, consisting of Vegetables, Grains and Fruits, which are found in great abundance and variety in this State. And it will be the aim of the Faculty, that all who spend any length of time at this Institute shall go to their home instructed as to the right mode of living, and the best methods of home treatment.

Potential patients were also assured that "WHATEVER MAY BE THE NATURE OF THEIR DISEASE, IF CURABLE, THEY CAN BE CURED HERE."

Adventists throughout the country began flocking to Michigan in pursuit of relief from ailments American medicine of the day could not help. Over the next seventy-five years, the institute would overcome a variety of financial and administrative obstacles and expand exponentially to become the Battle Creek Sanitarium, the largest and best-known health resort in the United States. The San, as it came to be called, would also become a model for modern American health spas.

To head up the institute, Ellen White appointed John Henry Kellogg, who would become the next major figure to spread Graham's vegetarian legacy and would forever change America's breakfasts. His work was cut out for him, because throughout the nineteenth century and even before, Americans had shown a prodigious appetite for meat. Frontiersmen had eaten such huge amounts of buffalo—as much as ten pounds a day per man—that the herds were in danger of extinction. And Americans ate meat at almost every meal. Pigs, first brought to the new world by Spaniards, had become immensely popular because the animals were relatively easy to care for and feed. Their slaughtered parts took well to curing, so that bacon and ham were staples that showed up regularly on the breakfast table. But beef, lamb, and game were also readily available and relished by Americans. Typical breakfasts could be six or seven courses including beefsteaks with sauce, ham, grouse, fried fish, fried potatoes, omelets, and an array of breads and fruit.

Such breakfasts are today seen mainly in hotel dining rooms, where they are served up as weekend buffet brunches and infrequently consumed in entirety. These days, the typical American breakfast is grain-based—usually cold cereal—along with fruit or juice and other beverages. This transformation of what Americans consume each morning has come about largely through the work of John Henry Kellogg.

Kellogg displayed the classic profile of the food reformer, experiencing chronic sickliness as a child that fueled a quest for ways to establish and maintain better health. His reading of Sylvester Graham created an epiphany, causing him to convert to vegetari-

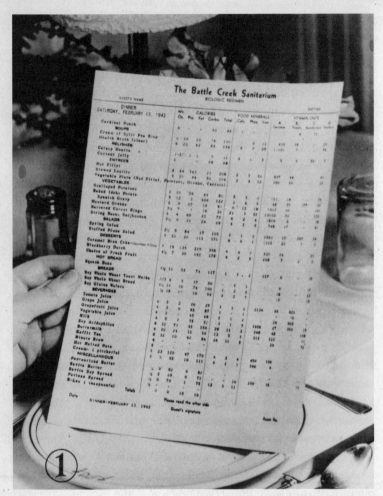

Bentley Historical Library, John Kellogg Papers

A vegetarian dinner menu from the Battle Creek Sanitarium.

anism and a largely grain-based diet. But to make the Kellogg Sanitarium in Battle Creek a broad success, Kellogg had to find a way of making the grain-based diet more palatable, so he invented or popularized some eighty grain and nut products, the most enduring being peanut butter and flaked breakfast food. Kellogg's first health treat is also still quite popular. Originally described as "a mixture of oatmeal and cornmeal, baked into biscuits, then ground to bits," it was first called Granula. The name was later changed to Granola when Kellogg was successfully sued by James Caleb Jackson, founder of the Danville spa, who had used "Granula" for his own, less pleasant-tasting health food. (Jackson's Granula was a stone-like wafer made out of Graham flour.) Besides borrowing product names, Kellogg was not above stealing innovations in natural foods developed by patients at the San. Among these was a Denver visitor named Henry Perky, who came up with little wheat cakes that he called Shredded Wheat. Kellogg dismissed the product, claiming it was "like eating a whisk broom." At the same time, he tried to develop his own version and came up with Granose, a flaked wheat product he later falsely proclaimed was "the first of the modern breakfast foods."

A number of Kellogg's other innovations were actually surrogates for food and drink forbidden to Adventists. These included Caramel Cereal Coffee, which Kellogg himself described as "a very poor substitute for a very poor thing," and two meat replacements: Protose, an unappetizing grain version of beefsteak, and Nuttose, a similarly unsatisfying imitation of veal. Kellogg's more successful nut product, peanut butter, is said to have been discovered at the San when an employee who was scolded by the doctor for ruining a peanut recipe angrily hit one of the nuts with a hammer and found that it turned into a palatable paste. That claim is thought to be untrue, for the product was already in use, and no one knows who invented it.

Kellogg's wife, Ella, played an important backstage role in the development of many of the grain-and-nut products served at the San and later sold to the consumer public. Stationed in an experimental kitchen, she was assigned the tedious job of endlessly testing grain recipes to ensure that they were dry enough to avoid becoming moldy but not so hard that they would break teeth. (One of the Spa's clients actually did break her dentures on a piece of zwieback toast.) Nor was operating this kitchen Ella Kellogg's only job. Though their marriage was famously celibate, the Kelloggs collected more than forty orphaned and abandoned children, whose care was largely the responsibility of Mrs. Kellogg. She effectively became a cartoon of what was expected of most nineteenth-century American women, chained to a kitchen that was also a laboratory and to a nursery that was actually a foster home and orphan asylum. One can only hope that among the many duties she performed for her husband, she was not the subject of an experiment in which Dr. Kellogg reported that he "found the application of pure carbolic acid to the clitoris an excellent means of allaying the abnormal excitement." (For promoting abstinence in men, the doctor recommended circumcision performed early on without anesthetic, "as the brief pain attending the operation will have a salutary effect upon the mind.")

ELLA KELLOGG'S SAVORY NUT LOAF
(From Science in the Kitchen, *1892)*

2 cups ground zwieback
1 cup ground walnuts or
   pecans

½ teaspoon salt
1 teaspoon dried herb (sage,
   mint, or celery seed)

Mix ingredients thoroughly and cover with boiling water. Allow to stand for a few minutes and add more water so that mixture is moist but not runny. Turn into a bread pan and bake at 350°F for one hour. Can be served hot with a tomato sauce or cold in slices, with a garnish of lemon sliced thin, or with lettuce salad.

Ella Kellogg's brown, dense, nut-based recipe is typical of what was found in vegetarian homes and restaurants before the 1970s. Mollie Katzen's popular *Moosewood Cookbook* (1977), with its appetizing use of fresh vegetables and fruits, brightened the image of vegetarian fare, a tradition advanced by Deborah Madison in subsequent vegetarian cookbooks.

Bentley Historical Library, John Kellogg Papers

The Battle Creek Sanitarium's hygienic kitchen serving dishes developed and tested by Ella Kellogg.

When not inventing new foods or advocating sexual repression, Kellogg was developing electrical or mechanical gadgets designed to improve health. One of his favorite innovations was an electro-mechanical exercise horse, a model of which wound up in the White House during the presidency of Calvin Coolidge. He also developed or adapted a number of vibrating devices for improving blood circulation and digestion, including a chair that oscillated twenty times a second and a vibrating belt that became a standard for years in weight-reducing salons. Other inventions included the

Dynamometer, a strength-testing instrument that helped determine appropriate muscular exercises, an arc-light battery that anticipated the modern tanning salon, and the first menthol inhaler used to clear nasal passages.

The contraption that may have been closest to Kellogg's heart was identical to a German automatic enema machine that could flush fifteen gallons of water though a human bowel in seconds. No aspect of the San has been more commented on or mocked by contemporary observers than the enemas Kellogg insisted be regularly administered to clients. These ritual purifications are featured in T. Coraghessan Boyle's novelistic treatment of the San in *The Road to Wellville* (1993) and the film of the same name, where Anthony Hopkins plays a bowel-obsessed doctor in a broad par-

Bentley Historical Library, John Kellogg Papers

Male guests in diaper-like apparel working out at the San on elaborate exercise machines.

ody of Kellogg. (The title of the novel and movie was actually a favorite expression of Kellogg's competitor, C. W. Post, and the title of a pamphlet Post included with his rival coffee substitute, Postum.) As Kellogg saw it, these purgings rid the body of the putrified residue of undigested meat. After each enema, oral and anal ingestions of yogurt, another natural food favored at the Spa, replaced what Kellogg called "the intestinal flora."

It is easy to dismiss Kellogg as an arrogant quack with a gift for public relations. In fact the San leader was also a physician and esteemed surgeon with a remarkable record of successful operations and postoperative dietary care. He is reputed to have performed over 22,000 abdominal operations in his lifetime, the last at the age of eighty-eight, with not one fatality in this long career.

Though he reaped rewards from his innovations in food, Kellogg resisted the temptation to turn himself into a full-time businessman and relied more for his considerable wealth on his income from the San, his copious writings and public lectures, and his gifts as a surgeon. In 1884 he offered the rights to Granola to the Adventist Church, telling Ellen White that the proceeds from sales of the product could support the entire work of the denomination. She rejected the offer on the grounds that it would interfere with the Church's primary mission of preparing for the Second Coming. A decade later she would also spurn Kellogg's offer of the rights to his best-known product, Corn Flakes, on the same grounds. It was only after Kellogg was removed as head of the San following a falling-out with the Adventists that the doctor allowed his younger brother, William K. Kellogg, to market his inventions aggressively. Too aggressively for Dr. Kellogg, it seems, for the brothers also had a bitter falling-out that lasted the rest of their long lives—both died at the age of ninety-one. William Kellogg named and eventually took over ownership and control of the Battle Creek Toasted Corn Flake Company that become the basis of the Kellogg cereal empire.

The principal inheritors of Sylvester Graham's legacy were the

Kelloggs and their great rival, C. W. Post, who not only built his own breakfast food empire but pioneered the promotion of his products through national advertising. Post had come to Kellogg's sanitarium to cure his chronic dyspepsia and he stayed long enough to learn the Kelloggs' formula for success. Post set himself up as a kind of mental healer who claimed he was able to cure not only his own ills but those of others by encouraging them to believe in the healing power of their minds. He would soon make the same claims for his products. Grape-Nuts, one of Post's earliest breakfast cereals, was marketed as a brain food that could also cure malaria and tuberculosis.

The efforts to cure oneself through diet would find more scientific basis in 1889, twenty years after the opening of the Battle Creek Sanitarium. In that year, a group of progressive Bostonians established the New England Kitchen as an attempt to uplift the poor by teaching them to eat food that was cheap, nourishing, and hygienic. By then, information about calories and the composition of foods had been discovered, leading to a movement toward "scientific cooking," the backbone of the newly developed home economics profession. The old days were over. Instead of inspiring people to take control of their dietary fates by prescribing quirky forms of abstinence, the new leaders were actually offering healthy food alternatives grounded in science. Whether these alternatives were accepted was another matter.

The founders of the New England Kitchen—chemist Ellen Swallow Richards, businessman Edward Atkinson, and Mary Hinman Abel, a domestic scientist—believed that the waves of immigrants entering Boston could be hastened in their assimilation by eating Yankee food. They worked hard to plan and raise funds for a take-out restaurant that offered at low cost such dishes as cornmeal mush, chowders made with pork, and casseroles of minced meat served with white sauce. Cheap, sanitary, and nutritious, these foods seemed to the founders entirely suitable for weaning immigrants from salami sandwiches and other garlic-laden foods repulsive to New England noses. No consideration was given to the attachments people had to their customary foods, let alone the fact that dietary laws would forbid immigrant Jews from even entering the decidedly nonkosher New England Kitchen. Not surprisingly, Boston's foreign-born and working poor chose instead to cook their own dishes in their own kitchens, dooming this experiment in social engineering. "The number of those who are intelligent enough to appreciate the nature of the food is too few," said the disappointed and disparaging Mary Hinman Abel. But the last word came from an anonymous Irish woman who said of the Kitchen's food, "I don't want to eat what's good for me; I'd ruther eat what I'd ruther."

Americans have always preferred to decide for themselves what foods they will eat. It was one thing to be persuaded into new choices by the fervent Sylvester Graham, but quite another to be manipulated by reformers who felt they knew best. Americans are still being persuaded that something is wrong with their eating habits, but these days, the emphasis is just as much on body weight and appearance as on questions of health. The modern heirs to Sylvester Graham are diet doctors, such gurus as Robert Atkins, Dean Ornish, and in earlier years, Irwin Stillman and Herman Tarnower, whose diet books periodically grace the bestseller list.

Just before Christmas every year, the ephemeral nature of these books comes home to me when I stage a book sale at the Schlesinger Library to sell off duplicate books, mainly cookbooks, donated by friends of the library who are happy to see us pull in some extra revenue. At the start of the sale, a mob of eager customers—most of them collectors and dealers—run in and snatch up classics they know have value, including anything by Julia Child, James Beard, or Elizabeth David. This gang is followed by a steady stream of holiday shoppers, who often find just the right cookie book for the aunt who bakes all her Christmas gifts, or a book about cheese for the cousin who is reputed to be a gourmet. By the end of the day, we are left with a pathetic heap of books that nobody wants, principally diet books and diet cookbooks, the latter of which are usually spinoffs of the popular diet books of the year before. The books invariably promise that each will be the last diet book anyone will ever need, yet publishers bring out still more of them every year.

Why are some of these books such successes? And more puzzling, why do the books keep coming when the diets of even the most popular of the books keep failing their hopeful buyers and finding their way to me? My guess is that a kind of double-think takes control of chronic dieters, allowing them to approach each new book with both battle-scarred skepticism and unquenchable hope for salvation from overweight. Just as Dr. Kellogg's patients in the San looked to him for better health through diet, diet book readers look for a new leader to show the way to a svelte body. But perhaps something else may be going on. "Just reading diet books relieves some anxiety about one's weight," observes the philosopher Richard Watson, noting wryly that the books provide "light reading for moderately heavy people." I would also add, since I freely admit being a habitual reader of diet books, that they actually provide a lot of fun and pleasure if you know where to look.

Diet books are wonderful barometers of popular culture. In recent years, for example, a number of the books have reverted to religion by offering weight-loss solutions that are part of a fundamentalist or evangelical view of life. They would have us dieting for Jesus or looking to Buddha for ways to abate a ravenous appetite. And New Age diet books now try to persuade us not to feed our inner child with junk food but to substitute meatlessness and meditation for McDonald's. The latest diet literature to date tends toward the psychological, offering techniques of behavior modification that encourage readers to take long walks or hot baths whenever they feel the need to raid the refrigerator. Either that or they will advise those of us who are overweight to forgive ourselves. The message in such therapy-oriented diet books is "It's not your fault!" That message is also implied, if not directly stated, in books that show readers how to tailor diets to their astrological signs or blood types.

Yet in essence all diet books are the same. The basic formula goes something like this: Establish your weight-loss credentials, provide a personal narrative, condemn competing books, make the pitch for your unique diet, provide motivation, present the actual diet (in four or five pages), and then summarize and promise success. Authors are generally doctors, nutritionists, psychiatrists or psychologists, medical journalists, or (my favorite) celebrities who have overcome their weight problems. To bolster their credibility, the books will include forewords and testimonials by colleagues, patients, or other celebrities who will invariably rave about the groundbreaking contributions being made by the authors to health, fitness, and beauty and how the diets have changed people's lives. Where the authors lack medical credentials, they will usually refer to some authority in the field, often praised as their guru.

For sheer reading pleasure, the best parts of diet books are the personal testimonials—what I like to call the fat narratives. This is where the authors, including some of the medical professionals, confess to past histories of obesity. They then offer up conversion stories about how they finally saw the light after years of battling their weight and explain why they now want to pass on their hard-won wisdom. The celebrity diet books have the longest and juiciest fat narratives and the least amount of bad science and psychobabble. Among this subspecies of weight-loss literature, I am especially fond of Renee Taylor's *My Life on a Diet: Confessions of a Hollywood Diet Junkie* (1986). Written by a comedy writer and actress whose dress size fluctuated between a short-lived size 6 and a zaftig 16, the book is essentially a show-biz memoir that is driven by Taylor's confession to a lifelong history of binge eating that she claims she was finally able to get under control.

Taylor describes herself as "a woman with the spirit of Audrey Hepburn and the appetite of Orson Welles." A compulsive overeater in a constant quest to become thin, she cannot completely hide the pain in her chronicle of failed diets, but it is alleviated by her irrepressible humor and her conviction, at least at the time the book was written, that she had her weight problem licked. This conviction frees her to offer us a hilarious review of her past attempts to get her appetite under control. She reveals, for example, that before attempting a new diet, she commonly staged what she called the Last-Meal-Before-Diet Binge, imitating the ritual reserved for convicted murderers awaiting next-day execution. Her version was an all-night feast of frankfurters, macaroni and cheese, jelly beans, and after-dinner mints, to mention just a few of her favorite treats. In describing these binges, Taylor compares herself to the marabunda, "those little red killer ants that invade the Brazilian jungle, eating everything in their path—foliage, cattle, even people."

Taylor's fixation on food is reflected in her interest in discovering what others like to eat, the first thing she asks when introduced to people. This has led her to the discovery that meat eaters are aggressive, lovers of sweets are benign, and overeaters like herself are utterly fascinating. Her obsession with food plays itself out in a bizarre story she tells about watching from another table as Fred Astaire ate his lunch in a Beverly Hills coffee shop. When he left the restaurant, Taylor, as a keepsake, snatched two packages of Ry-Krisps the dancer had left behind on his plate. Many years later, when she finally did meet Astaire formally, she said to him, "I have your Ry-Krisp crumbs." She reports, "He smiled at me politely and pretended I was telling him something normal."

Labeling herself a "diet slut," Taylor takes us on an odyssey of her adventures with all of the fashionable diets of her day, along with some she invented, in her desperation to lose the fifty or sixty extra pounds she always gained when she was not performing—weight she had to shed in a hurry when she was hired for a part. We hear of her encounters with the Army Air Force Diet, the Scarsdale Diet, Jack LaLanne's High Protein Diet and the Pritikin Diet, all of them low-calorie regimens she could not stick with. She jokes that one diet, the Champagne Diet, might actually have worked had it not led her into alcoholism. Her own innovations, the pizza diet and the ice cream diet, based on the principle of all-you-want-of-just-one-food, also ended in failure—but at least she was eating things she liked.

Her solution to perpetual bingeing, which she calls the Taylor-Made Diet, is a variation of the one-food-only principle. Under this plan, a different food is consumed each day, at mealtimes only, so that the week provides a daily rotation of fruit, grains, salad, fowl, vegetables, and eggs and meat, with desserts appearing at the end of the week. Taken as a whole, the diet provides balanced meals over the course of a week, but it is hard not to wonder what Taylor did on social occasions when her eccentric eating schedule collided with the rich food that is served at Hollywood

---

RENEE'S SPAGHETTI PRIMAVERA

To be eaten for dinner on an all-grain day—bagels for breakfast, pasta salad for lunch.

1 carrot, cut in strips	2 cloves garlic, chopped
1 cup broccoli	1 large fresh tomato
½ cup fresh or frozen peas	½ cup cream (not milk)
4 tablespoons olive oil	8 ounces spaghetti
½ large green pepper	⅓ cup grated Parmesan cheese
1 small zucchini	Salt and pepper

Steam carrot for 1 minute. Add broccoli and peas and cook 2 minutes longer. Drain and set aside. Heat 2 tablespoons olive oil in frying pan. Saute the pepper, zucchini, and garlic for 2 or 3 minutes until tender but still crisp. Add to the cooked vegetables. Chop the tomato.

Cook the spaghetti according to the package directions. Drain. Place in a bowl and mix with the cooked vegetables. Toss with the Parmesan cheese and cream and season with salt and plenty of pepper.

parties. Whether the diet works or not, the book is worth the cover price: strained through Taylor's comic sensibility, an obsessive eating disorder that is a serious problem becomes laugh-out-loud funny.

My second favorite book of this kind was written by Elizabeth Taylor, who also promoted a "Taylor-Made diet," a rather standard low-calorie plan that is the least interesting part of *Elizabeth Takes Off: On Weight Gain, Weight Loss, Self-Image, and Self-Esteem* (1987). More to my taste is the fat narrative that goes on for fully half of the book and is organized around her first five marriages (six if you count Richard Burton twice). As the media made almost everyone in the world aware of at the time, Liz Taylor was at her heaviest during her marriage to John Warner, the Republican Senator from Virginia—a period when the actress was living as a housewife away from her Hollywood milieu, with nothing to do and a workaholic husband who was practically never at home. She compensated for her loneliness and inactivity by caving in to her hearty appetite, telling herself that what she ate and weighed was no one's business but her own.

But of course her weight had always been everybody's business, particularly the tabloids and television comedians like John Belushi and Joan Rivers. Belushi, who suffered from a few addictions himself besides food, dressed up in drag for a *Saturday Night Live* takeoff that mocked the time the overweight actress almost choked to death on a chicken bone. Rivers, who took cruel glee in seeing this world-class beauty puff up, also took credit for the actress's turnaround, suggesting it was her vicious jokes about Taylor's weight that caused her to slim down. As Elizabeth Taylor describes it, the decision and the accomplishment were hers alone: she left Virginia and a marriage that wasn't working and started on a diet that restored her good looks, leaving us with a fat narrative that is also a heroic tale of self-respect. (That the author later fell into another unfortunate marriage and again gained weight matters not at all to our enjoyment of the book.)

What comes through in Elizabeth Taylor's diet book is what I and others have always found so appealing about the actress apart from her startling beauty—her directness, her resilience and zest for life, and her wonderful good humor:

> Someone told me that Debbie Reynolds kept a photograph of me taken during my fattest period on her refrigerator door. She said it reminded her of what could happen if she charged into the icebox. During the initial stage of my diet I thought, well, if it works for Debbie, maybe it will work for me. . . . If you think a picture of me as Miss Lard will inspire you, go ahead and put it on your refrigerator, I have no objection.

Beyond offering other amusing tips on dieting—like advising women never to allow their weight to go higher than their IQ—Elizabeth Taylor's book comes across less as a diet book than as a spiritual quest in which the actress went literally through thick and thin to retrieve her independence and self-confidence: "I believe my comeback is a victory for everyone who has ever felt unloved, unwanted and ineffectual." In other words, it was for us that Elizabeth Taylor gained and lost all that weight.

What would Sylvester Graham have thought of our country's fixation on fat? Since he singled out gluttony as the worst of the deadly sins, Graham surely would be appalled by the obesity afflicting more than half our citizens. But Graham, unlike the celebrities and psychologists, would link the problem to moral failure. Oversized bodies for him were proof not only of gluttony but of wickedness. (He would see the present-day popularity of coffeehouses as a sign of how far we have strayed, not to mention our national hamburger habit.) As for the diet books, he would surely mourn the loss of a religious foundation in most of them and abhor our selfish reasons for reading them—to look better, have better love lives, and "feel good about ourselves." Those books that limit or renounce meat eating or offer faith-based methods of weight loss may have met with his approval. But *More of Jesus, Less of Me* (by Joan Cavanaugh and Pat Forseth, 1976), a title that brings a smile to the faces of most people, would almost certainly not have amused the humorless Mr. Graham.

Is America beyond salvation? The fine quality of bread now available in America might have saved us in Graham's eyes, were he alive today. After years of packaged sliced bread as the only bread available outside of ethnic bakeries, we now can find honest loaves of crusty whole-wheat bread in ordinary neighborhood supermarkets everywhere. The renaissance of what is called artisanal bread is one of the great food stories of the late twentieth century, and one that certainly would have satisfied Sylvester Graham.

FOUR

The Harvey Girls

*Good Women and Good Food
Civilize the American West*

In the last two decades of the nineteenth century, Frederick Henry Harvey, an enterprising English immigrant, revolutionized food service in the American West by opening a series of railroad depot restaurants that offered food as good as one could get anywhere else in the country. The phrase "Meals by Fred Harvey" became a guarantee not only of delicious food in generous portions at a reasonable price but of outstanding service by welcoming, efficient, and impeccably groomed waitresses called Harvey Girls. From 1883 to the late 1950s, about a hundred thousand of these young women, who ranged in age from eighteen to thirty, were recruited from the East and Midwest. About half of them remained in the Southwest, where many of them married men connected with the railroads or with Western ranching, farming, and mining.

In mid-nineteenth century, before Fred Harvey's innovations, a traveler heading by rail from Kansas City to California was in more danger from malnutrition or food poisoning than from hostile Indians and desperate train robbers. The latter dangers had been dissipated by the U.S. Army and private law enforcement agencies like Pinkerton's, but little or nothing had been done to make rail transportation in the West the equivalent of Eastern trains, which stopped in populous cities where travelers had a choice of decent restaurants and hotels. Western railroads offered little food service and poor sleeping accommodations both on board and at stops along long, desolate routes. What passed for restaurants were nasty shacks that typically offered greasy fried meat, rancid bacon, and stale eggs that had been imported from the East. With the meals came hard, heavy soda biscuits that diners rightly called sinkers and a limited choice of beverages, usually cold tea or tepid black coffee. The food was generally served by surly, unkempt waiters on cracked and chipped crockery laid out on filthy tablecloths.

This level of food service had been a feature of rail transportation for almost half a century before Fred Harvey arrived on the scene. When American train travel began in 1830, speed was its main attraction. Amenities came later. From the beginning Americans loved the excitement and adventure of rail travel, and were willing to put up with appalling inconveniences. Less charmed were visiting English travel writers, who were used to a more mature rail system. These visitors were appalled at the carelessness of American rail transport. One such visiting Briton was surprised by how sanguine his fellow passengers were at a derailing caused by cattle on the tracks: "The locomotive was thrown off and plunged with its head into the gutter, and the baggage car, which followed immediately after, was also thrown off. But the passengers remained undisturbed except that one gentleman, in the fright, turned a summer[sault] out of the window." Not for nothing was a scoop-like metal device called a cowcatcher attached to the front of many early American locomotives.

The locomotives were uncomfortable enough even without accidents. The ride was jarring, the cars were filled with heavy train (or tobacco) smoke, and the floors were covered with spittle from chewing tobacco. Another English writer described the lengths to which passengers went to avoid putting their luggage down on floors that were "moist with expectoration." He had observed a woman who looked to weigh around 250 pounds hand over her carpet bag, which was "almost as plump as herself," to a good-natured gentleman who found himself carrying the heavy bag on his knees for the duration of the trip. The Englishman noted with some surprise that "ladies are used to such attentions in America." Not quite. In the years before Pullman sleeping cars were introduced, passengers slept in their seats or in uncomfortable communal bunks. Special cars that had been set aside for women in the early days of rail travel were later withdrawn so that the ladies were no longer spared the discomfort of tobacco smoke and spittle.

Worst of all, Americans and foreign visitors agreed, was the food served at train stops. Trains in the West covered such a large area that they could afford to pay little attention to the food needs of their customers. A train might move along for many hours without stopping to take on fuel, cargo, and passengers and then make three stops in quick succession. Still worse, at each of the stops, only ten or twenty minutes were allowed for meals, causing travelers to rush from the trains and bolt down what food was to be had at trackside eateries. What they often found were concessions rented by the railroads to anyone who could afford the price, including unscrupulous proprietors who were ready to take advantage of travelers.

Passengers at stopovers were obliged to pay for their meals in advance, making possible some notorious scams. One was to serve food that was too hot to be eaten in the limited time available, so that what travelers left behind could be reheated, scraped onto new plates, and sold to the next trainload of passengers. In a variation of this ploy, concessionaires would conspire with railroad conductors to blow their train whistles signaling departure just as food was being served. In fear of being left behind, passengers would rush to the train, leaving money and meals, the latter to be recycled for the next victims. To avoid this form of mealtime hijacking, experienced passengers would bring along bread, cheese, and fruit, or box lunches that typically consisted of fried chicken, cheese, hard-boiled eggs, and cake. Such meals had the disadvantage of spoiling badly in the summer and attracting masses of black flies, especially when a carload of rail travelers all ate at the same time.

Some of the railroads had dubbed roadside restaurants "refreshment saloons," an honorific that prompted this 1857 description in the *New York Times:*

> If there is any word in the English language more shamefully misused than another, it is the word refreshment, as applied to the hurry scurry of eating and drinking at railroad stations. The dreary places in which the painful and unhealthy performances take place are called Refreshment Saloons, but there could not be a more in-

Nevada Historical Society. Hornsilver, Nevada, c. 1908.

What passed for a restaurant in parts of the American West where Fred Harvey's innovations had not yet reached.

appropriate designation for such abominations of desolation. . . . It is expected that three or four hundred men, women and children . . . can be whirled half a day over a dusty road, with hot cinders flying in their faces; and then, when they approach a station dying with weariness, hunger and thirst, longing for an opportunity to bathe their faces at least before partaking of their much needed refreshments, that they shall rush out helter-skelter into a dismal, long room and dispatch a supper, breakfast or dinner in fifteen minutes. The consequences of such savage and unnatural feeding are not reported by telegraph as railroad disasters; but if a faithful account were taken of them we are afraid they would be found much more serious than any that are caused by the smashing of cars, or the breaking of bridges.

Fred Harvey may not have read this article, but his travels gave him firsthand knowledge of the pitfalls that awaited the hungry rail traveler in the mid-1800s, and he was able, in the course of a remarkable career, to raise the level of railroad food service dramatically throughout the American Southwest. Harvey would win the respect and gratitude of generations of passengers destined to travel by train between Kansas and California, a distance of more than fifteen hundred miles. At the same time, the Harvey Houses and the Harvey Girls would help to temper the popular image of the West as an uncivilized frontier where the denizens were distinguished by violence and vulgarity.

Harvey's introduction to food service began humbly enough in 1850 when he migrated from England to New York City at the age of fifteen and took a job as a busboy working for two dollars a week in a café. Several years later, stirred by the idea of his own restaurant, he moved to New Orleans, then as now known for its superior food. The city also exposed him to yellow fever. Sickness and bad luck would continue to plague Harvey after his recovery when he moved to St. Louis and opened his first restaurant with a partner in 1856. During the Civil War he contracted typhoid, restaurant profits suffered, and whatever money was left from the failing venture disappeared along with Harvey's partner. By this time Harvey was married with children to support, so he took on a series of jobs in shipping and train transport that eventually led him to Chicago's Burlington & Quincy railroad, where he became the general western freight agent. This position kept him traveling throughout the Midwest, where he soon got his fill of the wretched food and the unspeakable lodgings that passengers found in small towns along the tracks of train companies like the CB&Q.

During this period, Harvey still suffered from bouts of yellow fever and typhoid, and two of his children died from scarlet fever, so that he was exceptionally attuned to issues of health and hygiene. What he saw, and his earlier experience as a restaurateur, convinced him it was possible to provide decent food and lodging for hungry and tired railroad travelers. In 1875, while still working for the CB&Q, Harvey entered into a partnership to open restaurants along another rail line, the Kansas Pacific, but the scheme aborted when the partners could not agree on the high standards Harvey insisted were necessary. When the management of the CB&Q also rejected the concept, Harvey offered his plan for high-quality depot restaurants to Charles F. Morse, an officer of the Atchison Topeka and Santa Fe Railroad, then the most rapidly expanding rail line in America. Morse was as much impressed by the articulate and persuasive Harvey as he was by the Englishman's notion that decent food could dramatically improve the railroad business. The president of the Atchison agreed, and as a start, the lunch counter above the Topeka depot, the beginning point of the railroad line, was leased to Harvey.

Harvey picked the right horse in the race to open the West to railroad travel. The path followed by the Atchison was that of the Santa Fe Trail, one of the three famous Western paths (the others were the Oregon and Mormon trails). While settlers were more likely to use the latter two, the Santa Fe was the favorite of commercial travelers. Their loaded wagons could weigh from 3,000 to 7,000 pounds and were drawn by ten or twelve mules or six yoke of oxen, bringing manufactured goods to the West and returning with buffalo hides, furs, and precious metals. Such commerce opened enterprising Americans to the rich possibilities of train service along this route, and politicians and businessmen were opportunistic about securing land for railroads within Kansas and beyond. From 1855 to 1861 the population in Kansas grew from 8,600 to 143,000 as burgeoning railroads allowed farmers to bring their products to market. The rapid development of agriculture in Kansas became a financial base for the expansion of the Atchison Topeka and Santa Fe Railroad, which chose to sell off its land to farmers, thus ensuring even more business.

By 1872, the Atchison had reached the Colorado border, and by 1878 it extended as far as New Mexico. The company owned 7,000 miles of track a little over a decade later. It extended from Chicago to major cities in California. The Atchison brought prospectors to newly discovered silver and gold mines and settlers to newly opened western territories. Heading east, the railroad delivered Texas cattle to Kansas City and Chicago. New towns were formed all along the track, and the line would play a major role in the growth of such cities as Albuquerque, Los Angeles, and San Diego in the late nineteenth and early twentieth centuries. The Atchison (as it was known in the East; Westerners called it the Santa Fe) was clearly a company with big plans and enough vision to realize that providing good food was necessary for their success.

In fact, just before Fred Harvey made his proposal in 1876, the need to provide improved dining service had come vividly home to Atchison executives in the wake of a calamitous sightseeing expedition that was designed to celebrate the completion of a rail route from Topeka to Pueblo, Colorado. The railroad promised to serve only one meal during the journey, so that the 446 passengers, including 83 women, were advised to bring their own food for the round trip, which was scheduled to take a day and a half each way. Unfortunately, heavy snows, an unplanned layover, and other delays—in one case a snowplow running ahead of the train hit a cow—caused the excursion to arrive at Pueblo fully twenty-four hours behind schedule. By then passengers were half-starved and exhausted, having long since consumed their own provisions, the entire food supplies of one Kansas town the train stopped at, and whatever offerings they could find in a station agent's residence. Only the hospitality of townspeople in Pueblo saved the travelers from further suffering when they finally completed the first leg of their journey. The need for someone like Fred Harvey was clear.

From the beginning, Harvey was deeply concerned with standards for both food and service. In preparing his first venture, the room above the depot in Topeka, Harvey saw to it that the place was scrubbed clean and that English silver and Irish linen were purchased for his tables. The railroad had agreed to supply coal, ice, and water without charge—the latter being especially important, since water in the West was often available only in alkaline-laden streams and was a bad choice for drinking and making coffee or tea. Harvey also was assured of free transportation for his employees and for all the equipment and supplies his restaurant required. The result was that his first venture met with instant success, the more as Harvey was able to deliver ample portions of fresh and tasty food not only to passengers but to railroad workers and townspeople as well. A local joke had it that no one would ever leave Topeka, because the food at the depot was so good. The railroad went on to support Harvey in opening up many more eating establishments along the route, as well as a number of hotels. By the time he died of intestinal cancer in 1901 and left the business to his sons, Harvey's chain included fifteen hotels, forty-seven restaurants, thirty dining cars, and food service on the ferries across San Francisco Bay.

The railroad received enormous benefits in return for their support of the Harvey Houses and dining services. Harvey's reputation was so good that the Atchison used his name as a way to ensure that prospective customers would choose that railroad over others. Harvey's high standards also made it easier for the Atchison to recruit and retain employees along the routes served by Harvey Houses. His standards were so high, in fact, that his restaurants and hotels operated at a loss. But this did not faze the

*A fastidious Fred Harvey lunchroom in New Mexico in 1883
with Harvey Girls ready to serve.*

railroad: his good name and the good food he served made for advertising that other railroads would try to imitate but could never match. According to Lucius Beebe, who wrote many books on the topic of railroading:

> Harvey made no secret of the fact that he was giving more in food
> and service than he was taking in currency. At one depot hotel there
> had been a steady loss of $1,000 a month until an ambitious manager came along and, with an eye to gaining the good graces of his
> employer, cut portions and corners until the loss had been pared
> to a mere $500. Outraged, Harvey fired him at once, and started

looking around for a manager who would promise to lose the original sum.

Harvey's innovative approach to food service is worth looking into. To begin with, even when a Harvey House was established in a remote location, the staff was unusually large. According to Lesley Poling-Kempes, author of *The Harvey Girls*, "A typical house (with a lunchroom, a dining room, and without extensive hotel facilities) would include, in order of importance, a manager, a chef, a head waitress, between fifteen and thirty Harvey Girls, a baker, a butcher, several assistant cooks and pantry girls, a housemaid and busboys." Harvey also paid unheard-of salaries to key employees. In one instance, he awarded $5,000 a year to the chef in charge of his restaurant in Florence, Kansas, at a time when bank presidents earned that much. This particular cook had been the head chef of the Palmer House in Chicago and had the knowledge and experience to buy local game and to prepare it in a first-rate European style that brought a singular renown to the region. Relatively high salaries were also paid to hotel managers and to superintendents who regularly made inspection tours of Harvey Houses from Harvey central offices in Kansas City and Chicago. The Harvey Girls and other women who worked for Harvey fared less well than the men in both pay and opportunities for promotion, but their salary, working conditions, and perquisites were substantially better than those offered by competing employers. All of the employers discriminated against women, especially against Hispanics, Native Americans, and other local minority groups.

Nevertheless, the promise of a living wage was not the only reward for young women who came west to work as Harvey Girls. Harvey's employees were taught the value of offering excellent food beautifully served. Harvey took pains to see that menus rotated in such a way that train passengers could eat at his restaurants for four days without repeating meals. A system was also arranged with the train crews that saw to it that travelers would be fed properly within the limited amount of time allowed for train stops. Before arriving at a restaurant, a conductor would find out how many meals were required, and whether passengers preferred the lunch counter or the dining room. (As late as 1927, the going rate was seventy-five cents for the dining room and pay-as-you-eat at the lunch counter.) The numbers of diners would be telegraphed ahead, so that by the time customers entered the restaurant, the first course was already waiting for them on the dining room tables—fresh fruit cups or salads—and the rest of the meal could be served in less than half an hour. The method of service was equally impressive and efficient. The restaurant's manager would enter the dining room carrying a huge tray of meat, above his head, and then swiftly carve the roast into generous portions to be distributed by the circulating waitresses. Dessert pies were always on the menu, and the house rule was to cut them into four pieces rather than six, in keeping with Harvey's principle of making profit secondary to customer satisfaction.

No aspect of Harvey service has been commented upon more frequently than the way in which beverages were ordered and served. From as many as a hundred customers, beverage orders were taken by waitresses who were never seen to write the orders down or communicate them to anyone else. Nevertheless, within seconds, a line of servers would emerge from the kitchen carrying pitchers of coffee, tea, iced tea, and milk and would pour the drink that each customer had ordered. This baffling stunt was made possible by a cup code the waitresses followed that had been developed in the 1880s:

Cup upright in the saucer: coffee
Cup upside down in the saucer: hot tea
Cup upside down, tilted against the saucer: iced tea
Cup upside down, away from the saucer: milk

The only time the system was likely to fail was when customers unwittingly fiddled with their cups. Waitresses had no need to worry about serving alcohol; spirits could be gotten only in the sa-

FRENCH APPLE PIE WITH NUTMEG SAUCE

*Attributed to Henry C. Ibsch, head baker for the Los Angeles Union Station
and adapted from* The Harvey House Cookbook *by George H. Foster and
Peter C. Weiglin.*

8 cups peeled and sliced tart apples	½ cup all-purpose flour
1½ cups sugar	⅓ cup butter, at room temperature
Pie shell	½ teaspoon vanilla
1 cup graham cracker crumbs	Nutmeg sauce (recipe follows)

Place the apples in a saucepan with water to cover. Bring to a
boil and cook until tender, about 5 minutes. Mix in 1 cup of
sugar carefully. Arrange the apples in a pie plate lined with
pastry. Mix together the graham cracker crumbs, the flour,
½ cup sugar, and the butter and vanilla until the texture is
crumbly. Sprinkle over apples. Bake at 425°F for 10 minutes,
then reduce heat to 350° and bake 20 minutes longer. Serve
with Nutmeg Sauce.

NUTMEG SAUCE

1 egg yolk	½ cup milk
½ cup sugar	1 teaspoon ground nutmeg

Beat together the yolk, sugar, and milk. Heat in a saucepan
just until it boils. Remove immediately from the heat. Stir in
the nutmeg.

loons, where male bartenders poured an English whiskey blended
exclusively for Fred Harvey.

A glance at an 1888 Harvey House dinner menu indicates that
customers could order bluepoint oysters on the shell, fillets of

whitefish with Madeira sauce, or lobster salad. Entrées included capon with Hollandaise, roast sirloin of beef au jus, sugar-cured ham, duck, or stuffed turkey with cranberry sauce, and available side dishes included boiled sweet potatoes, Elgin sugar corn, asparagus, and peas. Desserts were apple or mince pie, assorted cakes, New York ice cream, oranges, and grapes, all followed by Edam and Roquefort cheese and coffee. Even in those days, seventy-five cents was cheap for such a meal.

The menu is quintessentially American. What made it remarkable was that the dishes used ingredients brought by rail from all over the country. Beef in those days was shipped up from Texas, slaughtered in Kansas City or Chicago, and then distributed by train to Harvey restaurants in places that had never known anything but buffalo and antelope meat. At the Harvey House in Gainesville, Texas, the son of the hotel's German-born chef recalled how meat was brought in from Kansas City: "It was top beef, brought in on the train in huge baskets that were two feet by three feet by two feet. Veal cutlets were brought in buckets. They weren't refrigerated but were shipped directly from the packing plant." Fresh vegetables that were not grown locally were shipped by train from the Midwest before they could spoil, and fresh fruit was refrigerated and shipped in from California when the rails reached that far west and sometimes from as far away as Mexico. Fish and seafood were transported in railway ice cars from the East or from the Gulf to Kansas and other landlocked areas of the West.

Success for Harvey bred more success. In 1882, with the cooperation of the railroad, Harvey went on to build and operate a resort hotel, the Montezuma, six miles west of Las Vegas, New Mexico. The Atchison had recently built a branch line that would deliver people to this massive wooden edifice, four stories high and over 300 feet long. To feed the hotel clientele, Harvey arranged for fresh produce to be delivered from Mexico during the winter months. The railroad would also continue to deliver such luxurious perishable foods as sea bass, shellfish, and live

GRILLED MARINATED SALMON

Attributed to Manfred Gunter Westerwelle, Chef, Victor Hugo Inn, Laguna Beach, California, and adapted from The Harvey House Cookbook, *by George H. Foster and Peter C. Weiglin.*

¼ cup salt	3 tablespoons sugar
1 teaspoon fresh ground pepper	12 stalks fresh dill, chopped
	6 salmon steaks, 1 inch thick

Mix together the salt, pepper, sugar, and dill. Rub into the salmon. Place in a bowl, cover, and refrigerate for 36 hours. Cook under a hot broiler, close to the flame, for 3 minutes on each side.

green turtles, causing one grateful customer to comment, "Without a butcher, or grocer, or gardener, within hundreds of miles, here was an elegant supper, which might be said to have been brought from the ends of the earth and set down in the middle of the American desert." Other resort hotels were to follow, all of them obedient to the concern for detail that was Fred Harvey's legacy to railroad dining.

Next to raising the standards for food consumed by American travelers, Harvey's most significant contribution to improving life in the West was his recruitment of female waitresses who would add not only efficiency but personal warmth and charm to his restaurants. The policy began in 1883 following an incident in Raton, New Mexico, in which waiters, along with their manager, were fired after a bloody knife fight. The new manager, Tom Gable, won Harvey's approval to replace the waiters with women, who were less inclined to get drunk and into brawls. "The waitresses were the most respectable women the cowboys had ever seen— that is, outside of their own wives and mothers," reported Gable. "Those roughnecks learned manners."

To find the female staff he desired, Harvey placed the following ad in Eastern newspapers:

> Wanted—young women, 18 to 30 years of age, of good moral character, attractive and intelligent, as waitresses in Harvey Eating Houses and on the Santa Fe Railroad in the West. Wages $17.50 per month with room and board. Liberal tips customary. Experience not necessary. Write Fred Harvey, Union Depot, Kansas City, Missouri.

The ads attracted immediate attention, mainly from the daughters of Midwestern farmers and railroaders. While waitressing was not a well-regarded profession for young single women—in the East it was less respectable than factory work—being a Harvey Girl promised something more than merely earning a living. Guarantees of job training, free train travel, and decent living conditions within a secure and supportive community made life as a Harvey House waitress seem very attractive to young women who were already accustomed to working hard. At the same time, going west in the latter part of the nineteenth century must have felt as liberating and adventurous for these young women as it did for the many men who heeded newspaperman Horace Greeley's call to "go West, young man." Fred Harvey offered a way for respectable young women to become part of the movement west other than as schoolteachers, missionaries, or mail-order brides (not to mention prostitutes and dance-hall girls).

Many of those who answered Harvey's ad were first-generation American women whose immigrant parents had set precedents for them by coming to this country to start new and better lives. Even the least adventurous could argue that finding a husband in the West was much easier than in the East. The 1870 census listed 385,000 men residing between the Mississippi River and the Pacific Ocean and only 172,000 women, a ratio of more than two to one. Lesley Poling-Kempes, historian of the Harvey Girls, points out in *The Duty of American Women to Their Country* that the reformer Catherine Beecher insisted that New England women needed to redress this imbalance: "To supply the bachelors of the west with wives, to furnish pining maids of the east with husbands, and to better equalize the present disposition of the sexes on these two sections of our country, has been one of the difficulties of our age." (Later, when Harvey Girls began to marry, writers quipped that Fred Harvey was running a matrimonial bureau.) According to Poling-Kempes, in 1928 the novelist Edna Ferber remembered that such marriages were met with approval: "My father used to say that those Western railroad brakemen and Harvey lunchroom waitresses were the future aristocracy of the West. " 'Fine stock,' he used to say." Harvey Girls had many opportunities to meet prospective husbands among the single men who worked for the railroad or rode it as passengers. "A woman could take her time selecting a spouse, knowing there would be no shortage of possible suitors, even as she neared and passed the age of thirty," Poling-Kempes concludes. "A sociologist could not have invented a better method by which the West could become inhabited by so many young women anxious to take part in the building of a new region."

But while Harvey came to sanction marriages, he first made sure that his waitresses worked hard. Harvey Girls were required to sign a contract promising to stay with the company for a stipulated period of six or nine months, and agreed not to marry during this time. The women also had to accept mandatory living arrangements with roommates in supervised Harvey dormitories, often above the restaurants, and to obey a strict curfew. They agreed not to fraternize with male Harvey employees, with violation grounds for dismissal. Their personal appearance was also outlined in detail by Fred Harvey, who decided upon a rather nunlike uniform so that they would not be mistaken for "fallen women."

Harvey Girls wore plain black dresses with high collars, heavily starched white aprons, and plain black shoes and stockings, and their hair was plainly done and covered with hairnets. (Jewelry,

makeup, nail polish, and gum chewing were strictly forbidden.)
The outfit was introduced in 1883 and scarcely changed over the
next fifty years. Each employee was given several changes of uniform, since soiled outfits were not tolerated. The slightest stain required a waitress to change at once. The railroad provided free
laundering service, but the women were responsible for starching
and ironing their own work clothes. In spite of this, there were few
complaints from the Harvey Girls about their uniforms or the
other rules.

Harvey's fastidiousness and the demanding nature of the work
itself combined with marriages to create a constant turnover,
though many Harvey Girls would remain with the company for
years, and a few with managerial skills would rise to the rank of
headwaitress. Staff were expected to work twelve-hour days for
six and often seven days a week, sometimes serving as many as
four trains a day with capacity crowds. And throughout it all they
had to maintain the style and efficiency that Harvey demanded.
When not waiting on customers, the women were expected to
clean the tables and chairs at their work stations and to polish sil-
verware, the mahogany counters, chrome-plated coffee urns, and
glassware, including pastry cases. One Harvey Girl remembered,
"It seemed as if everything in the dining room was silver or had
some silver on it. In later years when I was married, my husband
wanted to buy me a big silver service, but I said, 'No, I never want
to polish a piece of silver again as long as I live.' "

The hard work of serving travelers and maintaining the restaurants' facilities was lightened by the sense of pride the Harvey
Girls experienced. Poling-Kempes compares the role of the Harvey Girls in the settling of the West to the women mill workers in
Lowell, Massachusetts, in the 1820s and 1830s. Both were pater-
nalistic and highly regimented communities that nevertheless en-
sured respectability for the young women workers and offered
them cultural and economic opportunities they might never have
otherwise had. Both sets of women also enjoyed their days off and
the strong, sometimes lifelong friendships they formed. Typical of

the Harvey Girls who came from American farms was Gladys Porter, an Oklahoma girl who was hired in 1920 at the age of eighteen and stayed on for six years, in part to help support her large family but mostly because she liked the job and the people she lived with and met.

> I felt protected and looked after as a Harvey Girl in those days, which I needed being so young. The staff was like a big family to me. I was never homesick, but my family had moved to town by then and I could see them whenever I wanted. Because I had come from such a large family, I had no exposure to the nicer things in life. I didn't have any social skills and working as a Harvey Girl taught me how to be hospitable and caring. I also learned how to function in an elegant atmosphere I would never have been exposed to otherwise.

Gladys Porter's experience suggests the kind of opportunity the Harvey organization provided. Besides the advantage of free travel during vacations or visits home, the Harvey Girls also had the option of requesting a transfer to another location after their first year on the job. Some women would put in for choice assignments at well-located Harvey resort hotels, where, in addition to elegant surroundings, they could come in contact with affluent guests who tipped generously and might even be open to marriage with an attractive Harvey Girl.

Changes in the travel habits of Americans brought on by the acceleration of air and automobile travel inevitably led to the closing of the Harvey Houses. Initially, however, the Harvey empire was downsized by the development of faster trains that could cover greater distances, making many of the Harvey depot restaurants obsolete. Also, the growing popularity of dining cars on trains and Pullman sleeping cars gave passengers less reason to disembark, though Harvey's sons who took over the company were able for a time to supply trains like the Santa Fe with quality food and service in the Harvey tradition.

The Harvey Houses experienced a brief resurgence during the Second World War, when trains packed with servicemen crisscrossed the nation. But none of Fred Harvey's high standards could be maintained during this period when, in spite of food rationing, more than a million meals had to be prepared each month and even the smaller Harvey establishments served an average of two thousand traveling soldiers a day. One young bride from Ohio on her way to California to visit her soldier-husband reported having eaten nothing but baloney sandwiches at one Fred Harvey restaurant after another. Her complaint would have deeply grieved the long-departed Harvey. Allegedly, his dying words were a reminder to "never cut the ham too thin."

World War II also broke down some of the sexual and racial prejudices that affected Harvey hiring policies. Wartime factory jobs attracted women who might otherwise have become Harvey Girls. The Harvey Houses were required to drop their age requirements. They brought former waitresses out of retirement, hired married and divorced women, and recruited Hispanic and Native American women in New Mexico and Arizona. (Before then, when hired at all, minority women were behind the scenes working in kitchens or as maids in the hotels and resorts. Nevertheless, it is with Native American crafts that many older Americans associate the Harvey name, remembering the company's retail shops in the Southwest that sold handmade products like Navajo blankets and often employed regional Native American artisans to demonstrate their skills.) Dress requirements were also relaxed during the war, and short-term volunteers called "troop-train girls" were hired locally to fill the labor shortage.

From the outset, black and white railroad workers employed by the Atchison ate separately. African Americans, who served almost exclusively as porters, were seated not in the Harvey dining rooms with white train men but in designated areas where they were served by busboys rather than the Harvey Girls. Separation of passengers by race was abandoned temporarily in the early 1940s by the exigencies of wartime train transportation. Thus, before even the desegregation of the armed forces themselves, Harvey Houses stumbled toward equality.

Following the war, many of the Harvey Houses that had been

temporarily reopened to serve the wartime effort were closed for good. Their impact remained. In later years, the Harvey restaurants had served as homes not only to the women who worked there but to their children. The daughter of a widow who was a waitress would go to the restaurant every day after school. She remembers having been treated like royalty. "The baker kept the broken cookies in a paper bag for us and everyone was always giving us sweets and food. It was a big family, our family. The manager and his wife took care of us just like we were their own." At the same time she was provided with a working wage, the mother of this child had managed to find a community that provided an atmosphere in which her child could grow up in safety.

Fred Harvey's story is about the public success of an entrepreneur, and it is tempting to cast his restaurants as the forerunner of American fast-food chains. But Harvey's indifference to making a profit compromises the reality of such a legacy. Railroad subsidies allowed him to offer luxuries at reasonable prices, creating a standard that conventional businesses could not possibly follow. Today, the quality of the food in fast-food chains bears little resemblance to the meals Harvey served. His true legacy is the Harvey Girls. By bringing in thousands of respectable single women to work in new railroad towns, Harvey helped settle the West, for many of these women married and raised families in these places, helping to establish and build new communities.

FIVE

Home Cooking in the FDR White House

The Indomitable Mrs. Nesbitt

One of the unsolved mysteries of the Franklin Delano Roosevelt era in Washington is the question of why the White House continually served bad food. A well-known axiom said to have circulated throughout the capital during the twelve years of FDR's presidency advised all guests invited to a White House meal to eat first before leaving home. Few writers who have dealt at any length with the domestic life of the Roosevelts have failed to mention this gap in their otherwise gracious and generous hospitality. But the reason the Roosevelts continued to serve bland and mediocre meals throughout their tenancy in the White House has so far eluded scholars of the FDR administration, let alone anyone who knows anything about cooking and food.

What puzzled visitors at the time, and still seems puzzling, is why the President and his wife did not make a greater effort to feed world leaders well, not to mention other visiting dignitaries and themselves. The lack of decent cooking in the White House seemed all the more puzzling because the Roosevelts were high-born, and it was assumed that people who grew up with social advantages and wealth were supposed to know something about fine dining. It was likewise assumed that the President of the United States of America was in a position to employ the very best chefs in the country or from abroad, cooks who could be counted on to turn out sophisticated and delicious dishes for important visitors, if not for the Roosevelts and their children.

Instead, the preparation of White House food was entrusted to one Mrs. Henrietta Nesbitt, a Hyde Park neighbor of the Roosevelts picked by Eleanor to be the general housekeeper at the presidential residence. In this position, Mrs. Nesbitt was responsible not only for planning meals, but also for managing a domestic staff of thirty-two, whose duties included cleaning sixty rooms and twenty bathrooms and maintaining such extraordinary White House artifacts as the twenty-two East Room chandeliers, each of which contained 22,000 pieces of glass.

Mrs. Nesbitt's training for the job was limited, to say the least. Before coming to the White House as a fifty-nine-year-old wife and grandmother, Henrietta Nesbitt had never before worked outside of her home. In Hyde Park she had established a local reputation as a good baker and had also volunteered with the League of Women Voters. These two accomplishments, in the eyes of Eleanor Roosevelt, qualified Nesbitt sufficiently to run the White House domestic staff. Mrs. Roosevelt was further impressed by Nesbitt's ability to supply FDR's campaign with baked goods when he was running for governor of New York, and to continue to do so after he was in the governor's mansion in Albany. At the time, Mrs. Nesbitt was struggling to support her family by selling bread, cakes, and pies in her community, with the help of her husband Henry—or "Dad," as she called him—who like many other breadwinners hit by the Depression was unable to find outside work. One does not need to know much about Eleanor Roosevelt to know that Henrietta Nesbitt's plight must have moved her, just as

FDR Library

Henrietta Nesbitt (left), Eleanor Roosevelt, and Harriet Elliott (representing the OPA) with Mrs. Roosevelt ceremoniously signing a wartime pledge to conserve.

it prompted her to find jobs for her other former Hyde Park neighbors who had shown their loyalty to her and the future President. For Mrs. Nesbitt, the White House provided the ultimate employment opportunity.

Alas, Mrs. Nesbitt was in over her head. Among the many who spoke ill of her cooking and household management capabilities were the Roosevelt children, friends of the family, the inner circle of presidential cabinet officers, aides and confidantes of the Roosevelts, assorted journalists, and finally, the domestic staff itself. Yet even her many detractors had to admit that the job of running the White House during the FDR administration was more difficult than most people knew. Unlike the previous tenants, the Hoovers, who had been a formal, privacy-loving couple who lived an orderly life, the Roosevelts were spontaneous and openhanded in their hospitality, inclined to casually invite friends and family to come to the White House and allow them to stay for indefinite periods. One such visitor was Harry Hopkins, an adviser who had long been close to the President. After a long private dinner, the widower, who suffered poor health for some time before his death, was asked by the President to stay the night, an offer that stretched into three and a half years of residency. Hopkins's young daughter also moved in and was soon considered a member of the family. A constantly shifting part of the household were the adult Roosevelt children and grandchildren, who moved in and out of the White House according to the status of their various marriages. These comings and goings, often with little or no prior notice, unavoidably made more work for Henrietta Nesbitt and her household staff. She simply had to make adjustments—on top of the usual state dinners and receptions for the likes of Winston Churchill, Madame Chiang Kai-shek, and the King and Queen of England.

As far as her critics were concerned, these myriad demands were no excuse. They certainly did not lead Mrs. Nesbitt to seek solutions to her inadequacies as a cook but rather provided her with an ever-widening arena in which to serve bad food. The Roosevelt sons James and Elliott showed even less reluctance than others in speaking their minds about White House daily fare or citing their father's impatience with Mrs. Nesbitt's cooking. In a book about FDR, James included a memo of complaint from the President to Eleanor that was written shortly before America became involved in World War II:

> Do you remember that about a month ago I got sick of chicken because I got it . . . at least six times a week? The chicken situation has definitely improved, but "they" have substituted sweetbreads, and for the past month I have been getting sweetbreads about six times a week.
>
> I am getting to the point where my stomach positively rebels and this does not help my relations with foreign powers. I bit two of them today.

James also took pleasure in repeating White House speechwriter Robert Sherwood's opinion about one of Mrs. Nesbitt's omnipresent salads. Sherwood condemned them as gloppy and repulsive, much like the silly productions found at the time in flossy tea shops. Though the President and many of his guests regularly left this particular salad untouched, Mrs. Nesbitt continued to serve it meal after meal, year after year.

Open criticism of White House food became a favorite pastime among Washington insiders, a kind of in-joke that identified them as being close to the seat of American power. But there was more than a little cause for complaint. In his study of FDR, journalist John Gunther reported on the dreary repetitiveness of Mrs. Nesbitt's offerings: "Guests who stayed in the White House for long periods have told me that they could predict by the days of the week what they would have for lunch or dinner. The monotonous routine was like that of a boardinghouse—tongue with caper sauce on Mondays, boiled beef without any sauce at all on Tuesday, and so on." Likewise, in his diary, Harold Ickes, Secretary of the Interior in FDR's administration, described his disappointment in a formal dinner given by the First Family:

> The president and Mrs. Roosevelt gave their annual official dinner to the Cabinet last night. There were about eighty at table. I am bound to confess that the White House dinners are neither inspiring nor do they stand out as Lucullan repasts. I am not very fussy about my food . . . but it does seem a little out of proportion to use a solid-gold knife and fork on ordinary roast mutton.

White House tensions over food even reached the *New York Times* in a 1940 story headlined, "Housekeeper Vetoes Roosevelt on Menu." Describing a disagreement over the inaugural luncheon menu celebrating Roosevelt's election to a third term, the *Times* reported that although the President was "powerful enough to 'override' the wishes of Congress on occasion, [he] had little influence with the White House housekeeper." Mrs. Nesbitt had foiled the wishes of the Chief Executive, who had announced that chicken à la king would be served to the inaugural guests. Instead, they got chicken salad. Fearing that a hot dish for 2,000 expected guests could not be kept hot, Mrs. Nesbitt had made a unilateral decision to alter the menu, the rest of which included rolls without butter, coffee, and unfrosted cake. Especially in matters of food, Mrs. Nesbitt's parsimony was legendary. White House aide William Hassett recalled the results of one of her economies in his account of traveling with the President to Hyde Park for the weekend:

> With the President, besides Harry Hopkins and Grace Tully, were Mr. and Mrs. Morgenthau. . . . The President asked for orange juice for himself and friends; but Lucas, the faithful porter, said there were not enough oranges if the President was to have a glass of juice in the morning. Frugal La Nesbitt had carefully counted out for the trip not a dozen oranges but ten. So all went without.

The President's exasperation with Mrs. Nesbitt led him to say to his daughter Anna that one of his motivations for running for a fourth term was so that he could fire her. When he won the election, however, he could not follow through, because the running of the White House had long been ceded to Mrs. Roosevelt, who thought that Mrs. Nesbitt was doing just fine. FDR's only recourse was through humor, so that in addition to finding witty ways to criticize her cooking, he took pleasure in referring to the housekeeper as "Fluffy," the name she was called behind her back by many of the staff. The absurdity of the nickname is made plain by photographs of Henrietta Nesbitt during her White House years that reveal a short, compact, plain-featured woman in her sixties with a stringy neck and a determined look on her face. No one was ever less fluffy.

Another of Mrs. Nesbitt's detractors, Lillian Rogers Parks, was a White House maid who wrote a couple of gossipy backstairs books about her experiences. In *The Roosevelts, a Family in Turmoil*, she gleefully reports the President's impatience with Mrs. Nesbitt's cooking. "Mrs. Roosevelt complained to her husband about all the requests she was getting for things from all over the country, and mentioned that among them were hundreds of requests for White House recipes. Laughing, FDR said she ought to send some of Henrietta Nesbitt's recipes for brains and sweetbreads—"that would certainly dry up requests for recipes in a hurry."

As Lillian Rogers Parks tells it, no one on the White House staff much liked Mrs. Nesbitt, who had replaced an experienced housekeeper they had respected. Parks reports that Mrs. Nesbitt "always had to be right," and that her subordinates found her bossy, humorless, and prudish. The former maid describes an evening when the Hollywood film *It Happened One Night*, starring Claudette Colbert and Clark Gable, was brought into the White House for the enjoyment of the staff. "When Gable stripped to his underwear," she reports, "Mrs. Nesbitt got so indignant that she jumped up and left in a huff. We doubled over in laughter and it added to our already overflowing supply of Nesbitt stories."

The staff understood that they were stuck with the housekeeper, seeing that Mrs. Roosevelt had complete confidence in her and had neither the time nor the inclination to intervene in the running of the house. The strategy of the staff was to work around Mrs. Nesbitt—to ignore her instructions when they believed she was wrong—and live with the risk of being criticized and scolded. One such ploy had to do with the long-handled feather dusters the maids liked to use to clean the tops of highboys and chiffoniers, places that otherwise could not be easily reached. Mrs. Nesbitt had a decided distaste for feather dusters and forbade their use, believing that they just stirred up the dust without removing it. In the end, the maids smuggled in the dusters when their boss wasn't looking. (According to Cheryl Mendelson's recent and definitive book on housekeeping, *Home Comforts*, Mrs. Nesbitt was right about the cleaning method. "Do not use feather dusters," Mendelson insists: "They remove dust poorly and fling it into the air.")

Parks also comments on Nesbitt's disregard for the president's wishes, interpreting the household manager's high-handed behavior as an arrogant expression of authority. Upon being told by one of the White House staff that the President did not like broccoli, a feeling that would be shared years later by President George H. Bush, Mrs. Nesbitt told the cook to fix it anyway, making it clear that she knew what was best for Mr. Roosevelt. On another occasion, when the President was entertaining royal guests, he requested that hot coffee be served, knowing that his visitors preferred it, and was taken aback when the butlers brought in iced tea. Upon inquiring about the substitution, the president was told by the butlers that Mrs. Nesbitt had ordered the tea because she thought it was much better for them. (It is tempting to speculate that Mrs. Nesbitt was averse to hot foods of any kind.)

The almost unanimous feelings of hostility and resentment toward Mrs. Nesbitt were summarized by James Roosevelt: "Everybody was against Mrs. Nesbitt—everybody except Mother." The accumulated testimony of these witnesses and others gives us a picture of Mrs. Nesbitt as an incompetent cook, an overbearing household manager, and an arrogant and inconsiderate caretaker of her chief charge at the White House, President Roosevelt. But luckily for us, Mrs. Nesbitt was not the silent type. She left behind two published books that help set the record straight—one a memoir of her White House years and the other a cookbook. *White House Diary* (1948), based on the journal she kept while working for the Roosevelts, is a somewhat defensive account of how she faced and solved various challenges, showing that she was fully aware of the criticism she received. *The Presidential Cookbook: Feeding the Roosevelts and Their Guests* (1951) is a proud testament of what foods were cooked and served in the White House. Both books are rich, revealing documents that together go far to unravel the mysteries that surround the bad cooking of FDR's administration and the relationship between Mrs. Nesbitt and Mrs. Roosevelt.

The portrait one gets of Henrietta Nesbitt in her memoir is of a more complicated and connected person than the one-dimensional figure others were quick to criticize, although she does confirm some of their charges with occasional mean-spirited remarks about certain visitors and members of her staff. But the voice that speaks clearly for Mrs. Nesbitt in *White House Diary* is that of a no-nonsense, plain-speaking woman, capable of self-awareness, who never forgot where she came from.

> I've kept house all my life. It's as natural to me as breathing. I come of stock whose men are proud of their husbandry and the women take pride in housewifery. . . . A woman like myself was reared in a home, grew to love and tend that home, and left it for another where her married days were spent and her sons and daughters were reared. No matter how little there was in it, for women of my generation there was always the home.

Henrietta Nesbitt had been brought up by a Republican family who believed the slogan that "only saloonkeepers were Democrats." Nevertheless, she was able to see herself as living in a changing world with herself as a participant in that change. Nesbitt's experiences, especially in the League of Women Voters, where she was elected an officer and first met Mrs. Roosevelt, opened her mind to the world around her and led her to support Mrs. Roosevelt's husband for governor. She was appreciative of the fact that he was seen by affluent upstate New York Republicans as a traitor to his class, but she came to see the Roosevelts as friends of less fortunate Hyde Park neighbors like Henrietta and her husband, Henry, whom she called Dad.

Henry Nesbitt had come to the same conclusion even sooner because of an incident that had to do with chicken breasts:

> The chickens belonged to a millionaire Republican who had a Hudson estate close to the Roosevelts. He was one of the many Hyde Parkers who were so dreadfully perturbed at the thought of Mr. Roosevelt being made governor, but I didn't know anything about it at the time, not being used to politics. Anyway Dad was over at this man's place one day, and he was watching one hundred chickens being dressed for a house party he was giving. The ser-

vants were stripping off the breasts and throwing the rest of the meat away. Dad saw that all that good chicken was going into the garbage cans and thought it was a pity.

"Why don't you give it to people who work on your place?" he asked the owner.

"What, make beggars of them?" the millionaire answered sternly.

Henrietta noted that her husband was happy to find that the servants were saving the rest of the chicken meat in spite of the millionaire, and that the incident prompted him to join the local Roosevelt for Governor Club even before she had.

Elsewhere in *White House Diary* Eleanor Roosevelt's influence on Nesbitt seems clear when the housekeeper discusses her belief that the twentieth century was going to be a time for women, "that the man's world was coming to an end and the world of the female was starting . . . think of the progress women have made in the last eight years! Before then a woman couldn't call her second-best bonnet her own."

One begins to understand what Eleanor Roosevelt saw in Henrietta Nesbitt. Despite obvious differences in their social status, both women had to overcome personal limitations and call upon strong inner resources in order to meet unexpected and difficult challenges. Mrs. Roosevelt, an inherently shy woman, had to adjust to the increasing demands of being the wife of a world leader in the worst of modern economic times and later in the midst of a world at war. At the same time, Henrietta Nesbitt, who had no prior managerial experience, had to take charge of the White House under the glare of the national press.

The connection between Mrs. Roosevelt and Mrs. Nesbitt was forged during the worst of the Depression, when Mrs. Nesbitt was forced to call on her baking skills to help her family survive and provide employment for her husband, whose last few poor-paying jobs included making barrels and selling whale meat. Their best customers became the Roosevelts, who knew of their precarious financial condition when they bought baked goods for their campaigns, and later when they hired both Henrietta and her husband, whose duty it was to inventory the many packages received by the White House. Mrs. Nesbitt regarded the jobs as a lifeline that forever sealed her gratitude to Mrs. Roosevelt: "I don't know if she ever realized what it meant. I'm not one to talk much. But it was like a rope tossed out to the drowning, and I'll never stop being grateful."

Her indebtedness and respect for Mrs. Roosevelt doubtlessly prompted Mrs. Nesbitt to display only her best traits to her employer, in particular her loyalty and desire to spare the First Lady from most domestic concerns. While she occupied her position, the housekeeper did not give vent to uncharitable opinions she held of certain White House occupants, especially the Roosevelt children. But in her memoir she is not above making digs at the high divorce rate among the children. Nor does she withhold her disapproval of their continuous presence in the White House as adults, seeing them as mooching off their parents as they moved in and out of marriages. Mrs. Nesbitt also made snide remarks about unnamed White House guests who, in her opinion, were unreasonably demanding, unlike the most famous visitors, whom she always found easy to please. There was a bit of the bluenose and snob in Mrs. Nesbitt. But her memoir is unwavering in her respect and affection for the President and his wife.

When she first came to Washington, Mrs. Nesbitt did have doubts. In her *White House Diary* she discloses her initial anxieties about moving from her own small house in Hyde Park and taking over as chatelaine of the White House, a job she thought would last for only four years. On first viewing and circling around that imposing building, she counted the windows and tried to figure out the amount of time and labor it would take to keep them spotless. Here as elsewhere, her formula for making her new job manageable was to see each chore as a simple multiple of the cooking and cleaning jobs she had at home, never realizing, much less acknowledging, that the nature and magnitude of the work might require special training or a more professional approach. Void of experience in large-scale household management, she put her consistent rule of thumb to work and assumed that her new responsibility would essentially be like keeping house in Hyde Park, but instead of looking after six people, she would look after sixty. How was she to know that she would be getting last-minute memos from Mrs. Roosevelt informing her that five thousand people would be coming to tea?

From the start, Mrs. Nesbitt and Mrs. Roosevelt worked as partners, putting their heads together each morning to plan family meals as well as large social events. Even before the First Lady went off on trips, which accelerated throughout FDR's successive terms in office, Mrs. Roosevelt would send messages down to Mrs. Nesbitt concerning the President's meals. In describing their earliest planning sessions, Mrs. Nesbitt relates how the two women took the current national economy into account as they established what was to become, for want of a better term, the Roosevelt White House cuisine.

> I was going to spend my first year in the White House trying to match the need for saving with the swirl of entertaining. . . . But Mrs. Roosevelt and I had our economy program all mapped out and we were going to stick to it. With so many Americans hungry, it was up to the head house of the nation to serve economy meals and act as an example. I'd been trying to manage the best meals for the least money all my life.

It is clear from the *Diary* that what others regarded as ugly frugalities were part of a conscious effort to show that the First Family was willing to participate in the austerities required by the Depression and later by World War II. At the same time, Mrs. Nesbitt felt helpless to defend herself and Mrs. Roosevelt from routine attacks by the press that criticized the quality of White House food: "If we pinched the budget to give the guests something extra nice we were extravagant" and "If we tried to be an example and live economically we were not living up to White House standards and traditions. There was no in-between." Considering that living economically came as second nature to Mrs. Nesbitt, the statement may be disingenuous. But in trying to keep costs down, the housekeeper dealt with a problem caused by the Roosevelts themselves, who expected Henrietta to honor the need for Depression parsimony at the same time that they loved to entertain more frequently than any previous occupants of the White House.

The *Diary* is also at pains to point out that when it came to cooking the President's meals, Mrs. Roosevelt made it a priority that Mrs. Nesbitt protect her husband's health as well as try to please his tastes. As a paraplegic who had contracted polio in his late thirties, President Roosevelt had serious physical problems that were almost never discussed by the press or disclosed to the public. Before the illness that crippled him, he had been a robust and vigorous man who maintained his normal weight of around 190 pounds with little trouble. But confined to a wheelchair, he had to control his weight and be careful about what he consumed, as his doctors often told him. Mrs. Roosevelt and her housekeeper conspired to limit the President's calories by providing him with simple dishes that included more vegetables and less butter than he might otherwise have wished. Not surprisingly, Mrs. Nesbitt's part in the meal planning for the President became another target of the press, to which she offered a rejoinder:

> The newspapers took to saying I ruled the President with a rod of iron. Nonsense. I had an awful time getting vegetables down him.
>
> I've come to the conclusion men just don't like vegetables. They're meat eaters by nature. There was nothing Mrs. Roosevelt liked better than a nicely arranged salad, but the President always looked at anything with lettuce in it with a sort of martyrish eye, as if he knew it was good for him, but that didn't make him like it. Potatoes seem to be the male notion of a vegetable, even if the man is a president. So one of the hardest jobs Mrs. Roosevelt and I shared was trying to coax vegetables down the president of the United States.

One can begin to see how the President might become irritated with the results of Mrs. Nesbitt's gender-based theory of human appetite, still shared by many women today. To make matters worse, FDR was plagued with a series of health problems not directly related to his paralysis. As a dedicated cigarette smoker, he was subject to attacks of bronchitis and suffered from a sinus condition. And in his later years, he was diagnosed with high blood pressure, a heart problem, and serious indigestion. He was also given to bouts of depression. Even a less daunting list of ailments could account for his peevishness about what he was being served by Mrs. Nesbitt.

Certainly world problems affected the President's moods. The Depression and the construction of new social and economic programs preoccupied him for the first half of his administration, while World War II absorbed almost all of his attention during his last two terms of office. His task was to lead a divided nation past poverty and joblessness into a devastating war, a monumental responsibility that led FDR into mood swings, loss of appetite, and occasional emotional outbursts. The irritating domestic details of his life, always at hand, were easy targets for expressing frustration.

Indeed, Mrs. Nesbitt claimed that she could gauge how badly things were in Europe by the President's poor appetite or ill humor. At critical points in the war, he would stage what Mrs. Roosevelt quaintly referred to as a "tizzy-wizzy," in which he would angrily scratch things off menus and then reject whatever substitutes were put before him. "At first I'd just note the president was off his food, and feel responsible," Mrs. Nesbitt remarked. "Now I learned to look for the disturbing factor behind his upset, and could usually find it. The menu scratches were thickest in June, when news came of the bombardment of Paris."

Even the press found relief from world tensions by publishing human-interest stories about the President's refusal to eat any more spinach or accept another mouthful of liver and beans. Nesbitt felt that his complaints may have been amusing to the whole world, but as far as she was concerned, President Roosevelt needed just such nutrition. In keeping with her theory about male prejudices in food, she speculated that "food peevishness" was catching, and that the President was "too often surrounded by men who pushed their plates back and couldn't eat this and didn't like the looks of that, and it wouldn't agree with them anyway if they did."

Mrs. Nesbitt's reasons for restricting the President's diet may seem plausible, but to Blanche Cook, Eleanor Roosevelt's biographer, they are lame alibis that cover up sinister motives. Cook is convinced that Henrietta Nesbitt was Mrs. Roosevelt's secret weapon for acting out her passive-aggressive feelings toward her husband. In other words, the serving of bad food in the White House was Eleanor's unconscious way of getting even with the President and others for a variety of insults and injuries she had suffered in their marriage, including his extramarital affair.

Ingenious as this explanation might be, its validity depends on Eleanor Roosevelt's ability to distinguish between food that is tasty and delicious and dishes that are mediocre and dull. For the theory to hold, it would also have to be true that Mrs. Roosevelt had a high regard for good food and truly believed that eating well was important. Cook believes these things to be true. As proof, she points to the fact that the First Lady frequently took guests out to fine French restaurants, where she would often compliment the chef. In further evidence, the biographer notes that Mrs. Roosevelt had been educated in England by the redoubtable French schoolmistress Marie Sylvestre, who presumably knew a thing or two about fine dining.

This evidence is shaky at best, and is not supported by people who regularly shared meals with Mrs. Roosevelt and had first-hand knowledge of her appetite and food preferences. Those who did have such knowledge describe her as being indifferent to what was placed before her. That she took people to good restaurants and complimented the chefs is more a statement about her refined behavior than her capacities as a gourmet. And while Madame

Sylvestre may have had an appreciation for fine French dining, her taste would not necessarily have rubbed off on Eleanor Roosevelt.

Better witnesses of Mrs. Roosevelt's appetite and taste in food were Lillian Rogers Parks and James Roosevelt. Parks reports some rude remarks by one of the butlers "who used to kid that Eleanor must be extremely interested in sex because she certainly wasn't interested in food," prompting Parks to confirm that Mrs. Roosevelt did not care what she ate. As further proof, Parks noted, "one of the cooks had a theory that Eleanor had defective taste buds because she didn't notice any difference no matter how hard they tried to make something especially good. And so they some-

FDR Library

Mrs. Roosevelt at Val-Kill, Hyde Park, in 1938 in a rare cooking pose.

times just didn't care and quit trying." In the same vein, James Roosevelt described his mother's indifferent attitude toward fine dining and eating generally: "Now Mother is a wonderful woman and I yield to no one in my admiration for her, but, as she herself will tell you, she has no appreciation of fine food. Victuals to her are something to inject into the body as fuel to keep it going, much as a motorist pours gasoline into an auto tank."

In the face of such evidence it is hard to believe that Eleanor Roosevelt deliberately set out to serve bad food. The more likely explanation is that she was never very discerning about the flavors and textures of whatever was served but instead followed her impulses to offer her guests simple foods that appropriately reflected the hard times the country was experiencing, first during the Depression and later with wartime shortages and food rationing. Beyond that, she and Mrs. Nesbitt had good reason to believe that the President's uncertain health would be harmed if he was given what he wanted most.

While Mrs. Roosevelt may have been indifferent to food herself, she understood its value to others. Her frequent gifts of food suggest she knew the real and symbolic power it had to bring comfort and happiness to human lives. Henrietta Nesbitt agreed with this assessment of Mrs. Roosevelt's relationship to food, observing that while "she wanted plenty, enough for everyone, and some left over . . . she was too much interested in talk to care what she ate. She'd eat anything put before her." Nesbitt's diary makes it clear that Eleanor Roosevelt's thoughtfulness as a hostess would prompt her to send departing houseguests off with lunch baskets filled with fried chicken and fruit, while for herself she would make do with a lunch of crackers and milk before rushing off to catch a train.

Once the idea is dismissed that Mrs. Roosevelt would deliberately make her husband uncomfortable with food he disliked, we can better evaluate the First Lady's part in planning White House menus. That she took responsibility for those meals is made clear in a letter to James in which she tries to protect Henrietta Nesbitt from charges he had made about the housekeeper's cooking in a draft of his book:

> I know that the popular supposition is that food was always bad in the White House. I think the people who feel that way forget that all the time we lived there we were in the Depression years and felt we could not allow Mrs. Nesbitt certain extravagances. . . . I would like you to put a note where you begin your dissertation on Mrs. Nesbitt and say: "Mrs. Nesbitt, of course, always submitted menus to Mother. The responsibility for what she spent and for what she ordered was my mother's and my mother's alone. Mrs. Nesbitt carried out her orders and later when Dr. McIntyre controlled the President's menus she carried out the Doctor's orders."

Eleanor Roosevelt made no claims about her skills in planning menus and, despite her disclaimer, deferred to her housekeeper to select the dishes served. Henrietta Nesbitt evidently had a high opinion of her own culinary talents. Her cookbook's foreword announces that "food was her contribution to history." The question that remains, of course, is just exactly what was that contribution?

Mrs. Nesbitt's shortcomings in cooking game and terrapin were particular irritations to FDR, who favored these dishes. But her unfamiliarity with such fare is perhaps excusable. A better measure of her skills is more likely to come from her ability to prepare basic and simple foods like cooked vegetables. Here our suspicions are aroused when Nesbitt discloses that Mrs. Roosevelt sent her to Schrafft's in New York to learn that restaurant's method of preparing vegetables. Once there, Nesbitt was surprised to discover that each vegetable was cooked separately, in small amounts, by being plunged into rapidly boiling water for a short period of time. That this procedure came as a revelation to Mrs. Nesbitt leads us to believe that she was in the habit of cooking large amounts of vegetable for a long time in water not necessarily up to the boil—a technique that invariably results in overcooked, waterlogged, and mushy veggies of poor color and taste.

It is also telling that Mrs. Roosevelt singled out Schrafft's as a place for instructing Mrs. Nesbitt. This restaurant chain specialized in vegetable dishes, fancy salads, and rich desserts, food geared to the luncheon tastes of women. As a training ground, it would have reinforced Mrs. Nesbitt's gender-based approach to menu making. So despite evidence to the contrary, Mrs. Nesbitt continued to insist that "when men . . . worked up a food peeve, it was usually against vegetables, the one item that harmed them least and which they were supposed to eat," but that "ladies ate vegetable without protest, and it's well known that women live longer"—in her view a just reward for their nutritional good sense.

Nesbitt was convinced that women loved sweet potatoes, prompting her to serve them to the wife of the French president in a dish that included canned pineapple. (How much damage this did to Franco-American relations is unknown.) She also proudly served sweet potatoes at President Roosevelt's second-term inaugural dinner, this time mashed, seasoned with salt, sugar, and nutmeg, and then baked in a casserole with marshmallows on top.

Her recipes for salads justify their frequent criticism. Mrs. Nesbitt thought of salads as substitutes for desserts, offering such little tricks as making dressings out of the syrup drained from canned fruits, or covering green-tinted canned pears with a sauce made from cream cheese, candied ginger, and nuts. She also tells us that she "used pineapple cut in lengthwise sticks and rolled lightly in crushed peppermint candy as an opener for the meal." Mrs. Nesbitt belonged to a school that classified salad making as a decorative art. This distinctively American tradition comes down to us from Fannie Farmer and other early-twentieth-century cooking school teachers who applied the term "salads" to sweet and colorful cold dishes they created by mixing fruits, vegetables, and frequently gelatin. A particularly grotesque example of the art form is the recipe Mrs. Nesbitt gives for Ashville Salad, a concoction of canned soup, chopped vegetables, gelatin, cream cheese, and mayonnaise.

ASHVILLE SALAD

1 can condensed tomato soup
2 small packages Philadelphia
   cream cheese
2 tablespoons gelatin
1½ cups chopped celery

1 small onion, chopped
1 large green pepper, chopped
½ cup mayonnaise
Lettuce

Heat soup to boiling; add cheese; blend until smooth. Dissolve gelatin in 1 cup cold water; when soaked, add to hot soup. Add vegetables and stir in mayonnaise. Chill in individual molds or a ring mold. Serve on lettuce with dressing as a salad, or a ring mold may be filled with chicken or fish salad for luncheon meal. Serves 8.

Mrs. Nesbitt's treatment of meat and fish is less startling. Her recipes adhere to solid American standards, such as roast beef, roast lamb, and meat loaf, and rely almost solely on salt and pepper for seasonings. Only one meat recipe—for roast pork—uses garlic, the infrequency of which in her cookbook contradicts her *Diary*, where she insists that she does not trust people who do not love garlic. Her greatest emphasis in the chapter on meat is on resourcefulness in cooking with innards, and here her recipes reflect the war years, when choice cuts of meat were scarce. Her meals frequently included the sweetbreads and other foods FDR hated: calf's brains, lamb tongues (in aspic), veal kidneys, and pigs' feet. Such old leftover standbys and budget stretchers as chipped beef, croquettes, and ham loaf also make appearances.

When she did move outside of her American frame of reference, Mrs. Nesbitt was still predictable. Her Mexican corn dish included sliced green pepper and a dash of chile; her Spanish sauce had tomatoes, onions, and green peppers, with garlic making a rare appearance; and her Italian sauce included a dash of red wine. When feeding foreign dignitaries, Mrs. Nesbitt reports, she served mainly fish and vegetables to Asians, while South Americans got "a lot of sticky and colorful sweets, colored petit fours, tiny cream puffs with varied fillings, and always candy and sweet or salted nuts." Observing Moslem tastes, she offered Albanian King Zog's three sisters a lavish sweet display, and the Sultan of Muscat a dinner without pork or alcoholic liquors—"not even a light wine."

Mrs. Nesbitt was fond of referring to her cooking as simple, and believed that "the bursting high spirits of the Roosevelts came from the food they ate. They ate simple, vitality-giving foods because they preferred that kind." This has the ring of self-justification, a continuous thread in Nesbitt's memoir. But even if it were true that her cooking helped preserve the First Family's health and energy, her cookbook suggests that many of the complaints about what was served in the White House were fully justified. Her cooking cannot be characterized and dismissed as merely honest, uncomplicated American fare. At its best it was uninspired, but at its worst it was downright bad, epitomizing what was wrong with much of home cooking in America in the 1930s and 1940s: a lack of seasoning, a heavy reliance on canned goods, and a propensity for fad foods that included sweet, fussy salads and ingredients like pineapple and marshmallows used to doll up dishes.

Yet Mrs. Nesbitt's kitchen skills cannot be totally dismissed, and the competence and confidence she exhibits when writing about her baking encourages us to think that in some measure it might have made up for her lackluster cooking. It was her baking, after all, that first brought her to the attention of Mrs. Roosevelt, and when the housekeeper describes her background as a baker, she does so with convincing authority:

> My mother had taught me all her baking tricks. She had come from near Vienna, and her excellent pastry work was all in the Viennese tradition. . . . All the coffeecakes and pies I began baking for Mrs. Roosevelt came from my mother.

Nesbitt's disquisition on the making of apple pie is enough to make anyone's mouth water as she describes her thoughtful method of getting the pastry just right and selecting the best apples, and discloses such special techniques as lining the bottom crust with sugar before the apples are added and judiciously dribbling a spoonful of vanilla over the apples before the top crust is tucked in. We believe her when she says, "Put a slice of good apple pie before any human, and he'll melt." She then follows with a special Nesbitt touch by adding, "Maybe that's why greatness doesn't awe me so much as it does some."

FDR Library

FDR's fifty-second birthday toga party, on January 30, 1934, surrounded by staff and family and with a cake that may have been the fruitcake recipe Mrs. Nesbitt claimed was the president's favorite. (Unlike the others, he seems completely at ease in costume.)

She is positively lyrical at Christmastime, when she always prepared her family recipe for fruitcake, a great favorite of the President that also served as his birthday cake. The process of chopping up dates, raisin, almonds, citron, and orange peel was sheer pleasure for her.

> I defy any woman to chop up fruits like these, all pungent and sugary, and keep up any personal brooding. Fruitcake mixing can be heartily recommended as a cure-all for grouches and blues. For me, it always seems romantic, and reminds me of lines in poetry. "Dates and figs of Samarkand," and "lucent syrops, tinct with cinnamon."

Almost all of her recipes for cookies, cakes, and pies are appealing, and some are unusual. Honey drops, her standby cookies for White House teas, are not run-of-the-mill but include walnuts, honey, and chopped orange peel to give zing to the recipe. One ordinary batch makes twelve dozen cookies, as the practical Mrs. Nesbitt is quick to note.

When talking about baking, Mrs. Nesbitt exhibits none of the defensive language that is so apparent in her chapters on cooking. Instead she tells us "When I like people, I fix them an apple pie, and when I take a sugary, crusty pie from the oven and set it to cool, I feel the way an artist must when he's finished a picture."

Mrs. Nesbitt would probably have been more suitable as the White House baker and not the person in charge of running all aspects of a large, complicated household with little more than an American can-do attitude to help her succeed. Like the Roosevelts who had brought her to Washington, Mrs. Nesbitt was overwhelmed by the demands brought on by extraordinary historical events. The life she led at a time when most people her age were retired bore little resemblance to her old familiar life as an ordinary, small-town American housewife. In order to cope with the discrepancy, she had to persuade herself that her two lives were not really all that different from each other, that the dignitaries she served were not basically different from folks she knew in

HONEY DROPS

Adapted from The Presidential Cookbook, *by Henrietta Nesbitt*

½ cup butter
½ cup shortening
½ cup sugar
1 cup honey
1 egg
½ teaspoon vanilla
¾ cup chopped walnuts

½ cup chopped candied orange
  peel
3½ cups flour
2 teaspoons baking powder
1 teaspoon salt
½ teaspoon cinnamon

Cream butter and shortening. Add sugar and honey and beat until batter is smooth. Beat in egg. Add vanilla, walnuts, and orange peel. Beat in flour that has been sifted with baking powder, salt, and cinnamon. Dough should be slightly sticky but capable of being rolled into small balls using 1 teaspoon of dough. Bake in 325°F oven for approximately 18 minutes. Can yield 12 dozen cookies.

Hyde Park. And when the going did get rough, she could take comfort in what gave her most pleasure and pride—her mastery of baking, and the techniques handed down by generations of her family.

Mrs. Nesbitt's stiff ways made her an easy mark. But this bad cook should be given credit for her ability to stand up under fire. She did what her country required during some of the most difficult and demanding times in American history. Why did Eleanor Roosevelt insist on keeping Mrs. Nesbitt on throughout the uproar of constant criticism about her cooking? Perhaps because Mrs. Nesbitt's loyalty to the First Lady was reciprocated by Mrs. Roosevelt. And perhaps, even more simply, because Mrs. Roosevelt was comfortable with Henrietta Nesbitt.

SIX

Cooking Behind Barbed Wire

POWs During World War II

World War II in the Philippines was a conflict in which not only American fighting men but military noncombatants and ordinary American civilians became prisoners of the invading Japanese— captives suddenly in a country that had seemed to them a tropical paradise. Stories that have come down to us about such prisoners—U.S. Army and Navy doctors and nurses and overseas employees and their families—are compelling and more than a little frightening, even years after the events they describe. They remind us of how quickly and completely any of us can be deprived not only of our freedom but also of practically everything else that gives our lives meaning and value, to the point where mere survival—just getting enough to eat and drink—becomes our highest if not our only priority.

Stories of wartime imprisonment seem all the more painful and poignant when they are told by women, especially the mothers of young children concerned for their well being. Such stories also illuminate some important differences in the way men and women

World War II poster promoting defense production with captured American nurses unrealistically depicted in full regalia complete with caps, capes, white stockings, and pumps.

confront catastrophic changes in their circumstances, and how they adapt—or fail to adapt—to their loss of freedom and to scarcities of food and other necessities.

Although Hollywood has produced films about women imprisoned in the Pacific in World War II—*So Proudly We Hail* (1943),

Three Came Home (1950), and more recently, *Paradise Road* (1997)—history is better served by first-person accounts of those who endured internment by the Japanese. Especially valuable are diaries by Elizabeth Vaughan and Natalie Crouter, the wives of American businessmen in the Philippines, who were trapped with their families on the islands when the Japanese invaded. These accounts, along with a notebook kept by Commander Thomas Hayes, describe the appalling conditions of both military and civilian prisons. They also describe the experience of captivity, which for the women was often less frightening than boring, mean, and petty, but sometimes heroic and inspiring. From the food obsessions of these prisoners, much can be learned about the lives they longed for at home and would attempt to remake upon their return.

Before Pearl Harbor, the Philippines, which had been a Spanish colony until the 1898 Spanish-American War, had become a U.S. commercial outpost. In the midst of the Depression, men from the States with business and technical skills could go there to find high-paying jobs serving American mining and sugar-producing interests. The jobs offered high status in addition to high salaries, and the men's wives enjoyed a cadre of willing and loyal servants, including cooks, cleaners, laundresses, child minders, and gardeners. While their husbands were at their offices or away on frequent business trips, American married women in the Philippines had the time and leisure to gather at social clubs and play bridge or tennis, or occupy themselves in charitable activities.

When the Japanese began to occupy parts of Southeast Asia, many cautious Americans moved back to the United States. But others stayed behind in the Philippines, blithely believing that their country's armed forces would dissuade any enemy from invasion and that they could continue to lead their privileged lives. Two such victims were James Vaughan, a civil engineer originally from Mississippi, and his wife, Elizabeth, who was also from the South. They shared a hope of saving enough to buy a house back home in the States. Elizabeth Vaughan was trained before and after the war in sociology, which later allowed her to produce a doctoral dissertation that analyzed the trials that she and other captured expatriates suffered during the Japanese occupation of the Philippines. More widely read and praised, however, was the diary she kept and published of her experiences in WWII.

In *The Ordeal of Elizabeth Vaughan: A Wartime Diary of the Philippines* (1985) the author reports that she was never again to see her husband after he left their home in the provincial seaport city of Bacolod on a business trip to Manila on December 6, 1941. The next day the Japanese attacked the American naval base at Pearl Harbor, Hawaii, and the day after that Manila, where they bombed the Cavite Navy Yard and soon after overwhelmed the American military personnel. Unable to return to a family that included two young babies still in diapers, Jim Vaughan immediately joined the U.S. Army and was sent to Bataan, which along with Corregidor was where the remainder of the American ground forces in the Pacific had consolidated. Both places would soon be conquered by the Japanese. Military experts would later claim that the fall of Corregidor was the worst military defeat ever suffered by the United States, Vietnam not excepted. Jim Vaughan made it through this disaster and even survived the infamous Bataan Death March, only to die of dysentery in a Japanese prison camp in July of 1942. In the meantime his wife and two children became prisoners themselves, spending two years in captivity at Bacolod, and a final year in Santo Tomás, not far from Bilibid, where the Imperial Japanese Army had converted part of the University of Manila into a civilian internment camp.

Early in her diary, which she began as an extended letter to her missing husband, Elizabeth Vaughan succinctly captured the tragic irony of her situation in her description of how, just before her husband departed, she had acquired a potato ricer, an old-fashioned kitchen tool that had been hard to find in the Philippines.

Jim, remember how you wanted a potato ricer for the kitchen, for every time we had mashed potatoes, the cook, Consuela, left lumps

in them? So I ordered a ricer from Sears-Roebuck to please you. . . .
The ricer arrived a few days before you left for Manila—in the rush
of things, I didn't tell you. . . . [When] the war came, Consuela
rushed off without a word, the potatoes were exhausted, so here I
am, with a shining new ricer all the way from the States to please a
husband and a cook, and now there is no husband, no cook and no
potatoes.

Elizabeth Vaughan, who had always boasted that she would
never have to cook, was suddenly solely responsible for the care
and feeding of her two babies, with no servants to help and no
husband to give her moral support. In fact, she was fortunate to
have more food than most to cook, since unlike those in military
POW camps, civilian internees were able to hoard supplies they
had before the occupation and could receive food from the outside. Those like Vaughan who had sufficient cash or credit and
good connections to Filipino merchants were also able for a time
to supplement the meager fare from the camp kitchen where native foodstuffs and dwindling stores of canned food were prepared
in crude facilities. The possibilities for augmenting the food supply at Vaughan's camp continued until 1944, when worsening
shortages caused severe hardships for captives and captors alike.
These privations lasted until February 1945, when she was freed
by American troops.

The food shortages Vaughan describes were needless in a climate that could support sustainable agriculture. If the kind of
food Americans could stomach was hard to find, it was because
policies carried out during Spanish and American colonization
encouraged Filipinos to grow products for export—mainly sugar,
hemp, and copra (dried coconut)—and to rely on food imported
from the United States and elsewhere. But with supplies from
America cut off, POWs had to settle for the few available local eatables. Late in the war, even sugar became hard to come by.

Until then, sugar was the staple food of the POWs, who rarely
had enough meat and vegetables. Instead, they made fudge for all
occasions. Readily available sugar even served as a substitute for

alcohol, suddenly missing from the lives of many of the civilian prisoners. To compensate for the lack of liquor, POWs in the male quarters often carried around mugs filled with sugar that they nipped at to assuage their cravings for stronger stuff.

Throughout her imprisonment, Vaughan found it especially hard to find and prepare substantial food to satisfy her fussy children, Beth and Clay. In a May 1942 diary entry, she reports that precious bantam eggs were brought into the camp but that her children refused them for breakfast because they tasted of smoke after being cooked over wet tropical wood. They balked also at lunch, when she served them rice with tiny native tomatoes and green papaya. Finally she sifted out insects and worms from the little flour she had left and mixed it with heavily watered milk, a little chocolate, and some sugar, knowing that the sweetness would counteract the taste of smoke. Vaughan could only hope that the improvised blancmange provided the nourishment her children needed. In the same diary entry, she reports her determination to ration the dwindling canned goods she had on hand—evaporated milk, fruits and vegetables, canned sausages, and other canned meat—and rely more on native produce like mangoes and coconuts, realizing that the war would not end before her hoard of canned food was gone.

The same kind of rationing occurred more generally in September of 1942, when the camp kitchen's supervisor was found to be using too much canned food and throwing away local fruits and vegetables. The woman was replaced by a committee consisting of a trained hospital dietitian, a supervisor of home economics teachers, and a former hotel proprietor. Thereafter breakfast consisted solely of a large spoon of white or red rice, a bit of coconut honey, and a cup of weak coffee, with a pitcher of hot water available for those who needed a second cup. Vaughan's diary entry describes the rest of the camp's daily diet:

> Luncheon varies, but the main dish is always rice. At tea the first and main dish is rice and there is always a second helping for those who wish it. This is wonderful "chow" for Filipinos, but too much

starch for foreigners, and efforts to counteract this one-sided diet are seen in endless walking around and around camp buildings in an effort to take exercise and endless drinking of hot water and coconut milk (when the latter is available). Also a great rush for spinach juice on days this is served. There are almost no laxatives in camp and people must use other measures for common stomach and intestinal ailments. Children are allowed one cup of carabao [water buffalo] milk per day and no more canned milk is to be used. Carabao milk is delivered to the camp hospital where it is boiled. The milk is white but thickish and contains a much greater proportion of fat than most cows' milk. It has a strong taste. Clay drank the milk without noticing difference from Carnation, which also has a strong taste. Beth wouldn't drink the new milk (perhaps she noticed my turned-up nose as I gave it to her!) so I put a spoonful of molded locally grown chocolate and a spoonful of sugar in it, then she drank her chocolate milk.

Except for the difficulty in feeding her children, Elizabeth Vaughan somehow felt better when shortages finally beset the camp and she had to experience a measure of the deprivation she knew was being suffered by captured GIs.

Now that we have less food I enjoy it more. A surplus nauseated me—knowing that Jim might be starving in Manila and knowing that there are U.S. Army prisoners on this island who would grab and consume the refuse we would throw our pigs. . . . I want to go a little bit hungry if it means food for someone who is hungrier than I. We have been too fortunate in our food—since we're civilians the Japanese have made no effort to stop food supplies from coming in as long as we ourselves have to pay for it, cash or credit (all is on credit), but we all know this generous food supply can't go on indefinitely.

Vaughan was right. By November 1942, the dining room began serving unappetizing native foods that were listed derisively in Vaughan's diary:

poto—rice flour cakes, small puffy, snow white, gelatinous-like in
texture.

tinola—fish head soup, fish eyes glaring from pot, one head with
each serving, ghastly and nauseating to think of eating head and
wide-open eyes, but favorite dish of Filipinos, often served in
camp.

cincomas—tasteless, turnip-like white root, eaten boiled or sliced
and fried and called in camp "Dutch fried potatoes."

patola—a stringy, okra-like vegetable sliced and boiled in coconut
milk.

Complaints about food were most often directed at unfamiliar
ingredients that were made palatable to American tastes only
when presented in an accustomed form. Soybeans, not yet part of
the American diet, found acceptance when ground, mixed with
rice flour and water, and fried as fritters. Everyone loves fritters.

Coconut milk was also cut to one teaspoonful per cup of coffee
or tea, with carabao milk restricted to infants, children, and invalids. Only Thanksgiving brought relief from camp austerity,
with an ingenious substitute for the holiday bird and a cleverly
improvised dessert that took the place of pumpkin pie:

Promised something "special" in dining room. Dinner consisted of
native port, native sweet potatoes (camotes), a vegetable goulash
and squash pie without crust. The "special" was an awesome
"turkey" lying in state on a table in the center of dining room. A
large pumpkin-type squash, shaped surprisingly like the torso of a
fowl, had legs of long bananas fastened on with copper wire, which
also formed the feet sticking high in the air. The turkey's wings were
long, curved slices of camote, the neck was the stem of the pumpkin, painted darker than the rest of the body. The handsome fowl
lay on its back on a large platter of red rice which looked, at first
glance, like dressing.

For Thanksgiving tea there was chocolate coconut fudge for
everybody, made by some of the women of camp on an open fire for
several successive afternoons. Over one thousand pieces were

cooked so each of the 146 persons in camp was allowed a few pieces to take to his room.

In December, with the war in the Pacific a year old, shortages intensified drastically. Pilfering took place in the communal kitchen. Like coconut milk, sugar rations were cut to one tea-spoonful per cup of coffee or tea when the Imperial Army confis-cated the island's sugar stores for shipment to Japan. Salt and coconuts also became scarce, though Vaughan could observe a large coconut grove ripe for picking just outside the camp.

As bad as conditions were in Bacolod, they were worse in the cramped quarters of the Santo Tomás Internment Camp, a small section of the occupied University of Manila campus where Vaughan and some 3,500 internees spent the last two years of the war. Most objectionable to her here was the utter lack of privacy, especially in the communal showers and toilets. Dressing and un-dressing were also a public events, made worse by the constant spying of Japanese guards. Each adult's living space was about the size of a small bed, squeezed against another woman's identical small space. The only exception was "Shantytown," a collection of privately owned nipa-grass huts that those with money could build and live in with their families, albeit under strict supervi-sion. Otherwise, men were housed separately and conjugal visits were forbidden, in part no doubt to avoid births and the responsi-bility of even more mouths to feed.

Every daily function required internees to stand in long lines—getting meals, doing laundry, using toilets. The grim routine and tedium of life in captivity caused many of the women to become mean-spirited and selfish. Exactly one banana for each prisoner would be allotted each day and put in a pile on the center table in the dining room. But some would take more than their share, leaving the last to arrive without their daily ration. Vaughan's diary noted: "There is pushing in the food line and persons in camp act more and more like savages as life becomes less com-fortable and food less satisfying."

After the war, Elizabeth Vaughan returned to the United States and completed her Ph.D. at the University of North Carolina, where her doctoral dissertation interpreted her experiences at Bacolod and in turn became the basis of her book *Community Under Stress: An Internment Camp Culture* (1949). Here Vaughan provides evidence that women adjusted more readily to prison-camp life than men. Using such measures as percentage losses in weight and the comparative number of mental breakdowns, deaths from diseases, and suicides, she observes that men lost proportionately more weight than women, that 89.5 percent of the deaths from illness were male (in a prison population that was 61 percent male), and that all of the suicides were men. Vaughan concludes that the men's sense of themselves as protectors and providers was irreparably damaged by internment.

Natalie Crouter and Elizabeth Vaughan never crossed paths as they went from prison to prison in the Philippines. But Crouter, the author of *Forbidden Diary: A Record of Wartime Internment, 1941–1945* (1980) and a Boston-born wife of a former U.S. enlistee-turned-businessman, would have agreed with many of Vaughan's conclusions. Together with their two children, who were ten and twelve when war broke out, Natalie and Jerry Crouter spent the duration in a couple of Japanese prison camps, starting with the comparatively humane Camp Holmes, high in the scenic mountains of Luzon, and ending not far from Santo Tomás, in the civilian quarters at Bilibid, the infamous disease-ridden Manila prison that was also home to captured Allied soldiers.

Like the Vaughans' imprisonment, that of the Crouters took place in the wake of a U.S. State Department decision not to issue an official notice to American civilians to leave the Philippines. While the families of American military personnel had already been ordered back to the States, civilians and their dependents were left alone to decide if and when they wanted to repatriate. The Crouters decided to stay and soon found themselves trapped.

Although the Crouters all survived the war, its aftereffects were more debilitating than for Elizabeth Vaughan and her children.

Bureau of Surgery and Medicine Archives

Navy nurses—one of them too weak to stand—following their rescue from Los Banos prison on February 23, 1945. Their dresses were made in the camp from salvaged dungarees

Following the Crouters' return to the States in the summer of 1945, Natalie was hospitalized for dysentery and pernicious anemia. Her son, Fred, would suffer continued stomach disorders, and her daughter would belatedly act out adolescent rebellion but maintain the special bond with her mother that was formed in the prison camps. Her husband, Jerry, died within six years of the family's release. Though his health had been permanently damaged by wartime malnutrition, he returned to the Philippines a few weeks after the family's repatriation to start a new job. It was there in 1947 that he suffered a cerebral hemorrhage that caused him to come back to the States, where he would recover, but later die of liver disease in 1951 at the age of fifty-eight.

Temperament helped Natalie Crouter make it through, just as it did Elizabeth Vaughan. Before the war, Crouter had been a volunteer for a number of radical causes. Her concern for helpless minorities stemmed in part from the sense of weakness and dependency she experienced in childhood after she contracted polio complicated by meningitis at the age of nine. Memories of that experience surface in her diary, where she recalls the tireless care given by her mother, who for three and a half years took her daughter by coaster wagon and streetcar to a Boston osteopath for experimental treatments that succeeded in restoring strength to her paralyzed leg. These memories surfaced in relation to the care she gave to her own daughter, June, who was just entering her teen years when the Crouter family was imprisoned.

The closeness of mother and daughter is a consistent theme in the diary, with Natalie rarely failing to pass on her idealistic philosophy of life to her adolescent child. On Easter Sunday of 1942 she writes:

June has an onion sprouting in a little can. We talked about how dry it had looked, withered, yet that spark of life was there to come forth under proper conditions into lovely green points. I told her that everyone was like that and some day people would understand; there would be no more prisons, only hospitals or schools to correct abnormalities; society would try to correct unhealthy surroundings and malnutrition which warped people and covered their spark of life. As we went arm and arm to breakfast, she said, "Mummie, I just learned an awful lot. I never thought about people that way before. It's nice." Whether it is religion, idealism, socialism, art or some other creative expression, it must go with the bread. For those who have not been able to develop inner resources there must be outside help to draw forth their green shoots of hope and courage.

Natalie Crouter's world view was so humanitarian that she was able to identify with the families of her nation's enemies, or at least with some of them. "I can't help thinking of the mothers and wives back in Japan who will never know what happened to their men in the Philippine attack," she wrote.

This selflessness also found expression in how Natalie Crouter distributed a gift of native coffee that was sent to her for use in the camp. Rather than turn it over to the kitchen, where it was unlikely to be shared equitably, Crouter made certain that every overlooked group in the camp got a cup: "First the toilet-workers, next the towel-washers, then the women vegetable cutters, the porch groups, the British girls who get no packages, and so on." The same sense of fairness and concern for the common good caused her to criticize those in the camp who demanded special considerations. These included a group of Seventh Day Adventists who refused to eat pork when for a time it was plentiful but instead ate up all of the cheese, macaroni, and spaghetti, leaving none for others.

The camp forbade writing and journal keeping, rules Natalie Crouter flouted by writing on small scraps of paper she kept concealed in a can of food supplies, first covered with butter until it was consumed by her family, then in turn with brown sugar, beans, and peanuts. The diary itself is preoccupied with food. In its unedited version, it included descriptions of 3,785 meals, about two-thirds of which included camotes, beans, and rice. "The constantly hungry writer itemized every scrap of food she consumed during her entire incarceration," explained the diary's editor, Lynn Z. Bloom, who understandably eliminated this monotonous and repetitive account of daily meals but happily saved Natalie Crouter's many shrewd observations on the effects of food scarcity. "I still marvel at what food craving does to individuals," Crouter remarked.

> The strangest acquaintances—not really friendships—spring up.
> One who gets gifts or purchases attracts one or two others who have
> none, often odd combinations. In normal times they would not see
> each other. Lack of food changes people generally, makes insidious
> inroads in many directions of the personality.

Crouter's observations about the way others in the camp reacted to their changed circumstances are particularly shrewd and revealing. She accepted without complaint the menial tasks she was required to do, mopping up dirty floors, day after day, for she had noticed that the happiest people in the camp were the ones doing their share of community work. "Natures that withdraw take more of a beating in internment," she comments, "than those who adjust or melt into the group." She recognized early that it was her commitment to helping and establishing friendships with others that was sustaining her, although she did not discount her diet, which was rich in protein, fat, and B vitamins and included liberal helpings of garlic. "I'm getting a reputation for keeping as well as anyone in the camp," she wrote in May of 1942.

> People come to ask me how I eat my garlic. Part of my health is be-
> cause I don't feel down, find much to be amused at every day.
> Morale is highly important as good Nazis know. Otherwise it is rice,
> bananas, peanut butter, garlic and yeast tablets which do the trick.
> I'm practically a test case on garlic as an intestinal antiseptic.

The reference to Nazis is, of course, ironic, but Crouter was serious and has since been proved correct that garlic boosts one's immunity to infection. At the same time, she wondered why her husband, who ate the same food except for garlic, was faring less well, not realizing that his business losses and worry about the future were conspiring to depress him and damage his health. "It is strange that I, the weaker, continue to gain and escape the camp illness, while he the stronger, should have lost thirty-four pounds and contracted ailments. We are each doing more physical work than customary, both get the benefit of bananas, peanut butter and yeast tablets. Can it be the garlic?" It was more likely to have been Natalie Crouter's perpetual spirit of optimism.

As shortages started to become severe, Crouter showed concern but not despair.

We are not starving but we thoroughly crave *accustomed* food. There is a definite unbalance to our diet besides the fact of only two meals a day. We lack enough proteins, sugar and fat. The children have rice, syrup and a drink of hot water for breakfast; adults the same, plus weak coffee without milk or sugar. Strawberry jam on a piece of bread for lunch but no soup or tea. A radish for adults and a piece of O'Racca candy for the children. Gifts from the outside have satisfied my cravings for the moment but I'm still mad for a 24-hour soak in hot water, in a tub, solitary and alone—no fire buckets, no three others splashing cold shower in the small enclosure, all standing on one leg to dress.

Crouter's New England practicality made her dismissive of the efforts of many of the female prisoners to maintain their personal appearance and femininity by wearing satin nightgowns, putting up their hair in curlers, and using cold cream and lipstick. Like Elizabeth Vaughan and other women prisoners in the Philippines, Crouter used donations of cold cream to fry native edibles but found it "the ultimate low in cooking grease which browned food, even though its scent detracted from the dish." As for her hair, for convenience she allowed it to grow long and wore it in an easily managed braid that ran down her back. "My state of mind has no time for waves, rouge or lipstick," Crouter later wrote, "I cannot read or play cards when I am living this hard and I do feel it is a real experience, not a drop of which should be wasted or missed." As late as May 1944, Crouter was able to tell fellow inmates over dinner that they would one day look back with longing to Camp Holmes.

Release came at last in February 1945, with Crouter and her family overwhelmed with food, candy, cigarettes, and other kindnesses offered by the rescuing U.S. Marines, who themselves were a stunningly welcome and refreshing sight: "Huge, husky men, almost overpowering in their health and energy. They have such an American look: above all, secure and well fed." She was just as captivated by the sounds of American voices with their Southern, Western, and Eastern accents and by their fit bodies and undamaged souls.

After the initial euphoria of being rescued, the Crouters took stock and realized they were ruined financially. They had lost their home and possessions, which had either been looted or sold by them to pay for extra food while they were in the camp, and Jerry Crouter was without employment. The family returned to America, settling in Cleveland Heights to live with Natalie's sister while Jerry found work back in the Philippines, but he suffered illnesses and died in 1951. Natalie had to deal with intestinal parasites and a serious case of dysentery, but after recovering she began traveling extensively—to the Soviet Union in 1950 and to mainland China in the 1970s—and supported such liberal political activities as Henry Wallace's 1948 Progressive Party presidential campaign and the pacifist Women's International League for Peace and Freedom. Son Fred became a high school history teacher and later wrote a master's thesis based on his mother's diary. Daughter June, who eventually married and led a successful professional life, first had to deal with psychological problems brought on by her prison-camp experience. Her intensely close relationship to her mother during those years delayed the typical adolescent rebellion most children experience. With counseling, she moved on to a career as a social worker, but she retained symptoms brought on by the food deprivation she had endured during the war. She became an enthusiastic and accomplished cook who surrounded herself with an oversupply of food, alert and prepared for any unforeseen emergency that might otherwise lead to hunger.

Unmarried women—U.S. Army and Navy nurses—were also shocked to find themselves prisoners of the Japanese at the outbreak of the war in the Pacific. Typically, they were young women who had struggled through the Depression, attending nursing school before joining the service. To them, being stationed in the Philippines held the promise of adventure and romance—sipping long, cool tropical drinks and dancing under the stars with handsome army and navy officers. Their idyl ended abruptly when Japanese bombers attacked American military installations. Suddenly, nurses accustomed to taking care of mothers with newborns or dealing with the results of home accidents were serving the victims of a mass slaughter, injecting morphine into screaming patients, and helping doctors amputate crushed limbs.

Soon they were torn away from their patients and sent off to Santo Tomás prison camp, where Elizabeth Vaughan and other civilians were interned. With little money and few connections to supplement their meager rations, the nurses relied on food donations from civilians living outside the camp and, like the other inmates, tended the vegetable gardens that had been established in the camp.

Rations began to deteriorate by the late fall of 1943, when meat was impossibly scarce and fresh fruit and vegetables had become unavailable after a severe typhoon destroyed most of the prison's garden crops. In early 1944, control of the camp passed to the Japanese army. Outside contributions were banned and daily rations cut to fewer than 1200 calories. When American bombers became a threat, rations were cut even further to fewer than 1000 calories per day, and internees started to eat weeds or root for scraps from the kitchen. Deaths began to occur from starvation, and diseases such as beriberi, pellagra, and scurvy were rampant.

As a manifestation of their near starvation, the nurses took on "a recipe mania, a kind of psychosis of imagination" described by Elizabeth Norman in We Band of Angels, a book about the nurses' experiences as Japanese prisoners. They would copy recipes from magazines and cookbooks and compose fantasy meals, going so far as to consult with their dietitian to make sure that their imagi-

National Archives, U.S. Army Signal Corps

A view of shanties built by internees in the courtyard of the main building, Santo Tomás civilian prison camp.

nary menus were nutritionally sound. But in reality, they were suffering from emaciation and weakness, no better off than the patients they tried to care for.

When finally liberated from the camp, the nurses were treated by the GIs with food of every available variety, starting with K rations that the soldiers had long ago become sick of and were astonished to find the women relishing. Soon after, they were also regaled with the luxuries of American life, including chocolate, bread and butter, real coffee, and steak, which many of the nurses, sick from nutritional and tropical diseases, were in no condition to digest. Others with stronger constitutions bounced back more readily, among them a group of operating room nurses who were given four big cherry pies, which they ate with relish. One of them reports having eaten her share topped with cream and washed down with a healthy dose of bourbon.

LIBERATION CHERRY PIE

Most bakers would agree that the best cherry pies are made from fresh sour cherries. But their season is so short—a week or two at the end of June and the beginning of July—that those who want to eat this pie more than once a year have to settle for canned cherries. Since the nurses' pies were given to them in February, we can assume they contained canned cherries. [A note to the cook: If you can find 1-lb., 9-oz. jars of Morello cherries, available at Trader Joe's, use two of them.]

Crust

2 cups all-purpose flour

¼ teaspoon salt

⅓ cup butter, chilled and cut into small pieces

⅓ cup shortening, chilled and cut in small pieces

⅓ cup ice water

Filling

¾ cup sugar

3 tablespoons flour

¼ teaspoon ground cinnamon

4 cups canned cherries, drained

2 tablespoons butter

For top of crust

1 tablespoon milk

1 teaspoon sugar

To make the crust: Sift and mix together flour and salt. Cut the butter and shortening into the mixture until it is the size of small peas. Sprinkle 3 tablespoons ice water over mixture and blend. Add more water just until the dough holds together. Divide in two, one piece slightly larger than the other, and chill for several hours or overnight.

(continued on page 150)

To make the filling: Mix together all but 1 teaspoon of the sugar, the flour, and the cinnamon. Add to drained cherries and stir.

To assemble the pie: Preheat oven to 425°F. Roll out the larger part of the refrigerated dough and line a 9-inch pie pan. Sprinkle the 1 teaspoon sugar over bottom crust. Pour the filling into the prepared crust and dot with butter. Roll out the top crust and place on pie or cut into strips ¾ inch wide and weave into a lattice top. Brush the top with the milk and sprinkle with the sugar. Bake for 10 minutes, then reduce heat to 350° and bake for about 45 minutes longer.

That Crouter could look upon much of her experience as formative—and in some ways positive—proves she did not experience the worst of it. As bad as their lives had been in Santo Tomás, both the nurses and American civilians were always aware of the difference between their situation and that of the military prisoners held in nearby Bilibid. Nevertheless, Natalie Crouter, who had been separated from these men only by a wall, was shocked at her first sight of what remained of the 800 U.S. Army and Navy personnel in the converted Spanish penitentiary once it was liberated:

Collarbones stood out like shelves. Eyes were gaunt and hollow. Faces were drawn tight with nerves. Elbows were bony knobs. Arms and legs were literally pipe-stems. *There* was starvation and we felt that our troubles were nothing.

How these men arrived at this dreadful condition is described in *Bilibid Diary: The Secret Notebooks of Commander Thomas Hayes, POW, the Philippines, 1942–45*. The Philadelphia-born Hayes graduated from medical school at George Washington University in 1920 and four years later was commissioned a lieutenant (j.g.) in the U.S. Navy Medical Corps. After tours of duty in the States, Lieutenant Commander Hayes served on the USS *Milwaukee* until May 1941 and in August of the same year was assigned to the U.S. Navy base at Cavite in the Philippines. When the war began in December, he received a battlefield promotion to commander and became chief medical officer for a Marine regiment that defended the island bravely for weeks until being forced to surrender to the Japanese on Corregidor on May 5, 1942. With his medical unit, Hayes was sent to Manila's Bilibid Prison, where from July 1941 to December 1944 he served as chief of surgery and then as senior medical officer. With little food, medicine, and sanitary facilities, Hayes struggled vainly against the mounting death toll from nutritional diseases, dysentery, malaria, diphtheria, and pneumonia. His shrewd observations on the torturous daily activities of the camp were committed to a notebook, which he left with a fellow officer before he and many of his fellow POWs were packed aboard a so-called Japanese "hell ship" bound for Japan, where the captives were expected to work in labor camps. Hayes survived the sinking of this ship by American warplanes but died on another Japanese ship, also bombed and sunk by American aircraft.

Not surprisingly, Hayes's notebook chronicles his struggle to find enough food for himself and his patients at Bilibid. In a diary entry of July 1942, he described the psychological effects of malnutrition:

When food is denied, the sensation of hunger takes over. But this passes quickly. One adjusts readily to reduced quantities. However, when certain elements are withheld, a craving of the most painful kind will persist. This is often interpreted as hunger but it occurs when the belly is full. This state lasts a long time and some people never overcome the symptoms. Most often it is a craving for sweets—sugar is hard to do without. I have been through long sugar denials which were hellish, not only because my taste demanded it, but physiologically the old human machine was missing. Our blood sugar gets so low that we often fall asleep while eating or at work. It's during this phase of food denial that one becomes conscious of physical inefficiency, mental dullness, and the inability to concentrate. My memory becomes so bad at times that I can't recall the names of friends, or read a page from a book and hold the continuity.

As a man of science, Hayes is meticulous in his observations. He notes clinically that eventually the desire for food disappears altogether, along with the longing for particular foods: "I have forgotten desserts to the point where I no longer crave them. I can fill my emptiness with rice and my blunted gustatory senses are easily satisfied by the small quantities of supplementary items that we get occasionally." At this state, Hayes ate just to stay alive, a condition he found less preferable than hunger.

What Hayes and other Americans most disliked but ate nonetheless was the rice supplied by the Japanese. It was so infested with worms that one of Hayes's fellow navy officers removed his glasses whenever he ate so that he would not notice. The daily rice ration was made more attractive and palatable by mongo beans, tiny green granules about the size of shotgun pellets and with a pleasant lentil taste. They could be soaked, sprouted, and then stewed or fried and poured over rice. Ironically, it was at Bilibid Prison years before the war that nutritional experiments were performed to prove that mongo beans, which Hayes remarks were rich in vitamin B_1, could prevent beriberi when included in a plain rice diet. But even the availability of mongo beans did not prevent many of the prisoners from contracting this nutritional disease and suffering blindness or other related forms of impaired vision. Time and again, Hayes notes that were it not for outside contributions, he and others would have starved to death.

Food contributions came from many of the same sources that supplied Santo Tomás and other Japanese internment centers—Filipino friends and merchants, Japanese military entrepreneurs, and international humanitarians organizations like the Red Cross.

On Christmas of 1942, Bilibid received British Red Cross packages containing canned meat, soap, sugar, apple pudding, and jam. Shipments from the American Red Cross, however, were confiscated by the Japanese.

By May 1944, malnutrition, sickness, and overwork had killed hundreds in Bilibid and outlying labor camps and almost terminally demoralized the men who were left alive to care for the survivors. Hayes himself believed that if he and his fellow medical officers made it through the war and went back to America, they would find that their friends and families had gone on without them and would regard their return as an unwanted intrusion.

> I'm convinced that life at home has now gone on too long without us. We will never fit in again. Adjustments have undoubtedly been made and our loved ones have detoured their lives around the missing. We would be an ill-fitting part in the smooth running machinery of their daily routine. At times it seems silly for us to suddenly barge in and disrupt lives that have become used to being without us. Wade talks of going to Shanghai. I'm thinking of Singapore. Cecil says that Australia is in his future.

Why was Hayes so depressed when the women in nearby Santo Tomás were still optimistic? Perhaps because Vaughan and Crouter felt responsibility for keeping up the spirits of their children, and the very act of caring for children required them to believe in a future. Perhaps because, as women, they had more instinctive confidence that their relationships could survive the trauma of war. Though the women internees sometimes lost hope of being rescued, it never occurred to them that they might be forgotten. The extremities of the conditions suffered by Hayes and the others must have further distorted their sense of self-worth. Santo Tomás was no picnic, but its occupants were not subject to the "death camp" neglect and brutality that characterized Bilibid and other male POW camps in the Philippines. Tragically, Thomas

Hayes never got the opportunity to go home and be disabused of his fears.

Hayes's relatives were instead left with only his diary and another revealing book to which he had made a small contribution. *Recipes Out of Bilibid* was assembled by Colonel Halstead C. Fowler, who canvassed other inmates, most of them fellow Americans but also British, Dutch, and Filipino POWs who had been captured in the Philippines. The book includes dishes from all around the world, though most of the recipes came from the Americans and favored such basic comfort foods as pancakes, noodles, apple pie, and chili con carne. The preference among the malnourished prisoners at Bilibid was for rich foods of the kind they remembered eating at home in childhood or later with their wives and children. One can imagine the discussions that took place among the prisoners as they conjured up dishes they loved.

Recipes Out of Bilibid was compiled by Dorothy Wagner, the loving aunt of Colonel Fowler who had watched her West Point nephew leave for Manila with luggage that included a case of champagne meant to ward off seasickness. Forty months later, she met him on his return from the Philippines wearing borrowed clothes and carrying a bag that contained not much more than a little bundle of envelopes on which the recipes had been written. Fowler had miraculously survived the Bataan Death March and more than three years inside Bilibid prison camp, but came back emaciated, with three bullets still lodged in his body, and his vision severely impaired by beriberi. So moved was his aunt by the clutch of recipes that she decided to turn them into a professionally published book. In compiling the cookbook, Dorothy Wagner was able to visualize the suffering not only of her nephew and his comrades but also of the mothers and wives who were the ultimate sources for the recipes:

> Listening to Chick [Colonel Fowler] as he talked of the starving men who fed themselves on boyhood recollections, I tried to envisage the many kitchens in America and Britain, in Europe and China,

and scattered across the Pacific Islands that meant to each man the glowing heart of a beloved home. The women who presided over them must have brought love as well as patience and skill to their endlessly repeated labor of feeding their families, for only women capable of giving themselves generously to their work could have impressed the memory of those dishes so accurately on the minds of their boys.

Commander Hayes's contribution to *Recipes Out of Bilibid* is for a dish he calls "Fish Chowder." Fish and seafood chowder recipes fall into two camps—those made with milk, often called the New England version, and those made with tomatoes. The latter version often includes hot sauces and other spicy seasonings. Commander Hayes's recipe belongs to this camp. The absence of potatoes as well as milk would compel New Englanders to call this a stew, not a chowder, and the presence of curry powder suggests that the recipe was influenced by an Englishman with a fondness for curries. As a seafaring man, Commander Hayes was undoubtedly introduced to many different cultures, their people, and certainly their food.

Colonel Fowler identified the sources of his recipes whenever possible, giving some facts about the wartime accomplishments of these men and noting whether or not they survived the war. Just above Commander Hayes's recipe for Fish Chowder is this poignant note: "Contributed by Commander Hayes, U.S.N., who came from Tidewater, Virginia. He was among those who were lost aboard the prison ship that sailed on that tragic 13th of December."

At the same time that prisoners longed for home, civilians at the home front were preoccupied with the POWs and fighting men who were still risking their freedom and their lives. With the war effort the nation's priority, workers were encouraged to take jobs in defense plants, and women at home were asked to conserve resources. Home appliances would have to last until the war was over, and such desirable foods as meat, sugar, butter, and coffee

COMMANDER HAYES'S FISH CHOWDER
Adapted from Recipes Out of Bilibid

2 pounds fish fillets, such as
    cod
¼ cup peanut oil
1 large onion
2 cups raw oysters (optional)
6 tomatoes, peeled and
    chopped
2 hot peppers, minced

2 cups oyster or clam
    juice
3 cups water
1 teaspoon white pepper
¼ teaspoon Tabasco
1 tablespoon salt
¼ teaspoon thyme
Dash of curry powder

Sauté the fish in the oil until lightly brown. Remove from the pan. Chop the onion, oysters, and tomatoes, and add them to remaining oil in pan. Simmer for 30 minutes. Then place in a deep kettle, add the water and seasonings, and simmer for 10 minutes more.

SERVES 6

were rationed, invigorating home economists and food writers to instruct their readers on how to make do with less.

The United States government as well as food manufacturers issued pamphlets explaining vegetable cultivation and canning techniques so that people with backyards would grow victory gardens, allowing more commercially grown food to be shipped overseas. In this same spirit of patriotism, influential women's magazines ran stories all through the war giving tips for thrifty dishes that used few rationed ingredients. Alice Bradley, the principal of Miss Farmer's School of Cookery in Boston, dedicated *The Wartime Cook Book* (1943) to "Women who are cooperating in winning the war by using those foods of which we have an abundance in such combinations as to make themselves and their families strong." Bradley's wartime ideas included substituting soybean flour for wheat in thickening sauces and soups; using a pressure cooker to conserve heat and retain vitamins in vegetables; replacing sugar with honey or syrup in drinks and desserts; and cooking liver, kidney, sweetbreads, tripe, and tongue instead of the roasts and chops Americans preferred.

Housewives were taught to perk up leftovers with sauces (butterless and without cream, to be sure) or to extend foods by adding more breadcrumbs than usual to ground meat or by whipping a stick of butter with water and milk until it doubled in size. The efficient management of the home was billed as a form of patriotism, and homemakers were rightfully made to feel that they had a central role in the war effort. At the very least, they could spend money saved in the kitchen on war bonds. Typical wartime cookbooks had such titles as *Meatless Meals, Sweets Without Sugar, Thrifty Cooking for Wartime,* and *A Cook Book of Leftovers,* smacking of deprivation and a cheerlessness that people were conditioned to expect.

Intent on providing encouragement and practical tips, writers of those books were never given to speculate about the fix the world and all of its people were in. Such thoughts came from M.F.K. Fisher, who in 1942 brought out *How to Cook a Wolf,* a book about eating well during wartime in which she states:

> I believe that one of the most dignified ways we are capable of, to assert and then reassert our dignity in the face of poverty and war's fears and pains, is to nourish ourselves with all possible skill, delicacy, and ever-increasing enjoyment. And with our gastronomical growth will come, inevitably, knowledge and perception of a hundred other things, but mainly of ourselves.

Fisher instinctively knew that people under stress needed more from food than just basic sustenance. She knew that the frightening climate of a world at war was exactly the right time to be writing about appetite and the appeal of such simple dishes as polenta, spaghetti, and gingerbread. But she is discerning as she explains that the polenta must be made with the coarsely ground cornmeal available at the time only in Italian grocery stores, or enticing as she describes an economical recipe for gingerbread that "sends out a fine friendly smell through the house and is so good that it usually disappears while it is still hot, which is too bad because it is so good cold."

Unlike other wartime books about food, Fisher's *How to Cook a Wolf* never lost its audience. It is read today with curiosity and pleasure, for she captures our emotional and not just our physiological attachments to food. Like the wartime diaries and memoirs written by prisoners of war, her wartime cookbook captures the sensibility of a passionate observer who knew she was living through a momentous time.

SEVEN

Sachertorte in Harvard Square

Jewish Refugees Find Friends and Work

During World War II, as Americans fought fascism overseas, its victims came in waves from Europe to U.S. cities, where they were helped to adapt to their new country and in time were able to contribute something of their own culture—not the least of which was their cuisine. One of the most remarkable places where this exchange took place was the Window Shop, a gift store and Viennese restaurant near Harvard Square in Cambridge, Massachusetts. Here, for more than thirty years, New Englanders could enjoy such Old World delicacies as linzertorte, apple strudel, and kugelhopf, prepared early on by a largely refugee staff and later by a distinctive mix of refugees and native-born Americans.

The Window Shop came to national attention in May 1950, a little more than a decade after its opening, when Eleanor Roosevelt visited the place with a couple of her grandchildren, then attending nearby prep schools, to sample the establishment's celebrated Sachertorte. At the time, this surpassingly rich pastry, which immortalized the marriage of chocolate and apricot jam, would have been hard to find anywhere else in the Boston area, where Yankee tastes inclined to traditional local desserts like Indian pudding, a sweet but unsophisticated concoction that weds humble cornmeal and molasses. Mrs. Roosevelt herself was famously indifferent to food except as fuel to the spirit, so it was not the restaurant's superior baked goods that drew her to the Window Shop. Rather, the former first lady was impressed by the humanitarian effort that led to the shop's creation by a group of local women, most of them Harvard faculty wives of Protestant background, who had determined to help Jewish refugees in their flight from Nazi persecution and genocide.

With a loan of less than a hundred dollars in "pocket money" from its volunteer founders, the shop opened in 1939 as a small dry-goods exchange on Church Street in Cambridge. There, for a few months, it occupied a couple of rented rooms with a large window that gave the shop its name.

The founders of the Window Shop saw it as their special mission to help some of the hundreds of European Jews who had recently arrived in the Boston area. These were refugees who had little or no money and few, if any, resources for learning a new language, finding new employment, and adapting to their new country. Many of these displaced people came from upper-middle-class families in Germany and Austria, where husbands enjoyed successful business and professional careers and wives oversaw prosperous households with servants. Men from Rhineland countries who had been doctors, lawyers, professors, and merchants found their European credentials useless in the New World. Some took lower-paying jobs, often with consequent damage to their self-esteem; others sought to retool themselves by enrolling in one of the many local colleges and professional schools. Women refugees also sought to support themselves and their families with whatever work they could find during difficult economic times—at best as teachers and translators, more often than not as cleaning women, housekeepers, and governesses. It was these women newcomers especially that the Window Shop was designed to help.

Though the Window Shop would receive help from Jewish and Christian charities in New England, especially from the Boston Jewish Committee for Refugees, it was designed from the first as a bootstrap operation that would sustain itself by the sale of inexpensive American-made dry goods and handmade and home-baked items produced on consignment by refugee women. The inexperience of the founders in running such an enterprise caused the Window Shop to get off to a shaky start. Some of the volunteers who had contributed to the shop considered that the contents of its cash box essentially belonged to them and could be used whenever they ran out of money while shopping in Harvard Square. The result was a bookkeeping nightmare that was made worse by the complexities of consignment retailing, a system that

Schlesinger Library

The Window Shop Coffee Room in 1940.

proved hard for the volunteers to handle and even harder to explain to the refugees. Some refugees in reduced circumstances also created resentments by reminding everyone concerned that the work was beneath them. "There was strong criticism of them," said one of the Harvard wives, "and, under the surface, feelings of anti-foreigner, anti-Semitism, anti-newcomer."

Nonetheless, the Window Shop persisted. If the faculty wives who started it were not entirely free from such prejudices, they could nevertheless feel sympathy for women whose social and economic background was similar to their own but who had been torn abruptly from their comfortable middle-class lives. Among the most deeply devoted to helping victims of war were two volunteers who later served successive six-year terms as president of the Window Shop board of directors, from 1942 to 1954, guiding the enterprise through its most significant period of growth and development. These volunteers were Elsa Brandstrom Ulich, known as the Swedish Angel for her heroic work as a nurse in World War I, and Alice De Normandie Cope, a crusader for most of her long life for displaced families and children. Both of these women had firsthand experience with Nazism, as did two Austrian-Jewish refugees, Mary Mohrer and Alice Perutz Broch, whose efforts as paid employees were critical in the Window Shop's gift shop and, later, its bakery and restaurant.

Mary Mohrer was the first refugee employee of the Window Shop and the only one whose career spanned its entire thirty-three-year history. In Vienna, this daughter of a Jewish factory owner was a teacher who had earned an advanced degree in art history and was conversant in English and four other languages. When the Nazis came to power, she narrowly escaped to Switzerland, where she helped her father buy his way to freedom in England. She also persuaded the United States consulate in Zurich to grant her an American visa that allowed her to come to New York City in 1938 at the age of twenty-seven. In New York Mohrer worked briefly as a translator for the National Council of Jewish Women, a group that was struggling to save the lives of refugees still trapped in Europe—"a terribly depressing experience," as she

later recalled. At another translating job in the city, the young refugee got her first taste of American anti-Semitism when she was
told by another otherwise friendly physician that the only thing he
liked about Hitler was the German leader's attitude toward the
Jews.

Disheartened by her New York experience, Mohrer moved to
Cambridge. Here she found welcoming members of the Harvard
community who shared her cultural and intellectual interests,
took her into their homes, and put her in touch with the women
who were opening the Window Shop. "I met wonderful people,"
she recalled. "I mean the wonderful experience of this was the in-
credible openness, frankness and generosity of people. Really
lovely. It was invaluable."

It was Mohrer's idea to sell goods produced by local refugees,
allowing them to receive money for their work instead of charitable donations, which she knew would compromise their dignity.
One woman Mohrer recruited offered tiny umbrellas made out of
handkerchiefs that sold well at thirty-five cents apiece, while others made leather flowers that found disappointingly few customers. Still another woman baked cakes that sold for ten cents a
portion. Besides handling everything connected with the goods
and services sold by the shop, Mohrer also offered social-work services that she recalled were needed round the clock by her refugee
clients:

> People came with their personal problems, housing problems, psy-
> chological problems of husbands who had had big positions and fi-
> nally got a position here but their ego was so damaged that living
> with them was practically impossible. That could happen at mid-
> night. You could get a phone call, and you would walk over to Ox-
> ford Street and sit and talk with them, and there are millions of
> stories like that.

For several years Mohrer received $12 a week for her work, but
during its first few months, the gift shop could rarely pay her more
than $7, of which she often had to pay a dollar or two to consign-

ment workers. "When there was money," she recalled, "I had frankforts and beans for lunch. When there was not money, no frankforts—maybe no beans."

Though she had no experience in retail selling, Mohrer became an adroit salesperson, and her language skills allowed her to widen her network of refugees. Before long, she was able to increase profits from an expanded inventory of handmade items that included sweaters, gloves, and belts, as well as flowers, cookies, candies, apple strudel, and other baked goods. The quality and variety of goods produced by the refugees continued to improve under Mohrer's leadership. After Eleanor Roosevelt visited the Window Shop in 1950, she described the gift shop's offerings in her syndicated newspaper column. "They have embroideries such as are learned in other lands. Artists hand-block some of the materials used. They have blouses, frocks, coats, skirts, hand-knit sweaters and painted scarves done by a Russian woman of 65, and hand-made toys and glass and pottery."

Mrs. Roosevelt's visit was not the first time the Window Shop received widespread attention. On a particularly hot August day in 1939 Mary Mohrer came to work in a dirndl, the regional costume of Salzburg characterized by a full skirt gathered at the waist, and worn with

Schlesinger Library

Dressed in a dirndl outfit, Mrs. Schiffer, a Window Shop employee, rolls out dough.

a tight-fitting blouse. Young and lean, Mohrer must have looked fetching in the outfit, for she caught the eye of a photographer for the *Christian Science Monitor*. Accompanied by a brief article about the shop, Mohrer's picture in the *Monitor* coincided with an unlikely craze for dirndls that was started by the Duchess of Windsor. When the Window Shop became besieged with demands for the garments, Mohrer managed to find refugee women who were able to stitch them up. In short order, Harvard Square was able to witness the bizarre spectacle of Cambridge women of different sizes and shapes decked out in a costume not flattering to a stout figure. They were trying in vain to look like the Duchess of Windsor, who in turn was trying to look like a Tyrolean peasant, one can only suppose without success.

The sale from such items in the gift shop helped hundreds, and attracted a large and dedicated group of loyal patrons. But with the Window Shop, Mohrer was doing much more than simply selling clothing and baked goods. She became a one-woman social service agency, finding jobs for some refugees, and Mohrer sometimes even helped by dissuading others from serving at the Window Shop. The latter were women who had studied to become professionals of one kind or another in Europe but were prepared to work as cooks, waitresses, or salespeople in order to make ends meet. A Romanian woman with a degree in chemistry who applied for a job in the kitchen was persuaded by Mohrer to enroll instead at MIT, where she went on to earn a doctorate. Mohrer gave similar advice to a recently divorced Polish woman who worked in child care. At Mohrer's urging, the woman enrolled at Tufts University's Fletcher School of Diplomacy and later found a job more suited to her interests at Wellesley College.

In making these recommendations, Mohrer exhibited the wisdom and generosity that had been shown to her during her first days in Boston by a local baker she later called the Man with the Golden Heart. Desperate for work just after she arrived from New York, she had applied for a job with a Jewish bakery. The owner warned her the position was unsuitable for an educated woman of her background, but he promised to keep the job open for two weeks and give it to her if she came back before the end of that period. It was during those two weeks that Mohrer was guided to the Window Shop.

Mohrer arrived at the shop and started work there largely through the efforts of Mrs. Howard Mumford Jones, the wife of the distinguished man of letters who served for many years in Harvard's English department. In the fall of 1939 Mrs. Jones—Bessie, as she was called—oversaw the move of the Window Shop into larger quarters on tree-lined Mount Auburn Street. Mrs. Jones also began to establish standards and procedures that would allow the gift shop to become a better-organized and profitable business. Among other reforms, she arranged for members of MIT's Business Administration Department to set up an adequate bookkeeping system.

It was during the period of Bessie Jones's participation that a decision was made to entice more customers into the shop by adding a small bakery and tea room. A sum of $300 was allotted to hire refugees who could bake Viennese delicacies and transform the basement of the relocated Window Shop into a lunchroom, the forerunner of the restaurant that would become a favorite Harvard Square eating place.

In charge of the lunchroom operation was Alice Perutz Broch, another Jewish refugee, from Austria, who—legend has it—was given a wealth of recipes by her cook just before she and her family boarded a plane to flee from the Nazi threat. As the story goes, the cook assured Mrs. Broch (then Mrs. Perutz) that if the recipes were followed faithfully, they could be prepared even by someone who did not know how to cook. Mrs. Broch, like many well-to-do Austrian women of her class, was such a person. Fortunately, she did know how good food should taste and was willing to work hard to learn how to create it.

Mrs. Broch came to the United States with two sons, her first husband, and her husband's mistress, a peculiar arrangement but one that seemed to Alice Cope to have been undertaken to help ensure the safe escape of the entire group from Austria.

They all came together—she and her husband, and her husband's lady, and the Perutz' two boys, but they weren't divorced then, and very sensibly. I wouldn't be surprised if it was Alice Perutz who saw to it that they didn't get to this country unless they were all one family. And then they could get a divorce. I don't know this for a fact, but that's what I suspected. Then when they were divorced, very quietly she and this lovely Mr. Broch got married and it was months before anybody knew anything about it. One day someone said, "You know Mrs. Perutz isn't Mrs. Perutz any more. She's Mrs. Broch." I said, "What? How did *that* happen?" So I took myself down to the kitchen, and I said, "What's this about your having gotten married again?" "Oh," she said, "just two old things getting married."

Initially, cooking at the Window Shop was left to Mrs. Broch and another refugee, a Mrs. Schiffer, who was conscientious enough but far less accepting of her diminished social status. Marion Bever remembered the women and their approach to life and work:

An unlikelier pair you never saw in your life! Mrs. Schiffer was kind of a prickly, upper middle class, Jewish lady whose husband was at the Harvard Law School, and who had two children here, and who worked very hard but who always felt, I think, that it was somewhat beneath her. But she kept right at it. Mrs. Schiffer was always trying to be a lady on the side. Whereas Mrs. Broch would just roll up her sleeves. She didn't care. She was just working hard, and she was always a lady anyway. They were quite different.

Fortunately, Mrs. Broch had great patience and a gift for settling disputes. As Marion Bever put it, "Mrs. Broch could get along with anybody."

Though Mrs. Broch helped to set up the Tea Room and Bakery at Mount Auburn Street, she only became its manager in 1942 after a succession of American-born managers had come and gone, each one failing to understand the refugee employees and their special problems. That part of the job came easily to Mrs. Broch, but she was not ashamed to enroll in a local cooking school, where, among other things, she learned how to convert European weights into American measures. She also learned standard techniques for running a restaurant to ensure that meals were prepared efficiently and at minimum cost.

While the Window Shop's food operation had problems common to all restaurants—managing staff, getting good ingredients, controlling inventory, establishing a rational price structure—the Tea Room and Bakery had some unique difficulties that it struggled to overcome. During the first two years of its operation, for example, no cooking was allowed at the Mount Auburn Street location for fear that the smells might annoy apartment dwellers who lived above the basement lunchroom. As a result, hot dishes had to be transported by car in double boilers from a nearby home kitchen, while guests waited impatiently for their orders. (Volunteers later admitted that the procedure probably violated every sanitary code in the city of Cambridge.) Problems were also caused by the basement lunchroom itself, which was subject to occasional flooding and mealtime visits by a rat the staff named Charlie.

Even when the Window Shop later moved to larger and more convenient quarters, the Tea Room and Bakery would continue to employ many part-time workers with little or no experience, requiring complex planning and scheduling. Volunteers among the Harvard wives were willing to pitch in when paid members of the kitchen staff absented themselves to satisfy competing responsibilities of children, sick or aging parents, and demanding husbands. But Broch had also to deal with a refugee staff who needed ongoing help as they adjusted to America. Besides psychological problems, many of the refugees and their families were also plagued by illnesses caused by poor nutrition and lack of medical care during their flight from Nazism and their early years of poverty and neglect in the United States.

Despite these obstacles, the Tea Room and Bakery attained

creditable efficiency under the leadership of Alice Broch. During the war, Broch found ways to use leftovers that satisfied customers and invented new recipes that took current food shortages into account. Austrian cuisine relies heavily on meat, a rationed food during the war, so that supplies had to be stretched through the ample use of breadcrumbs mixed with leftover boiled beef to make mock cutlets, or the mix was stuffed into green peppers and served with tomato sauce. Dumplings filled with small amounts of ground meat, cheese, or bread replaced choice cuts of steak on the menu, as did noodle dishes or savory strudels.

Alice Broch's relationship with employees was such that they willingly brought butter and other needed supplies they had purchased with their own ration coupons. Largesse also came from the Cambridge commercial community, with whom Mrs. Broch at all times maintained strong connections. The story goes that during the war a truck driver making a delivery remarked on the "funny crowd" at the Window Shop, where everyone talked with an accent. After being told about the background of the refugees and what the shop was, the driver returned the next day with a pound of butter. It was a gift from his employer, Mr. Sage, who ran family-owned grocery stores in several Cambridge locations.

Following its next and last relocation in 1947, the Window Shop expanded its food offerings from a few delicate pastries to full meals based largely on Mrs. Broch's recipes. As a full-size restaurant, it began to attract customers not only for desserts but for such dishes as Wiener Schnitzel (veal scallop), Backhendl (fried chicken), and Gekochtes Rindfleisch (boiled beef). For displaced Eastern Europeans especially, such dishes provided solace and satisfaction, a taste of home, and a reminder of better times, even if the shop's offerings did not completely match the meals they remembered from the Old Country.

By 1950 the restaurant was solvent and running efficiently. Two years later it was able to boast that it was employing 75 people with a payroll of over $92,000 and decent health insurance and pension plans. This was a complete turnaround from when the

GEKOCHTES RINDFLEISCH
Boiled Beef

Boiled beef, usually eaten with horseradish, is an Austrian specialty made with different cuts of meat. It was said to be the favorite dish of Emperor Franz Josef I. Many Viennese followed his example by eating it for lunch every day, varying the meal by the cut of beef and such garnitures as sauces, salads, and pickles.

3 pounds boneless beef (bottom round, rump, or chuck)	3 carrots, cut into large chunks
3 pounds bony chicken parts (wings, backs, necks)	4 stalks celery, cut into large pieces
1 or 2 beef soup bones	1 leek
2 quarts water	3 tablespoons chopped parsley
Salt	1 bay leaf
3 tablespoons cooking oil	8 black peppercorns
2 cups large chunks of onions	3 whole allspice
	Horseradish, for serving

Place the beef, chicken parts, and beef bones in a large soup kettle. Add the water and salt. Bring to a boil, making sure the water covers the meat. Skim. Heat the oil in a skillet. Add the onions, carrots, celery, leek, and parsley and cook until lightly browned. Add to the soup kettle and continue to boil. Add the bay leaf, peppercorns, and allspice. Cover and cook at low heat for about 2 hours. Test meat for tenderness and cook longer if necessary. Remove the beef from the pot. Skim the fat from the soup and strain, making sure that the vegetables are pressed for that last bit of flavor. The soup can be served separately before the beef is sliced and served with horseradish.

modest Tea Room and Bakery ran in the red and drained the proceeds of Mary Mohrer's profitable gift shop.

Elsa Brandstrom Ulich, who became the head of the Window Shop in 1942, was more responsible than anyone else for the change. This remarkable woman was born in St. Petersburg, the daughter of a Swedish military attaché. During World War I, she became a Red Cross nurse and almost single-handedly cleaned up a camp for 8,000 prisoners at Krasnajarask, Siberia, where captured German soldiers were dying in great numbers from typhus. Afterward, she traveled to Germany to keep a promise she made to find the families of prisoners who perished in Siberia and see to it that their orphaned children were cared for and educated. In the course of this work, she met and married Robert Ulich, a German educator with progressive political beliefs, and settled in her husband's country until Hitler came to power, when they made their way to Cambridge. There Robert Ulich started work at the Harvard School of Education and Elsa Ulich began another phase of her work on behalf of victims of war. Though she rarely mentioned her experiences in Russia, her reputation followed her to Cambridge, where refugees knocked on her door and often stayed for weeks while Mrs. Ulich found them friends, homes, and jobs.

Throughout the half-dozen years she worked on behalf of the Window Shop (until her death from cancer in 1948), this strikingly handsome woman became the face of the restaurant, serving as hostess, greeting customers, and directing them to their seats with characteristic graciousness and ease. She also established the unique hiring and salary policies of the Window Shop, which required the nonprofit enterprise to pay competitive wages and provide employment for as many refugees as possible. This meant tailoring jobs to the refugees' abilities rather than the reverse, and dealing with constant turnover when newcomers could not adjust to the work or found more appropriate employment.

Ulich also saw to it that the Window Shop was managed by the refugees themselves, giving Mary Mohrer and Alice Broch the independent authority they needed to choose merchandise and menus, and to hire, train, and manage employees. Under Ulich's leadership, the Window Shop became one of the first businesses in Cambridge to hire and pay equal wages to African Americans. American-born workers with disabilities were also hired during this period so that they could work alongside displaced Europeans, each group learning to accept the other.

Ulich spearheaded the move of the Window Shop to its final home on Brattle Street at a site made famous in Longfellow's poem "The Village Blacksmith." The location could hardly have been more fortuitous. Brattle Street leads from Harvard Square, with its array of shops, to a classically beautiful neighborhood, with stately houses set far back from the street and fine gardens, the homes of many of the city's most affluent citizens. The building Mrs. Ulich determined to buy, called the Dexter Pratt House after Longfellow's blacksmith, dated back to the beginning of the nineteenth century and had undergone various incarnations that included the smithy, a glue factory, and a restaurant called the Cock Horse. Though the structure was in considerable disrepair and badly in need of an exterminator, Ulich persuaded the Window Shop board to vote for the purchase of the house. At an emergency meeting, she assured the board that the Cambridge Trust Bank was ready to grant a mortgage, and that $40,000 could easily be borrowed from friends to restore the building and equip the restaurant and gift shop. Ulich's successor, Alice Cope, later described the board's favorable decision, following which one member was heard to say, "I don't know why we had to have a meeting for all this. Mrs. Ulich would never have accepted anything but yes." He was, of course, right. Once she saw the possibility, nothing stopped her, and the needed money was borrowed in less than a week at 4 percent interest, to be repaid in full in ten years. One husband, when consulted, told his wife, "Give the money, but don't lend. You'll never see it again." Imagine the satisfaction of the board when the money was repaid before the ten years were up and that skeptical husband had to eat his words!

In its new location, the restaurant occupied rooms on two

floors joined by a beautiful but narrow staircase, which customers and waiters had to negotiate with care. However, these inconveniences were overcome by willing workers and a growing number of regular patrons happy to find delicious European food in Harvard Square. With an expanded restaurant and a bigger gift shop, the Window Shop started to become profitable enough to pay its debts and fulfill its mission of employing more refugees. Between December 1942 and December 1946, before Ulich began to decline from her illness, the shop's cash surplus had already quadrupled, from about $11,000 to almost $44,000. Profits would continue to increase, and Window Shop salary figures would also be able to grow from $8,400 in 1942 to $241,000 in 1967. That year it employed between 75 and 100 people and accommodated from 300 to 800 customers every day.

At Ulich's death in 1948, Alice Cope, wife of a member of the Harvard Medical School faculty and a former volunteer, became the head of the thriving Window Shop enterprise. Like Ulich, Cope had seen the effects of persecution close up and so brought a special sensitivity to the plight of Jewish refugees. Not long after her marriage to a doctor, she accompanied her husband to Germany, where he had arranged to train with a renowned Jewish pathologist, Ludwig Pick. The couple witnessed the repeated destruction of Dr. Pick's laboratory in 1933 by Nazi thugs determined to do away with "Jewish science." Sometime afterward, Pick himself was arrested and sent to a concentration camp, where he died. For as long as they could, the Copes remained in Germany, using their Quaker connections to try to help Pick and other victims of the Nazis. When this work became too dangerous, the couple moved on to London, where Alice continued to help refugees, and eventually back to Massachusetts, where she became interested in the Window Shop and served as a volunteer.

Many of those Alice Cope worked with at the Window Shop would later remark on her resourcefulness and compassion. She lived at a time when women from good families were expected to marry well but not to work outside the home. Instead, they were

encouraged to give their time to causes and organizations they believed in. Reflecting on the unexpected course her life had taken,
Cope observed:

> You see, I never went to college. Nobody ever thought it was worth-
> while for me to go to college. Every step I took I took because I saw
> something I wanted to do, and I couldn't do it unless I had some
> kind of further education. In the end, of course, I got the strangest
> kind. Nobody would give me a degree for it but probably it was the
> best I could ever hope for.

When Cope took over, the Window Shop was doing so well that
it had even started a scholarship fund, which disbursed thousands
of dollars to diverse groups of people. After World War II, the shop
expanded the populations it was serving by taking in refugees
from Communist-dominated Central Europe as well as immigrants from India, Greece, Iraq, Israel, and Taiwan. But the Cold
War was diminishing the number of Eastern Europeans being
allowed to come to the United States, and at the same time, the
McCarran-Walter Act was imposing entry quotas on those seeking
to relocate.

In 1952, Alice Cope was invited to speak before the President's
Commission on Immigration, testifying to her belief that the re-
settlement of refugees and displaced people should be accomplished on a nonsectarian basis. Besides backing federal funding
to aid state and private agencies for resettling immigrants, Cope
suggested sending teams of physicians and social workers to Europe to select candidates for admission to the United States. "The
money would be well spent," she argued, "and would be returned
a hundred times over in terms of people who are settled happily
and who are contributing their full share to our way of life."

Her recommendations were not followed. In those Cold War
years, immigration was largely restricted to people who could
prove that they were political refugees from Iron Curtain countries. During this period, too, the Window Shop became less effec-

tive as a vehicle for resettling newcomers to the United States. The same volunteers who helped displaced people during and immediately after World War II were not as interested in helping newcomers from Hungary and Cuba. A few of these new refugees found employment in the Window Shop, but most found more compatible communities outside of Cambridge and developed their own networks for finding jobs and family services. In consequence, the Window Shop board of directors changed its longstanding policy of helping only those who planned on becoming American citizens and started to give aid also to refugees who wanted to return and be of help to their own countries.

These changes in the mission of the Window Shop, combined with changes in the constituency of its staff and transformations in Cambridge itself, forced the place to close in 1972. By this time, Mrs. Broch and other Window Shop veterans had retired and Mary Mohrer had indicated that she wished to. Refugees who could replace these women could not be found. The board of directors determined instead to call upon professionals to run the food operations of the Window Shop, a decision that Cope later recognized was doomed to fail.

In hindsight one can see that some of the same problems which beset the Window Shop at the beginning beset it at the end. The people who knew most about it were not consulted. American-trained restaurant managers were engaged. Ordinary business methods were instituted where only extraordinary methods had been successful before. They all failed because the special ingredients which had made the shop such a success were no longer understood.

In 1974, Cope summarized the reasons for the board's decision to close.

Atmosphere, caring, even hard work could not prevent the Window Shop from being affected by changing times. Many people have asked why the shop was closed. It has been hard to explain, for on the surface everything seemed to be going along in the same old way. Our devoted friends and customers did not see the effect of the serious problems brought on by the changes in Harvard Square. It must be remembered that the Window Shop was the first to provide European merchandise and European food. When it started, it had little competition. Gradually, this competition became strong indeed, and, while it was healthy and easily met by both departments of the shop, the competitors were not running a philanthropic enterprise. When times were bad, they could lay off workers, while the policy of the Window Shop was to keep every possible position filled at all times.

Though Cope and other Window Shop volunteers and employees were saddened by the closing of the shop, they considered it fitting that the property on Brattle Street was sold to the Cambridge School for Adult Education, with its own mission of outreach. Part of the site was also saved for a restaurant called the Blacksmith Shop, which would retain bakers from the Window Shop and continue to sell Viennese pastry until 1989. Today the Blacksmith Shop houses the Hi-Rise Bakery, run by an accomplished baker who makes fine breads and specializes in such classic American desserts as lemon meringue pie and chocolate chunk cookies. Preserved from Window Shop days is the summertime terrace and the narrow staircase leading to a second-floor dining room.

Today, young people around Harvard Square have never heard of the Window Shop or its unique fare. What matters, however, is that the shop became a place where desperate foreign-born people could find the resources they needed to become proud, self-sufficient Americans. And if, as a byproduct of this noble endeavor, Cambridge residents learned about the wonders of Viennese pastry, who could disagree that this too was a notable achievement?

SACHERTORTE

Sachertorte is reputedly the only cake that caused a major lawsuit over who had the right to call its product the genuine one. Created in 1832 by Franz Sacher, Metternich's chef, the cake was the subject of a dispute between Demel's, Vienna's most renowned pastry shop, and the Sacher Hotel, owned by relatives of the chef. Demel's had bought the right to bake and sell the authentic Sachertorte (stamped with an official seal) from a descendant of the creator. The Hotel Sacher based its case on the family connection. The only difference between the cakes produced by the two litigants had to do with apricot jam. Demel's spread it over the cake before covering it with icing; the Hotel Sacher split the cake into layers, spread the jam between the layers, and then frosted the cake. The courts decided in favor of the hotel, prompting Demel's to call its cake the Ur-Sachertorte (the very first version). Squabbling aside, this cake is a wonderful treat.

The Cake

6 ounces good-quality semisweet chocolate (Valrhona, Côte d'Or, or Scharffen Berger)
1 stick unsalted butter
¾ cup sugar
6 large egg yolks
6 large egg whites
1 cup flour

The Apricot Jam Glaze

1½ cups apricot jam
1½ tablespoons lemon juice

Icing

1⅔ cups sugar
8 ounces good-quality semisweet chocolate
½ cup water

(continued on page 178)

Preheat the oven to 350°F. Prepare a 9-inch springform pan by buttering it and lining the bottom with parchment or wax paper. Butter the paper and dust the pan with flour.

For the cake: Melt the chocolate in a double boiler. Allow to cool. Cream the butter and sugar for 3 minutes. Beat in the egg yolks one at a time. Beat the egg whites until stiff peaks form. Add chocolate and blend well. Fold carefully into the sugar mixture. Add the flour gradually, carefully folding it into the batter. Spoon the batter into the prepared pan and bake for 50 minutes in the middle of the oven.

For the glaze: Allow the cake to cool; remove from the pan. Heat the jam with the lemon juice and boil for half a minute. Strain through a sieve. With a pastry brush, cover the top and sides of the cake with the glaze. Allow it to set.

For the icing: Cook sugar, chocolate, and water in a heavy saucepan, stirring constantly until it comes to a boil. Using a candy thermometer, cook until 225°F. Remove from the heat and stir with a wooden spoon for a minute. Test by pouring a spoonful onto a cold plate. It should set and have a shiny surface. Keep stirring until it sets. If it is grainy, add a few tablespoons of boiling water to the mixture and cook briefly until smooth. Test again.

To finish the cake: Place the cake on wire rack over a clean pan. Pour the icing all at once onto the top of the cake, allowing it to cover all surfaces. Help it along by tilting the cake. It should have a shiny surface and set up immediately. Do not attempt to patch it or you will ruin the smooth look of the cake.

In Vienna, a bowl of whipped cream *(schlag)* would be offered along with the cake.

EIGHT

Food Keeps the Faith

African-American Cooks and Their Heritage

The search for the roots of African-American life in the wake of the American civil rights movement has generated a series of remarkable cookbooks that show how food has always been a successful way for black Americans to keep their racial past alive and preserve their sense of common identity. Some of these cookbooks are by an older generation of black women who survived poverty and discrimination to achieve degrees of fame and financial success as cooks, caterers, and restaurant owners in parts of the United States as far from each other as Tulsa, Oklahoma, and New York City's Harlem. Other recent recipe collections have come from African-American women who have never or only briefly been professional cooks but have traveled around the country and abroad to rediscover the food of their forebears, tracing it back to the American South or further back to Africa. All these books blend family history and regional American history to account for the ways in which African Americans have contributed to a rich and distinctive cuisine that is now widely known and appreciated beyond black communities for the delight and variety of its flavors.

A cookbook that vividly recalls the lives and culinary contributions of African Americans in the American southwest is *Cleora's Kitchens: The Memoir of a Cook & Eight Decades of Great American Food* (1985). Born in 1901, Cleora Butler traced her ancestry to former slaves who became landowners first in Texas and later in Oklahoma. Before the Civil War, her great-grandmother, Lucy Ann Manning, served for many years as a house cook on a large plantation near Waco, Texas, where she and her husband Buck had migrated with their owner from Mississippi. Following emancipation, the plantation owner gave a large tract of land to Buck Manning, who in turn gave fifty acres to each of his seven children. (Only parenthetically is it mentioned that Manning's former owner was also his father, suggesting how common was the practice of plantation landlords begetting children by their household slaves.) Besides working his land, Cleora Butler's grandfather, Allen Manning, put to use some of the kitchen skills he had learned from his mother while his wife attended to their eleven children, the oldest of whom, Mary Magdalena, or Maggie, would become Cleora Butler's mother. "It was natural that, as the oldest, Maggie was required to assist in the Manning kitchen and, in time, to take full responsibility for it," her daughter observed. "Maggie was quick in developing the talent that established her as one of the finest cooks in northeast Oklahoma."

At twenty, Maggie Thomas accepted the proposal of a local farmhand, Joseph Thomas, and married him three years later, in 1898, over the objections of her father, who was reluctant to lose his oldest daughter: "The one (mind you) in charge of the cooking," Cleora Butler noted. The couple moved into a three-room house provided by their employers, a young Waco doctor and his new wife, for whom Maggie Thomas began doing the cooking. It was here that the Thomases' first child, Cleora, was born as part of the first generation of African Americans who had no personal recollection of slavery.

Council Oak Books

Cleora Butler.

For her parents and other African Americans in the Southwest, the newly opened Indian Territory held additional promise of free land and further liberty and independence. In 1902 the young girl left Texas with a large wagon train that included her parents, her widowed grandfather and his new wife, uncles and aunts, and a number of other farmhands, all hopeful of new opportunities in what would soon become the state of Oklahoma.

Most of the migrators settled in Muskogee, where Maggie Thomas made dresses and other garments for wealthy families in the area and she and her husband built and settled in their own house. There, at the age of five and a half, while her mother was giving birth to a baby brother, Cleora made her first attempt at cooking dinner from leftover slices of pork liver. At ten, the young girl baked her first batch of biscuits, using a new baking powder and cookbook supplied by Calumet, a feat that was followed by many more kitchen forays inspired by her mother's success in baking and selling cakes.

When I was twelve, the time spent in the kitchen at my mother's side was the most precious to me. I watched as she magically mixed liquids and powders, added dashes of pepper and salt (plus assorted and crumbled leaves that I learned were called spices), placed them inside or atop the stove and produced marvelous concoctions that invariably tasted yummy. The apparent ease with which she cooked convinced me that turning out cookies and cakes must be a pushover.

Her mother's inspiration notwithstanding, the child's first attempt at baking a cake was judged by her brothers to be a disappointment and was buried in the backyard in what Cleora Butler would call "the dough patch," a graveyard for her failed experiments that included "the molasses caper."

My efforts at blending sorghum molasses and flour to make cookies resulted in a solid sheet of gummy residue. My tasters, Walter and Joey, refused outright to even smell it. So adamant were they that they snitched to my mother about the secret dough patch. Mother was furious. She started out giving me a tongue lashing, but somewhere in the middle of it began to laugh and laughed till she was weak. She told me to stick to making good biscuits and to experiment only when she was there to guide me.

The girl could hardly have had a better or more willing guide to baking bread and pastry. The popularity of her mother's bread was so highly esteemed in Muskogee that she could charge twenty-five cents a loaf when the going rate for bread was a nickel. Maggie Thomas also staged "cook-ins" during the winter months, in which she would ask Cleora and her brothers what kinds of cookies or desserts they wanted and then see to it that sons and daughter alike were taught how to make the treats properly. "Learning to be self-sufficient, especially in the kitchen, was something Mother insisted upon for all of her children," Cleora Butler declared. "We didn't mind it a bit. After all, it was a family tradition."

Though the young girl also learned from her grandfather, who had a special talent for preparing hog meat and making pork sausages, her special bond was with her mother, whose work began to win awards and led her to be hired by some of the best hotels in Muskogee.

> Throughout my young life, she filled me with confidence and taught me that cooking was a fine art. Foodstuffs were but raw materials— the sculptor's stone, the artist's paint, the musician's instrument. Mastering the art of cooking rested on following the basic directions of a recipe (reading it four or five times if necessary), then improvising where desired. I learned early that "dumping and stirring" could be hazardous to your results.

In 1923, after formal training in cooking at Muskogee's Manual Training High School and a year at Oberlin Junior College, Cleora found her first job as a cook for a family in Tulsa. "It was *the* place to be," she recalled. "One black entrepreneur had reportedly moved to Tulsa and opened a bank account with $75,000 in cash! Everybody was caught up in the high style of living that was characteristic of the entire nation." In 1925 Cleora's parents also moved to Tulsa, to which her father had been commuting as a cook, he too following the family tradition. Once settled in, Maggie Thomas, who had been coming to the city occasionally and sewing for her daughter's employers, began to work as pastry chef for the newly opened Ambassador Tea Room.

Barely mentioned in Cleora Butler's account of the prosperity that characterized Tulsa in the twenties is the infamous race riot that scarred the city two years before she first arrived there. But she does describe the economic booms and busts that were a part of Oklahoma life and helped to make her employment so irregular. She cooked sporadically at farewell parties for Tulsans whose fortunes were lost before she found a permanent job in 1932 with the family of a busy oil worker who was able to purchase one of the city's most elegant houses. Here she served hundreds of meals and prepared or supervised countless parties until 1940, when she married George R. Butler, a hotel worker who had been courting her for several years.

Cleora Butler's most vivid memories of the Depression are not so much of economic struggle but of the sense of solidarity she and her family shared with fellow African Americans in Tulsa.

> Tulsa's black community had felt the effects of the financial crash long before October of 1929. Money had already become scarce on the north side of town, where most blacks lived, and unemployment had been growing since 1927. Still everyone loved parties and a good time as much as they ever did, even though few could afford to throw a bash for even four or six friends. Our way around this was for everyone to bring something. We'd get together and brew our own beer. Then each would bring his or her share of ingredients for the planned menu. It always turned out to be an exciting evening.

Butler observed that during the Depression such BYOB parties also became popular even among the wealthier white population. "Their parties were perhaps more grandiose than those we had, but I know they were never more fun."

For African Americans, one of the most memorable events of the era was the World Heavyweight Championship bout in June 1937, when Joe Louis, "the Brown Bomber," knocked out Max Schmeling in the first round. "The blacks of North Tulsa literally danced in the streets," Butler remembered. "This was a most special occasion. We didn't often get a chance to cheer about anything, let alone a hero of our own." The victory was celebrated with a feast of fried chicken, all the trimmings, and homemade ice cream. Other special occasions included visits of members of the Cab Calloway band, in which Butler's brother played saxophone. Walter Thomas would regularly bring Calloway to his parents' home for meals, and the popular bandleader never stopped raving about the cooking skills of Maggie Thomas and her daughter. The home of Maggie Thomas also became a favorite destination of other black musicians and entertainers, who often ate in private homes when traveling through the segregated South and Southwest.

Though Cleora Butler stopped working full-time after her marriage, her cooking skills were called upon regularly when World War II began and naive victory euphoria gripped the country:

In 1942 Tulsa was gearing up for war. There were parties galore, especially in the beginning when most everyone thought the whole thing would be over in a matter of months if not weeks. When sons and daughters, fathers, uncles and aunts were going away, people said, "Let's have a party!" so I did a lot of catering during that period. I've always felt it was a little like returning to the roaring twenties. There were parties all over the place. Parties for departing soldiers and sailors and a lot of parties for no specific reason at all.

In 1944 Cleora Butler again took steady work for a prominent Tulsa family, for whom she prepared sophisticated dishes, including imported trout, boned squab, and steamed fig pudding, as well as specialties of her own. She graciously shared her recipe for coconut torte with butter sauce with Mrs. Waite Phillips, wife of the Tulsa oil magnate and philanthropist. Fulfilling as it was, Cleora was forced to leave this job when she was called upon to take care of her father-in-law, who had developed cancer and required constant care.

In the early fifties, apart from her nursing duties and occasional catering, she took up another enterprise that had begun a decade before when she experienced racial discrimination at a hat sale in an exclusive downtown Tulsa department store.

While society in the 1940s had changed to the point where blacks could shop in a few white establishments, it was not usually permitted for one to try on clothing, especially hats and shoes. Occasionally, you might be permitted to try on a hat, but you were given a hand mirror and shown to a back room where "preferred" customers could not see you trying on your selection.

The hat I wanted was exquisite, so despite the horrible treatment, I purchased it. In fact, I bought two, but left the store infuriated and totally resolved never to buy another hat as long as I lived. Because of my continuing passion for hats, however, I found a way out of my problem.

Butler's solution was typical of her can-do attitude. She found a correspondence school in Chicago that allowed her to master the millinery craft and was soon able to supply her North Tulsa friends with hats she could sell for as much as $50 each.

In the mid-fifties, she took a job as a stock clerk in a dress shop, where she learned the rudiments of running a business and became friendly with a broad spectrum of Tulsa society. When the store closed in 1961, Cleora Butler decided to start her own business. In April of the following year, with a loan from the Small Business Administration, she and her husband opened Cleora's Pastry Shop and Catering in North Tulsa, the African-American section of the city, where her cooking was already well loved. Like her millinery venture, the pastry shop had been hatching in her mind since the 1940s, when she supplemented her family's income by selling small pies for five cents apiece in her father-in-law's billiard parlor. With her mother's help, she had baked some 150 pies a day in her own kitchen. Later, just before she opened her shop, Cleora gained additional experience in production baking when a contact from the dress shop resulted in orders for her to bake batches of tarts each week for a lunchroom in South Tulsa. With this experience and her husband at her side, Cleora Butler felt ready to run her own business.

The couple expected that the work would be hard but they were not prepared for the long hours involved in running a food operation with limited assistance. Nevertheless, their enterprise was successful and a source of great pride to Cleora Butler.

My husband and I arrived at the shop at six a.m. every day (to open at eight) and usually did not get home until nine p.m. However, business was terrific. Among the equipment we purchased was a donut maker. The big shiny machine occupied a prominent spot in the front window and my husband was so busy that before long he became an expert at making donuts. My assistant and I baked pies and cakes in the kitchen at the rear of the shop. After all these years I was now employer rather than employee.

Take-out chili and hamburgers were added to the shop's bill of fare, and bread soon followed at customers' insistence. Sour-dough French bread became a popular favorite after one customer supplied Butler with a "starter" and taught her all she knew about baking the bread. Cleora recalled that one regular customer bought the bread as part of a weekly ritual:

> One of my North Tulsa friends would come into the shop every Thursday evening, just as our bread for the next day's sale was coming out of the oven, to purchase a loaf of our sourdough bread for the family for whom she worked. Each week she would also buy a second loaf for herself, but before she would let us wrap it, she'd break open the top of the loaf with her fingers. Reaching into her purse, she would withdraw a stick of butter, push it down into the still warm loaf and hand the bread back to us for wrapping. This, she allowed, was her weekly treat to herself.

Customers cut across every class in Tulsa. As orders of food poured in from work crews building the Turner Turnpike through Oklahoma, the catering side of Butler's business expanded, with accounts with the Tulsa Opera Guild and the Tulsa Philharmonic Auxiliary. For five years the little shop supplied delicious baked goods to Tulsa, and it was only when it became obvious that her diabetic husband could not keep up the pace that the enterprise shut down in 1967. As she had with his father, Cleora nursed George Butler until he succumbed to his disease in 1970. Subsequently, she rebuilt her catering business, serving food first to a local school and church, and eventually remodeling her kitchen to accommodate the increased business that her reputation had attracted over the years in Tulsa and throughout the Southwest.

Cleora Butler was able to grow and develop as a cook, so that her account of her eight decades in American food includes not only traditional regional dishes of the Southwest but stylish meals of the 1970s and 1980s that introduced new ingredients and combinations of food into American kitchens. Her earliest recipes were for dishes she learned from her mother—hickory nut cake (with nuts that were gathered on the mountain behind her grandfather's house), burnt sugar ice cream, grated sweet potato pudding, and corn fritters. Her dinners of the 1930s featured appetizers such as toasted pecans seasoned with Worcestershire and Tabasco sauces, pickled shrimp, and oysters wrapped with bacon. She also offered an eggplant soufflé made with chopped pecans and aged cheddar, a fresh pork and bean casserole, peach cobbler, and an apple pudding made with chopped pecans and graham cracker crumbs for dessert. By the 1940s, Butler was using ingredients like artichokes, avocado, and bleu cheese in her recipes and was preparing garlic bread and a dish called Enchiladas de Acapulco. In later years, she cooked rice pilaf with pine nuts, buckwheat cakes with chicken livers, tomato-mozzarella salad with red onion and anchovies, jalapeño corn bread, and a macadamia nut chess pie. Baked fudge was a popular dish in her pastry shop and later became a favorite at the Garden, a popular Tulsa restaurant.

When Cleora Butler describes her food memories, she speaks about how dishes tasted and smelled as well as how they looked. She vividly describes the fragrant yams she ate in childhood and how they oozed syrup as they came from the oven. She recalls her grandfather supplying the children in his family with the sugar cane they loved to suck, and how on butchering days he made special strips of meat he called "melts" that he would grill and give to the waiting youngsters. For Butler, food continued to be both a sensual pleasure and a way of sharing love with the many people who mattered in her life. Her most vivid adult recollections of food are tied to family and friends. A few years before her death, Butler looked back on seventy years of cooking and felt that the most memorable affair she ever catered was the twenty-fifth an-

BAKED FUDGE

Adapted from Cleora's Kitchens

4 eggs

2 cups sugar

1 cup (2 sticks) butter

4 heaping tablespoons cocoa
  powder

4 rounded tablespoons flour

1 cup pecans, broken into
  large pieces

2 teaspoons vanilla

Whipped cream, for serving

Preheat the oven to 325°F. Beat the eggs well, add the sugar and butter, and beat well again. Sift the cocoa and flour together. Add broken pecan meats. Fold into butter mixture. Mix in vanilla. Pour into 9 × 12 × 3-inch Pyrex dish or tin pan. Set pan in a pan of hot water (enough to come ½ inch to 1 inch up on the sides of pan). Bake for 45 minutes to 1 hour. The fudge will have the consistency of firm custard and will be crusty on top. Serve with a dollop of whipped cream on each piece.

SERVES 9 TO 12.

niversary party of her former high school cooking teacher. "The menu called for nothing extraordinary, but it was prepared with the greatest affection and appreciation."

If not for her cookbook, which was published by a small local press, the long, rich life of Cleora Butler might well have been forgotten. Only recently, in fact, have cookbooks like *Cleora's Kitchens* commemorated the lives and achievements of representative African-American women like Butler and her mother, who cooked for a living but always put the needs of their family ahead of their own. Filled with memories of family and community meals and of the people who prepared them, these cookbooks help to rescue black cooks of the past from the anonymity in which they were consigned by white cookbook writers of the post–Civil War period, who almost never named individual African Americans as the source of their recipes. Instead, these writers often created condescending caricatures of black women cooks as bandanna-headed mammies or as kindhearted but formidable servants too ignorant to be able to help their employers translate their cooking knowledge into formal recipes. Typical is the introduction to *The Blue Grass Cookbook* (1904), where John Fox Jr. is full of nostalgia for his old Kentucky home and the black women who cooked there, whom he describes as "broad, portly, kind of heart, though severe of countenance." Of the 300 recipes that follow in the cookbook, not one is directly attributed to "that turbaned mistress of the Kentucky kitchen" that Fox so admired.

Among contemporary cookbooks by African-American women, *Cleora's Kitchens* is unusual in that it was written by a talented black cook who never aspired to leave her native Oklahoma and bring her talents to an American city known worldwide for its food. This was not the case with Edna Lewis, who was born a decade or so after Cleora Butler in Freetown, Virginia, but went to New York City and eventually became nationally recognized and honored as a cook and author of classic works on country cooking that include *The Edna Lewis Cookbook* (1972), *The Taste of Country Cooking* (1976), and *In Pursuit of Flavor* (1988). Freetown, where Lewis was raised, was a small farming village that was settled by her grandfather and other former slaves shortly after the Civil War. In this pastoral community, she learned from her mother and other women to prepare and preserve a rich variety of fresh fruits and vegetables from local fields, orchards, and woodlands, and to take full advantage of local livestock, farm-bred fowl, wild game, and freshwater fish. Lewis's strong respect for the land was what nurtured an early desire to go to college and become a botanist, an ambition she had to forgo when her mother died and she was left to care for her youngest sister. Lewis took the girl with her to New York City, where she worked as a file clerk and imagined she might become a designer after a job sewing costumes for the Christmas windows of the Bonwit Teller department store. Instead she was steered into a career in food by friends who admired her cooking.

In 1947, Lewis accepted an offer to partner in the Café Nicholson, which occupied the ground floor and garden of a brownstone on East Fifty-eighth Street in Manhattan. Intended as a place where truck drivers might eat, the restaurant soon attracted the city's elite and visiting Southerners like William Faulkner, who assumed from the quality and variety of the food that they were eat-

Reproduced by permission of Alfred A. Knopf Inc.

Edna Lewis.

ing in a French restaurant. (In all likelihood, the Café Nicholson featured a mixed menu of continental and country dishes, much like Lewis's first cookbook, which offers recipes for Crêpes Suzettes, Quiche Lorraine, and Meringue Torte, as well as for Southern Spoon Bread, Roast Pork Ribs, and Baked Virginia Ham.) Illness forced Lewis to give up her interest in the restaurant and turn briefly to raising pheasants with her husband on an organic food farm in New Jersey. Then in 1967, she opened her own restaurant on Seventh Avenue near 125th Street in Harlem, where she served authentic food of the South. Here, too, her cooking received high praise, but it could not make up for poor financing, and the place went bankrupt in January of the following year. By this time, however, Lewis was known as an authority on country cooking, and she was able to start a new career as an author, teacher, and visiting chef.

In *The Taste of Country Cooking*, her most admired book, Lewis celebrated the food of Freetown, describing her early life and the food-related rituals that defined each season of the year. In the remembered world of her youth, spring planting was associated with the taste of salads that featured regional ingredients only available for weeks at a time.

First spring meals would always be made of many uncultivated plants. We would relish a dish of mixed greens—poke leaves before they unfurled, lamb's-quarters, and wild mustard. We also had salad for a short period made of either Black-Seeded Simpson or Grand Rapids, loose-leaf lettuce which bolted as soon as the weather became warm. It was served with thin slices of onion before they begin to shape into a bulb—the tops used as well—in a dressing of vinegar, sugar, and black pepper. It was really more of a soup salad. We would fill our plates after finishing our meal and we adored the sweet and pungent flavor against the crispy fresh flavor of the lettuce and onions.

In the same way does Lewis recall how fall celebrations were always accompanied by special meals. So, for example, on Race

Day, the first Saturday in November, when the whole county would turn out for a yearly horse race in Montpelier, Lewis's family would stoke up on a breakfast of griddle cakes topped with blueberry sauce, sausage patties, biscuits, and pear and Damson plum preserves. Emancipation Day likewise called for a special dinner of guinea fowl, wild rice, green beans, tomatoes, Parker House rolls, and a purple plum tart and special cookies for dessert. On Christmas morning, breakfast included pan-fried oysters, pork sausage, and what Lewis calls "thin-sliced skillet-fried white potatoes," more commonly known as home fries, a comforting dish that can turn up at any meal.

Along with Christmas, hog butchering was the other major event of December in Freetown, where it was understood that the carcasses had to be chilled to firm up their meat before they could be cut up properly. The winter rite included the erection of scaffolds for hanging the hogs and lighting big wood fires to heat the iron drums of water needed for scalding and cleaning the animals after they were slaughtered. After the hogs hung for three days, the butchering would be carried out by an itinerant butcher who specialized in the task. The women would then render the lard and make the sausages, while the men prepared the hams and bacon by hanging them in the smokehouse for several days over smoldering green hickory logs and sassafras twigs. Wrapped in white bags and securely tied, the smoked meats could last a year and be used in any number of ways, which explains why Virginia hams in particular would become a permanent and important part of Edna Lewis's culinary vocabulary: "Ham held the same rating as the basic black dress," she claimed. "If you had a ham in the meat house any situation could be faced."

Other foods that were served throughout the year were the relishes, pickles, chutneys, jams, and jellies that women in Freetown joined in canning and preserving at harvest time. It was from these women and especially her mother that Lewis learned to become both a good cook and good baker, picking up tips she continued to follow even after she acquired such modern gadgets as an oven thermometer. A striking example of how Lewis was taught to connect with food with all of her senses occurs near the end of *In Pursuit of Flavor*, where she offers advice on how to avoid overbaking a cake.

> You have to know the moment the cake is ready to be taken from the oven. I use a cake tester but I also listen to the sounds of the cake after it has cooked for 25 minutes. When it is still baking and not yet ready, the liquids make bubbling noises. Just as the cake is done, the sounds become faint and weak, but they should disappear. Sometimes when I take a cake from the oven, I'll think the sounds are not quiet enough, and so I put the cake back for just a minute. And then all the sounds will be gone after that minute!

In 1993 Lewis moved to Atlanta, where she helped organize the Society for the Revival and Preservation of Southern Food, and the following year was named as one of America's Top Black Chefs. Called "the Dean of Southern Cooks" by *Gourmet* magazine, Lewis has also been honored by the James Beard Foundation, which conferred their first Living Legend award on her in 1995, and by Les Dames d'Escoffier, which named her a Grand Dame in 1999.

Leah Chase, a Creole from Madisonville, Louisiana, came from a tradition that was a mixture of black, Spanish, and French influences. She married into the family that owns Dooky Chase, now a landmark New Orleans restaurant. But it was her know-how and ambition that turned the restaurant from a popular local eating place into a destination for visitors from all over the world.

Dooky Chase started in 1941 as a po' boy stand where sandwiches and lottery tickets were sold to people living in the neighborhood. During the civil rights struggle, it became a meeting place for black activists, and it later expanded so that it could serve lunch to African Americans who were finding jobs in New

Orleans offices and needed a comfortable place that served familiar food. In 1946, Leah married Dooky Chase Jr., the musician son of the restaurant's owners, and began to take an active role in its management and overall development as soon as the couple's children reached school age. Leah Chase fought with her in-laws to change the furniture, the decor, and especially the menu, introducing such esteemed Louisiana fare as crawfish étouffée, deep-fried oysters, Creole jambalaya, and red beans and rice to satisfy the tastes of its customers. In *The Dooky Chase Cookbook* (1990) she took credit for adapting the cuisine of the restaurant to the city's new racial and ethnic mix in the post–civil rights era.

> It wasn't until I changed the whole Dooky Chase's menu to Creole that I really got acceptance from everybody. People got excited when I put stuffed chicken breasts on the menu and went back to veal. The customers really began to feel my presence then. Up till then there had been no integration. The blacks were eating at home and they were happy with their fried foods. But when integration came, it was a whole new ball game because they were able to go all over then. You had to start changing to keep up with the pace.

Like other African-American women of her generation who became successful restaurateurs, Leah Chase grew up in farming country, one of eleven children, but never claimed that her early life prepared her for a career in food beyond teaching her some cooking basics. Her mother was a talented baker but preferred to pursue her passion for fishing, which gave her time away from her brood. (It may also have caused her death after she was soaked by the wash of a motorboat and contracted pneumonia; she never completely recovered from its effects.) Chase freely admits that her mother hated daily cooking, and that she herself developed a distaste for growing her own food after working in the huge vegetable garden her father planted when he was not working in the fields or in local shipyards before World War II. "If you have ever grown vegetables yourself," she later declared, "you don't care if you grow another one in your life. I'd just as soon go down to the French Market and buy it off of some vendor."

From the time she was sent to a Catholic high school in New Orleans, Leah loved the city, with its wide availability of food sold in open markets and eating places, in one of which she started work as a waitress at the age of eighteen. Though she had seldom been inside a restaurant, Chase found the job more attractive than work in local clothing factories or laundries, the other main alternatives that were open to black Creole women in the New Orleans of 1942. She soon advanced to short-order cooking, improvising a popular hot lunch of Creole wieners and spaghetti that sold for sixty cents. It was the first time she found some commercial use for what she learned about cooking in Madisonville, and Creole home cooking would become part of the mix of cuisines served at Dooky Chase.

The Dooky Chase Cookbook reflects some of the preferences of her family, who used onions, rather than expensive spices, as the main source of flavoring and ate sweet potatoes as regularly as others ate bread. "Getting used to eating so much meat in New Orleans was hard for me at first," Chase admitted, and in many of her recipes, like one for red beans, meat is mostly a flavoring or an accompaniment, as it had to be among poor farm families in Louisiana. "In the country, Mother would get up and cook this big pot of greens and put pork chops on the side." Yet her cookbook also reflects the colorful extravagance of New Orleans with a series of recipes from a Wild Game Dinner that started in 1978 and has since become a traditional annual event for local politicians. The event was initiated when the wife of Mayor Dutch Morial insisted he remove forty ducks from their freezer, whereupon the mayor brought them to Dooky Chase's restaurant to be cooked and served at a party for his cronies. Even when the mayor left office in 1986, invitations went out and ducks were cooked and served to more than 350 invited guests at a banquet room in the city's Municipal Auditorium.

Chase's cookbook briefly goes against the grain of rich Louisiana cooking with a short chapter of eight recipes for low-sodium, low-cholesterol dishes, but quickly returns to vegetable recipes that commemorate the greens, okra, and onions that her father grew in the family's garden. The book ends with dessert recipes that are prefaced by Chase's confession that unlike her mother she really doesn't like to bake or make desserts. The confession, like other comments in her cookbook, identifies Leah Chase as the kind of restaurateur whose success comes as much from driving ambition, hard work, and good business instincts as from a natural talent for cooking and love of food. Chase's account of her winning struggle to bring Dooky Chase's up to date and expand its clientele is a tribute to her intellectual curiosity and desire to develop through research and reading.

> Dooky Chase's was my mother-in-law's whole life, but she didn't know how to grow in the restaurant. She wasn't the type to go out and seek change, but the place would suffer for it. I go out to see what other restaurants have and see if I can do that too. I learn as I go. You grow as you go to different places and read books.

Perhaps the best-known African-American woman who has achieved success as a restaurant owner is Sylvia Woods, whose expanding soul food enterprise in Harlem is internationally renowned and a destination for foreign visitors as well as New Yorkers and tourists from all over the United States. Like Leah Chase's, Sylvia Wood's ambitions required her to abandon her rural background and test her talents in a great American city. In Woods's case, however, she had the consistent help and support of her mother and her husband and never lost touch with her home community as she launched her restaurant and shared its success with the next generation of her family.

Sylvia Woods was born in 1926 in Hemingway, South Carolina, another black farming community that she later boasted had "more cooks per square inch than you would find in most cooking schools." When Sylvia was three, her widowed mother went north for five years to earn money as a laundress in Brooklyn, New York, and left her child in the care of her grandmother, a hardworking independent woman who was Hemingway's only midwife. Woods especially remembered her eighth birthday, when her mother returned and threw a party with standard South Carolina fare for the child's teachers and classmates. "I can't remember exactly what she made, but I can guess there was chicken and rice perlow, fried chicken, stewed butter beans and okra, candied yams, collard greens, and probably a coconut cake or an apple cobbler."

It was in Hemingway too where the girl met her future husband, Herbert Woods, when the two were children, and where the couple married when they were still in her teens. Their long, loving and mutually supportive union was interrupted only briefly in the mid-fifties, when Herbert served in the U.S Navy and Sylvia followed her mother's example and went to New York City, where she found work as a waitress in a small Harlem luncheonette. Like Leah Chase, the young woman had rarely visited a restaurant, much less worked in one, but in 1962, when the owner decided to sell his place, Sylvia managed to buy it and expand into larger quarters with money her mother supplied by mortgaging her South Carolina farm. The restaurant began—and would remain— a family affair, with Sylvia overseeing the cooking of the quintessentially Southern food and her four children helping in different ways as they came of age, while her husband took charge of shopping, building maintenance, and real estate expansion in Harlem. Within thirty years, Sylvia Woods would be known worldwide as the Queen of Soul, and would compile her recipes for the food that made her famous in *Sylvia's Soul Food: Recipes from Harlem's World-Famous Restaurant* (1992).

In her second cookbook, *Sylvia's Family Soul Food Cookbook* (1999), menus include all parts of the pig, such country favorites as backbone in gravy, pigs' tails, barbecued pigs' feet, and chitlins. Side dishes—black-eyed peas, collard greens, and sweet potato and rice dishes—are featured, as well as biscuits and corn bread. Many of the recipes in the book came from South Carolina friends and relatives as a result of a cook-off Sylvia staged in the Jeremiah Church in Hemingway. Like Sylvia, the women had learned from their mothers and grandmothers, and the book represents much of the accumulated cooking knowledge of generations of black South Carolina cooks.

The cookbook is also a memoir and family saga in which Sylvia Woods details her rise to fame and takes special pride in the success of her long marriage and the accomplishments of her children. Here she describes how her family expanded a little restaurant, where one could get a "roll and a bowl" (of soup) for sixty-five cents, to a Harlem establishment that now takes up much of a city block, with a branch restaurant in Atlanta. In 1979, Sylvia's Restaurant received a rave review from Gail Green in *New York* magazine that helped make soul food fashionable. Now, as well as serving regular Harlem customers and visitors from around the world, Sylvia's Restaurant offers catering for off-site parties, a popular option for New Yorkers. With her oldest son, Van, a trained and experienced businessman, Sylvia has also introduced a line of specialty soul food products—bottled spice mixes, sauces, and canned vegetables, such as turnip greens and collards—that are available nationally in supermarkets and shops. Widowed in the summer of 2001, Sylvia Woods has carried on, knowing that her family represents the future of her restaurant enterprise and expecting them to continue its expansion and innovation even as they keep faith with the food of old friends and kinfolk in South Carolina.

For these black cooks and restaurant owners who have won some measure of fame, cookbooks have become more than a means of publicity or promotion. They are a natural and appropriate way of recording personal and family history. But cookbooks have also become a vehicle for urbanized black Americans who have wanted to reconnect with their rural origins by journeying around the country and gathering recipes from older relatives and family friends. One such odyssey that took place in the 1970s is described in *Spoonbread and Strawberry Wine: Recipes and Reminiscences of a Family* (1978), a family history cookbook by sisters Norma Jean and Carole Darden, New York City professional women who traveled throughout the South and Midwest in search of ancestral memories and especially memories of food.

> As children, we had always been intrigued by the women in our family as they moved about in their kitchens, often preparing meals for large numbers of people. Each one worked in a distinct rhythm, and from the essence of who they were came unique culinary expressions. They rarely measured or even tasted their food but were guided, we guessed, by the aroma, appearance, and perhaps some magical instincts unknown to us.
>
> We felt it was time to capture that elusive magic, strengthen family ties, and learn more about our ancestors' history and tradition.

The sisters were able to trace their family back only as far as their paternal grandfather, Charles Henry Darden, a former slave who had settled in the small town of Wilson, North Carolina, not long after the Civil War. Charles Darden turned out to be a remarkable community leader and entrepreneur who established successful businesses in Wilson and saw to it that all of his ten children were educated. Three of his seven sons became doctors, two were lawyers, and two morticians; two daughters were teachers and the other a nurse. Though he was a teetotaler, Papa Darden, as he was called, was famous for making wine that he sold in his general store, and the first recipes in the book are for wine made from strawberries, dandelions, peaches, plums, and watermelon as well as grapes. Charles Darden's wife, Dianah Scarborough Darden, was a seamstress by trade who taught her daughters the arts of dressmaking and needlepoint as well as other homemaking skills that included canning, pickling, and preserving, her favorite domestic activities. "She felt the whole process just seemed to pull her into the rhythm of the universe," the sisters reported. "She'd plant her seeds in the spring, pick and prepare the vegetables and fruits from the earth in summer and fall, and serve them in the winter." In tribute, the authors provide family recipes for pickles, preserves, relishes, jellies, and jams made of peaches and other local fruit. Their grandmother instilled in her children what was then called "race pride," which combined self-reliance and community service as a way to resist second-class citizenship in the Reconstruction period, when Southern blacks were being intimidated and prevented from voting by the Klan and local white authorities.

A sense of family and racial pride was also passed down from the maternal side of the sisters' family and in particular from their mother, who was a teacher in the Deep South and became an active community leader in New Jersey after marrying one of the doctor sons of Charles Darden. From their mother, the Darden sisters also learned what preparations were needed when African Americans traveled in the South in the days before desegregation. As children, when the girls were sent alone by train to visit relatives, their mother saw to it that they had packed meals, since dining cars were off limits. Arrangements were also made with black porters to watch over the children as they traveled at night in sleeping berths to avoid the humiliation of having to sit at the rear of cars as soon as the train went south of Washington, D.C. The sisters also had strong recollections of later family motor trips through the still segregated South when their mother had prepared supplies of fried chicken, peanut butter sandwiches, chocolate layer cake, and a thermos of lemonade.

Aunts Maude and Lillian are particularly memorable members of the Darden family. Maude, from Alabama, was ninety-four when *Spoonbread and Strawberry Wine* was written, and knew the most about the family history, guiding the Darden sisters on their search. For years, she had regularly sent the girls shoe boxes full of pecans and candy on Saint Valentine's Day, and the sisters were able to see that her candymaking skills were undiminished in her advanced years, when they watched her make such old-fashioned treats as peanut brittle, divinity fudge, and molasses taffy. On the other hand, the Darden sisters' elderly Aunt Lillian of Virginia had little to tell them about the family's past and had nothing to contribute in the way of favorite family dishes. "Sorry dearie," she told her nieces. "I can't even remember how to cook." Lillian's specialty turned out to be beauty foods that she was introduced to by her sister Nell, whose flawless complexion lasted until her death at ninety. In Aunt Lillian's refrigerator were the fruits and vegetables she used to make her own natural cosmetics, such as cucumber or watermelon rind to soften and smooth skin, sliced tomatoes to neutralize oily skin, and grated white potatoes for bags under the eyes.

Looking for recipes, the Darden sisters shook loose family stories that had been nearly forgotten. Artelia, the youngest of their aunts, had been known as the spunkiest girl in the family, the one who had "inherited her mother's staunch pride."

When she was seven, a new minister in town stopped by her father's store and requested that she deliver some string beans to his home at a later time. However, when she arrived, he refused to let her in the front door and ordered her to go around to the back door. Many seven-year-olds would have been intimidated into obeying this order from a man of the cloth, but Artelia never cared much about public opinion. She knew she'd been insulted, and she marched home, taking the beans with her.

An inveterate tomboy who hated to study, Artelia nevertheless managed to get through college and surprised her family by becoming not only a responsible mother and housekeeper but "a most inventive cook who had a knack for making anything taste good." Her children especially remember that she sang and hummed in the kitchen as she made bread:

When they heard her sing out, "Take two and butter them while they're hot," they knew it meant that she, an accomplished baker, had prepared one of her best breads. Muffins, biscuits, and fruit loaves were her specialties, and one thing is for sure—no one could stop at just two.

AUNT MAUDE'S PECAN BRITTLE

Adapted from Spoonbread and Strawberry Wine, *copyright © 1978*
by Norma Jean and Carole Darden. Used by permission of Doubleday,
a division of Random House, Inc.

1½ cups pecans, halved or in
  pieces
¼ teaspoon salt
1 cup sugar

½ cup light corn syrup
½ cup water
1½ tablespoons butter

Sprinkle the nuts with salt and warm them in a 300°F oven. Mix the sugar, corn syrup, and water and heat slowly, stirring until the sugar is dissolved. Continue cooking over moderate heat. The mixture is ready when a small amount dropped in a cup of cold water becomes brittle (260°F on a candy thermometer). Remove from the heat and stir in the butter and warm nuts. Pour immediately onto a buttered cookie sheet. As soon as cool enough to handle, cut in strips and wrap in wax paper. Or wait until completely cooled and break into irregular pieces.

YIELD: ABOUT 1 POUND CANDY.

AUNT LILLIAN'S PEACHES, CREAM, AND HONEY MASK

Whip up a little heavy cream (¼ cup), mash ½ peach, and mix with 1 tablespoon honey. Apply to face and leave on for 15 minutes. Enjoy licking your lips! Stored in refrigerator, remainder will last for two weeks. [We're not sure what this will do for us besides cheering us up.]

The middle-class Darden sisters came from suburban New Jersey and visited the South to reclaim their culinary heritage and chronicle the eventful lives of African Americans who might otherwise have been lost to history. In contrast, another black cookbook writer, Vertamae Smart-Grosvenor, was born in coastal South Carolina and never stopped identifying herself with the food of her rural birthplace, even after her mother brought her north to Philadelphia when the girl was ten and she afterward lived and worked as an adult in Europe, New York, and Washington, D.C. Her identification with South Carolina is clear in the subtitle of her earliest cookbook, *Vibration Cooking, or the Travel Notes of a Geechee Girl* (1970), Geechee and Gullah being the names of the dialect and culture of black Americans from the Sea Islands of South Carolina and Georgia. As Smart-Grosvenor tells it, her ties to this part of the country went so deep that it was not until she was sixteen that she noticed that not everyone in Philadelphia ate rice each day.

> Us being geechees, we had rice everyday. When you said what you were eating for dinner, you always assumed that rice was there. That was one of my jobs too. To cook the rice. A source of pride to me was that I cooked the rice like a grown person. I could cook it till every grain stood by itself.

Smart-Grosvenor would do further justice to her native cuisine in *Black Atlantic Cooking* (1990) and go on to become the popular host of a series of award-winning public radio and television programs that focused on the food of Africa as it found its way around the New World and into its indigenous cuisines. Spun off from these programs were two cookbooks that are also filled with family lore, *Vertamae Cooks in America's Family Kitchen* (1996) and *Vertamae Cooks Again, More Recipes from America's Family Kitchen* (1999).

Taken together, these cookbooks give us a picture of the young Vertamae as a mischievous, fun-loving child who barely survived her birth as a premature baby but grew into a gangly six-foot girl who learned to hunt and drink corn liquor with her father. In Philadelphia, she was a latchkey child whose experiments in cooking while her mother was at work came close to burning down their rented home. Her love of adventure carried over to early adulthood, and at nineteen, she left Philadelphia to pursue a bohemian life in France, where her circle soon included American and European artists, intellectuals, and radical political activists. She broadened her culinary horizons by shopping in Paris markets and learning to cook and dine in the manner of the French. Among other sophisticated refinements, she learned to eat fruit with a knife and fork but quickly unlearned the practice the minute she found herself back in South Carolina, where she picked some figs and stuck them directly in her mouth. "I didn't dare tell anyone that I had been eating prosciutto and figs rolled together with a fork."

The hope of a theatrical career brought Vertamae Smart-Grosvenor back to the United States and to New York City. Here she struggled to find work as an actress while supporting two children and enduring the hardships and racism she found in the city. Not suited to nine-to-five work, Smart-Grosvenor took odd jobs, sometimes in funky restaurants where her eclectic cooking skills stood her in good stead. While studying drama, she cooked in a theater commissary, whipping up such budget dishes as spaghetti with sausages and meatballs and a Mexican ground beef dish made with corn, tomatoes, onions, and green peppers. In the 1960s she also cooked for SNCC fundraisers and other Harlem parties, serving what she called classic soul food—neck bones, chicken feet stew, biscuits, greens, and grits. Her idea of a good time during this period was to fry up a batch of chicken for her friends and serve it with potato salad and a couple of gallons of wine, with music by James Brown, Otis Redding, or Aretha Franklin playing in the background. Together with her love of food, Smart-Grosvenor's nostalgia for her South Carolina past would finally blend with her natural showmanship and start her in a career that has now lasted more than a quarter century as a cookbook writer and media correspondent on African-American cooking and community life.

In her books and widely enjoyed television and radio programs, Vertamae Smart-Grosvenor has certainly done much to bring wider public attention to the contributions of African Americans to the food of the Americas. In particular, she has taken pains to rescue her South Carolina ancestors from the anonymity in which they were left by earlier cookbook writers. Even in a collection like *200 Years of Charleston Cooking* (1930), where African Americans are acknowledged as talented cooks and the source of many popular dishes, the women are portrayed by the editor, Lettie Gay, as hopelessly superstitious and resistant to enlightened science:

> Her cooking instinct knows no rules, no measures. She is far more likely to conjure her oven than to use a heat control device. She wouldn't know what to do with a thermometer, but by hunches she knows when to take a boiling syrup off the stove. To translate hunches, a fine mixture of superstitions and a real knowledge of cookery, into intelligible recipes is no easy task.

The Charleston cookbook is filled with food identified with South Carolina cooking—okra, rice pilafs, and a number of dishes made from yams—but nowhere are any of the recipes traced back to named black women whose training at the hands of other women more than made up for their lack of experience with level measurements. Nor is there any recognition of the fact that many of the ingredients used in the recipes came from Africa.

Only in recent years has serious scholarship been done to trace the African-American contribution to South Carolina cuisine and to show how the food of Africa was spread throughout the Americas during the African Diaspora. And not surprisingly, some of this scholarship has also taken the form of recipe collections. Karen Hess, a white researcher, has provided an absorbing history of South Carolina rice and its origins in *The Carolina Rice Kitchen: the African Connection* (1992). Particularly notable is the work of Jessica B. Harris, who has been definitively tracing the effects of the African Diaspora on the food of all the Americas in a growing number of authoritative and richly illustrated cookbooks. These include *Iron Pots and Wooden Spoons: Africa's Gift to New World Cooking* (1989), *The Welcome Table: African-American Heritage Cooking* (1995), and *The Africa Cookbook: Tastes of a Continent* (1998).

These books—and others by black cooks, family historians, and food historians—have done much to recover recipes for authentic African-American food and to give names and voices to talented black cooks of the past who would otherwise have been forgotten. The same books have also helped to eradicate demeaning images, perpetuated for years by American popular culture, of black women cooks as ignorant or comical figures. Now at last past generations of African-American women can be seen as the originators of popular regional food, as imaginative cooks who added much to the richness and diversity of our country's food and to the flavors of the world's cuisines.

NINE

Growing Up with *Gourmet*

What Cookbooks Mean

Cookbooks were one of my favorite forms of reading long before I had professional responsibilities for collecting them or thoughts of writing about them. I remember sitting on a Cape Cod beach years ago with M.F.K Fisher's *The Art of Eating,* a title that drew stares from other vacationers whose notions of summer reading were more along the lines of novels by Agatha Christie, Danielle Steel, or Robert Ludlum. At the time, I felt special, in the know, a holder of secret knowledge about a vast, unappreciated literature that told me things about people and their lives and times that I could not always find in novels or histories and biographies. I had not yet realized the extent to which others found meaning and pleasure in reading and collecting cookbooks, whether or not they cooked from them.

The realization hit me later when I became a professional collector of cookbooks as Curator of Books at the Arthur and Elizabeth Schlesinger Library on the History of Women in America, where I am regularly contacted by people who want to donate cookbooks and food magazines they have been hoarding over the years. The gift most frequently offered is an accumulation of twenty or thirty years of *Gourmet* magazine. In almost all cases, the owners have long ago given up the idea of trying out all the recipes that looked appealing but find that putting the collection out with the trash is more than they can bear. The would-be donors are grievously disappointed when I tell them I cannot accept their gift, for the Library already has a complete, bound set of *Gourmet*. To solace them and let them know that they are not alone in wanting to find a suitable home for their magazines, I describe a *New Yorker* cartoon I keep on my office wall. It shows a woman dressed in mourning speaking to a lawyer who says, "That being your mother's wish, I see no reason we can't arrange interment with all her old copies of *Gourmet*."

Not all such collectors divest themselves of their food magazines and cookbooks when their supply gets out of hand. One woman I know rents commercial storage space to hold most of her 15,000 cookbooks, and another has turned her home and her books into a research library for the use of anyone in her small town and beyond. Some collectors try to limit what they buy, but even those that are interested only in French or Chinese cookbooks, for instance, or books about Mediterranean cuisine, can easily run out of room as cookbooks proliferate in their field of special interest. I know people who buy cookbooks as souvenirs of their travels and people who read cookbooks instead of traveling—lavishly illustrated books about the foods of exotic countries that satisfy their taste for adventure but do so without great risk and expense.

Cookbook collections can reveal secrets about their owners. One such donation came my way from an elderly woman who shared the family home with a brother who had just died. To her great surprise, she had found in his bedroom closet hundreds of cookbooks, not one of which had ever come down to the kitchen. The books were a welcome gift to the library, for unlike many cookbooks we receive, the pages of these contained no butter stains or traces of cake batter. The collector, it turned out, was on a restricted diet and read the books as a substitute for eating the dishes that were off limits to a man with his particular health problems. Instead of food stains, what I found on the pages were lovingly composed wish lists he had written of forbidden foods such as chocolate and peanut butter desserts. As I read his lists, sometimes written in a wavering hand, I envisioned a scenario in which he would eat a real meal of lean fish or breast of chicken, steamed vegetables, and a dry salad, and then go up to his room to read his recipes and fantasize about steak and home fries, onion rings, and a salad with Roquefort dressing.

A similar picture came to mind when I examined the cookbook collection that had belonged to Ella Fitzgerald, the great jazz singer who died of complications of diabetes. Her books reflect a hearty appetite and reveal that she was a lover of soul food and other rich ethnic cuisines. It was clear that she had cooked from her oldest cookbooks, where many recipes had her marginal commentary or little checkmarks she used to register her approval of a dish. Recipes for pork stew, biscuits and gravy, chopped chicken liver, kreplach, and lasagne also had telltale stains to show that a real cook had been at work. But her newer books, acquired after the onset of her illness, were without blemish. Like our earlier donor, Ella Fitzgerald seemed to have read these books in order to bring back memories of bygone meals or vicariously enjoy the taste of new dishes she was not permitted to eat. Evidently, she was reading recipes the way trained musicians read music and hear melodies in their mind's ear.

Recipes are a link to the past, and many of us find special meaning in dishes that bring back memories of family and friends or of ourselves in younger days. The first cookbook I ever bought retains a strong connection to my teenage years, and though I have rarely cooked from it, it occupies a sentimental spot on my shelf. It is the original *Gourmet* cookbook that I had given my mother for her birthday when I was an adolescent. For me, that thick brown classic with its gold lettering represented a sophisticated, elegant world of food that could easily have been available to our family if only my mother applied herself and learned to prepare the recipes. When weeks passed without the appearance of "gourmet dishes," I asked what was holding her up, and my mother defensively replied, "I don't understand this book." In a great, obnoxious show of arrogance and impatience, I shut my eyes, opened the book at random, and with arm held high overhead zoomed my index finger down on the page and read where it pointed: "Marinate the ham of a bear for five days in cooked red wine marinade . . ." Dumbstruck, I looked at my mother, and she looked me in the eye and said, "See?" in that victorious voice she used for such triumphs over her pretentious daughter. The notion of my mother cooking anything that had to be hunted down in a forest struck us both so funny that we exploded into uncontrollable laughter—that rare shared kind that goes on and on, fizzles, then starts up again when the laughers look at each other, and only stops when they are too weak to go on.

Much later, I understood the meaning of that episode and why we laughed so hard. I was at an age when I felt qualified to improve my mother, while she had every right to stand her ground and protect her received wisdom. I wanted "gourmet" meals, while she wanted to protect what she had learned from her mother, recipes for tasty meals that were served in a steady weekly rotation of roast chicken, pot roast, meat loaf, lamb chops, steak—the usual Midwestern American fare. Only much later, when I began research in food history, did I discover that the recipes I was trying to impose on my mother were intended for an Epicurean male readership more likely than my mother to confront and cook wild beasts. The earliest issues of *Gourmet* magazine, from which the recipes in my birthday present had been gleaned, were never intended for a female audience. The illustrations of boars' heads, shotguns, and fishing rods make it clear to me now that the magazine was geared for a readership of men who fancied themselves intrepid sportsmen.

The machismo of the old *Gourmet* was the first hint I had that cookbooks could have definite gender biases and reflect society's different expectations of men and women. Conventional thinking of that time had it that daily meals were understood to be the work of women and that any man who was interested in cooking had better be a well-paid executive chef. Outdoor barbecuing was the exception. Male cookbook writers could write about everyday home cooking and still retain their self-respect and sense of superiority as long as they first established their firemaking credentials and found some way to set themselves apart from women. This was especially true of cookbooks that came out between the 1930s and the 1960s and were filled with guy talk designed to coax likeminded men into the kitchen. As part of the inducement, the writers had to prove that male cooks were creative and adventurous, not held back as women were by fretting over level measurements or fussing about the nutritional content of food.

In his book *The Best Men Are Cooks* (1941), Frank Shay declares, "Women have reduced cooking to a science while men cooks are working to restore it to its former high estate as one of the fine arts." He snidely refers to the British Mrs. Beeton, the most famous woman cookbook author of her day, as "the nineteenth-century lady who put the blight on English cuisine." Shay takes a strong stand on salads, insisting that they be composed of such greens as romaine, chicory, endive, and cress, and that concoctions "made with mixtures of nuts, fresh or canned fruits, soft cheeses and leafy greens have no place in male gastronomy." Expectably, Shay shows no interest in planning family meals, baking cupcakes, or catering to the food preferences of children. He prefers the dangerous world of old-style barbecue, complete with pit men to watch over the fire. "No one ever expects the women to do the cooking at a barbecue," he insists. "That task belongs exclusively to certain fire-scorched men of experience." The clambake is another all-male cooking bastion Shay defends, dominated as it should ideally be by overlords who supervise the women as they gather driftwood and seaweed, collect rocks, and maybe even dig the trench where men will cook the clams and lobsters.

Despite the humorous bluster of his male persona, Shay's work is a collection of honest recipes suitable for any home cook. The book includes recipes for polenta and risotto, dishes now in vogue that were not found in most other American cookbooks of the 1940s. There are also fine recipes for all sorts of dessert pies, which apparently had some status with him as guy food, but not a single recipe for cakes or cookies, girly sweet stuff that requires unmanly exact measurements. Though it is mostly a put-on, Shay's masculine posturing disguises the fact that he wrote a good home cookbook, and it is a sign of his times that to do it he had to put women down.

Frederic Birmingham, author of *The Complete Cookbook for Men* (1961), is another writer who makes fun of women in order to establish his authority and his right to produce a cookbook. He sets himself apart from women in the usual way by trying to show that men are more imaginative and take more risks in the kitchen while women, obsessed as they are with following recipes precisely, are uninspired and predictable. As a long-time editor of *Esquire* magazine, Birmingham was groomed to stroke male egos, and he too latches onto outdoor cooking as an inveterately male prerogative, inventing prehistoric precedents in which cavemen clubbed animals over the head and cooked them over roaring flames while women stood safely on the side and watched. Birmingham also comes up with a method-acting school of outdoor cooking in which he puts himself in the place of a steak or double lamb chop and intuitively knows when it is time to turn over.

These amusing books are period pieces that illustrate the ludicrous posturing that men had to go through in order to be comfortable writing about food. Women, too, since the nineteenth century had to strike certain poses when writing cookbooks and domestic manuals and hide the fact that they may have been more interested in politics and social justice. Lydia Maria Child, known in her day as a prominent writer and abolitionist, published her most popular book, *The Frugal Housewife* (1829), to stay afloat while she and her husband Calvin, a man with no visible income, continued their work as reformers. Child knew about frugality firsthand and passed on economical tips on cooking and household management to her reading public, who evidently found them useful, for by 1832 the book had gone into seven editions. and was published in England as *The American Frugal Housewife*.

Child sets a sober, cheese-paring tone as she recommends feeding the family with scraps and inexpensive cuts of meat that would otherwise have been directed to the garbage pail. "Calf's head should be cleansed with very great care," she explains. "It is better to leave the wind-pipe on, for if it hangs out of the pot while the head is cooking, all the froth will escape through it." The book. projects an image of the author as a middle-aged housewife with a large brood of children. In fact, Child was only twenty-six when the book was published, remained childless her whole life, and lived a public life at a time when women were routinely relegated to the kitchen. For her, writing about food was a means of economic survival. Her real interests lay elsewhere.

Most other female cookbook writers of the nineteenth century accepted the common wisdom of the day that men and women occupied separate spheres, with women destined to run the home and stay out of the workplace. At the same time, promoting the party line created successful professional careers for women like Sarah Josepha Hale, editor of *Godey's Lady's Book,* a traditional nineteenth-century women's magazine, and for Marion Harland, author of the immensely popular *Common Sense in the Household* (1871), who made a fortune instructing women on the proper care of hearth and home. Less well known but among my favorite cookbooks of the period are novelized household manuals that had something of a vogue in the late nineteenth century. These are recipe collections crudely disguised as fiction, with plot lines that present early married life as an idyl of domestic bliss made possible by the young bride's good cooking and sense of economy. The books are clearly influenced by other sentimental fiction of the period that was written by and for women, and that was famously condemned by Nathaniel Hawthorne, who complained that

"America is now wholly given over to a d——d mob of scribbling women."

Catherine Owen, who also wrote conventional cookbooks, wrote fictional accounts of women rising above straitened circumstances by earning money through their skills as cooks. Her books *Gentle Breadwinners* (1888), *Ten Dollars Enough* (1886), and *Molly Bishop's Family* (1888) are morality tales that advise women to be prepared for whatever life may dish out—loss of inheritance, dying husbands, economic downturns. Her main characters rescue themselves from poverty by opening boardinghouses or by selling baked goods commercially, playing out Owen's philosophy that superior domestic skills give women a fallback position in the event of financial catastrophe. Despite her didacticism, Owen's books are charming and delightful to read. But they are not nearly as much fun as *A Thousand Ways to Please a Husband* (1917), written by Louise Bennet Weaver and Helen Cowles LeCron. This novel centers on a year in the life of the impossibly happy newlyweds Bettina and Bob. Each short chapter revolves around a meal the couple share or one of the parties they frequently give, with lessons in domestic management shining through. Here they are having their first meal together as man and wife:

> "Say, isn't it great to be alive!" exclaimed Bob, as he looked across the rose-decked table at the flushed but happy Bettina. "And a beefsteak dinner, too!"
>
> "Steak is expensive, dear, and you'll not get it often, but as this is our first real dinner in our own home, I had to celebrate."

As she is fond of reminding Bob at every opportunity, Bettina knows a thing or two about economizing, although this does not stop her from indulging her husband's sweet tooth. He loves her cookies and soon learns to make his own sweets, as we learn in chapters called "Bob Makes Popcorn Balls" or "Bob Makes Peanut Fudge." The two seem more like convent-school roommates than a married couple as they cook and eat together. Reading their story, I cannot help but picture Bettina and Bob on their tenth anniversary, each heavier by fifty pounds, as they struggle to sit side by side before their fireplace toasting marshmallows or waddling off together to a picnic with a hamper so heavy it takes both of them to lift it. Their real fate is unknown, however, for while the authors went on to write three more Bettina books, I was disappointed to find that they are not novels, only collections of recipes.

I am reminded of the Bettina books whenever people approach me to confess a guilty pleasure—that they read cookbooks "as though they were novels." I assure them I understand their appeal, have the habit myself, and tell them about cookbooks that are in fact novels. But there are also cookbooks that were written by novelists or have respectful prefaces by famous novelists. Far and away, the most high-minded example of the latter is the preface Joseph Conrad wrote for *A Handbook of Cookery for a Small House* (1923), his wife's cookbook.

> Of all the books produced since the remote ages by human talents and industry those only that treat of cooking are, from a moral point of view, above suspicion. The intention of every other piece of prose may be discussed and even mistrusted, but the purpose of a cookery book is one and unmistakable. Its object can conceivably be no other than to increase the happiness of mankind.

Jessie Conrad knew great writing when she saw it. When she published another cookbook thirteen years later, she reprinted her husband's words, explaining, "Although this preface was written for my first little book of cookery, I feel that the sentiments expressed in it apply equally well to this its successor."

A lighter note is sounded in Truman Capote's brief foreword to Myrna Davis's *The Potato Book* (1972), a fundraising cookbook for a Long Island school. Capote offers his tribute to the potato with a recipe he calls "my one and only most delicious ever potato lunch." His first ingredient, a chilled bottle of 80-proof vodka, assures us that this is the real Truman Capote talking. He pairs the vodka with a potato that is baked and slathered with sour cream, then topped with spoonfuls of "the freshest, the grayest, the biggest Beluga," a dish Capote insists "is the only way I can bear to eat a potato." I was happy to learn about this preference but somehow doubted that Capote would have turned up his nose at a plateful of hot, crisp French fries, even if they were bereft of caviar.

That Marjorie Kinnan Rawlings, author of *The Yearling*, wrote a cookbook would not surprise readers of *Cross Creek*, her memoir of life in a remote corner of north central Florida, for *Cross Creek* is full of passionate descriptions of food. What may be surprising, however, is that her editor, the legendary Maxwell Perkins, famous for his brilliant nurturing of Ernest Hemingway, F. Scott Fitzgerald, and Thomas Wolfe, provided that same service for Rawlings's book on Florida cuisine, *Cross Creek Cookery* (1942). In one of his letters, Perkins told her that she had "done a wonderfully fine piece of work," that the book "as a whole is delightful, and something altogether new." In another letter he said, "You have been wonderfully ingenious in blending the practical directions with the anecdotes, and in a way which sets all against the background. It is a most charming book."

So it is. Rawlings here brings together her talent as a cook, storyteller, and provider of local color, and spices her cookbook with her ready wit and readier opinions. She speaks throughout of Dora, her irreplaceable Jersey milk cow that produces cream that "rises to a depth of three-quarters of an inch on a shallow pan of milk" and is "so thick, when ladled off into a bowl or pitcher, that it is impossible to pour. It must be spooned out." But like so much of what is most desirable in life, Dora and her incomparable milk came with a price. Dora was the daughter of a mean-spirited cow, and she too had a vile disposition and never stopped glaring evilly at Rawlings, who responded in kind. Dora had a sister that Rawlings named Atrocia, who was even more sinister but who was sold off before she could cause much harm.

I found that reading this cookbook by so gifted a writer would be delight enough even if the recipes were not as tempting as they are. Rawlings describes her black bottom pie as "so delicate, so luscious, that I hope to be propped up on my dying bed and fed a generous portion. Then I think that I should refuse outright to die, for life would be too good to relinquish." Rawlings took care to include dishes that were true to the region, the so-called "cracker" food that local people loved. She gives several recipes for swamp cabbage (hearts of palm), a vegetable found at the core of immature trees and cooked to accompany campfire fish or game dinners. Armed with her .22 rifle, Rawlings blasted away at quail, dove, rabbit, and squirrel, which she clearly knew how to cook. She also knew how to prepare alligator tails and bear meat, although she never claims to have hunted the animals down. More conventional are her recipes that transformed the tropical fruits that grew so abundantly on her property into grapefruit marmalade, kumquat jelly, and mango chutney.

It came as no surprise to me that Rawlings was on the plump side, or as one of her acquaintances put it, "She looks like a woman who is a good cook and enjoys her own cooking." Dora had something to do with it. After a passage in which the writer proudly claims to reject desserts at the end of large meals, she concedes that for her, some desserts *are* meals: "I like to sit down on a summer afternoon and eat a whole quart of Dora's ice cream. I like to sit by the open hearth-fire on a winter's day, about four in the afternoon, and eat a quarter of a devil's food cake, with a pot of tea or coffee."

Lillian Hellman, the well-known playwright and memoirist, was another writer who compiled a cookbook, the last work she was able to write. Published posthumously, *Eating Together: Recipes' Recollections* (1984) was cowritten with a close friend, Peter Feibleman, whom she first met in New Orleans when she was thirty-five and he a child. "Lillian was the only person I had met who didn't talk down to children," he later said. "She asked me how old I was and when I told her I was 'only ten,' she nodded and her face didn't change. 'I don't know what you mean by "only." Ten isn't so young,' she said and turned away."

The cookbook reveals another side of Hellman, who was famous for being outspoken, acerbic, quarrelsome, mendacious, and a troublemaker. Here we see her better qualities—her wit, strong ties to friends, love of laughter, love of food, and stubborn courage in the face of death. Feibleman reports one of their last conversations when she was legally blind, partially paralyzed, and unable to walk.

"I'm no fun anymore," she said . . . trying to sit up in bed. After a long pause she added: "But I was fun. Wasn't I?"

I was reading a book by the window and asked her to shut up till I finished the page I was on.

"I'll shut up," Lillian said, "on one condition. When we talk, we talk about something important."

"Such as?" I said.

"Such as," Lillian said, "what are we having for dinner?"

Food, for someone with Hellman's combative disposition, proved to be an exquisite battleground, for it gave her a lot to fight about: what to cook, how to cook it, how to serve it, and with whom to share the meal. Hellman loved to cook, and she maintained an ambitious vegetable garden on Martha's Vineyard, where she also loved to go fishing in the dinghy she kept on the beach. She spent sociable summers there cooking for dinner guests at least twice a week, a custom she preserved long past the time that failing health would have stopped others.

Working on the cookbook kept her occupied the last year of her life and in constant touch with Feibleman, whom she loved but fought with as much as any other people she was close to. The book was conceived, Hellman says, "as a tribute to an old friendship." It is divided in two, "Her Way" and "His Way," with each author presenting favorite recipes accompanied by anecdotes. Her recipes relate to good times with friends—meals shared in Paris with Janet Flanner, or the veal dish she and Peter ate at a favorite Los Angeles restaurant where they swapped funny stories about Dorothy Parker shortly after the writer had died. Hellman gives us a wonderful recipe for Bolognese sauce given to her by the mother of a chauffeur that director William Wyler once hired in Rome. (Hellman is never above name dropping.) And sometimes she just squeezes in an anecdote whether or not it relates to a recipe. With the mention of Paris, for instance, she launches into a tirade against Simone Signoret, whose French production of *The Little Foxes* left Hellman in a lifelong rage.

For his part, Feibleman demonstrates that he too is a dedicated cook, offering such tips as never using water in a recipe when stock, wine, or beer are at hand, or using prosciutto bones instead of salt for soups, stews, casseroles, and even some vegetable dishes. His recipes relate to New Orleans and to Spain, but most of all they relate to Hellman, for whom this book was a way of feeling alive. He describes one of the last times he saw her, just after their cookbook had been turned in to the publisher. Met at the door by a nurse, he was told that Hellman was getting weaker, that her memory was fading, and that she was dying. Moving on into her bedroom, Feibleman asked, "How are you?"

> "Not good, Peter," Lillian said.
> I asked why not.
> "This is the worst case of writer's block I ever had in my life," Lillian said. "The worst case."

How like Hellman to have perceived the end of her life as writer's block.

The intimate power of cookbooks to make connections between people came home to me most recently when a college class was sent to the Schlesinger Library to seek out and write about cookbooks that corresponded to their backgrounds. As they roamed the shelves, I heard sporadic squeals that told me that students were finding cookbooks they could relate to—Irish, Italian, African-American, Jewish cookbooks with food familiar to most students from the Boston area. I noticed, however, that one young woman seemed at a loss. Speaking with a distinct Russian accent, she explained that she was new to America and had no hope of finding a book that spoke to her. I handed her a copy I found of Anya von Bremzen's *Please to the Table: the Russian Cookbook* (1990) and moved on to help someone else. But the next thing I knew the young Russian was awash in tears because she had come across recipes from Odessa, the city she had recently left. All of her pent-up homesickness broke loose when she read these recipes from her native land.

Another student I helped that day was struggling with the assignment, because, as she described herself, she was a "plain-vanilla Midwesterner of English, German, and Scandinavian background" and was sure no cookbook could speak to that. I handed her some community cookbooks from her home state, Iowa, books typical of the kind that are compiled to raise money for churches, schools, and other organizations. To her amazement, the young woman found that one of the cookbooks was from a neighboring county and she was able to recognize the recipes and the names of the some of the contributors. She too had found her place and her people in a cookbook.

ANNOTATED
BIBLIOGRAPHY

1. FEEDING THE GREAT HUNGER:
The Irish Famine and America

Allen, Darina. *The Complete Book of Irish Country Cooking: Traditional and Wholesome Recipes from Ireland.* New York: Penguin, 1996. The recent renaissance in Irish cuisine owes much to this book and its author, a cooking teacher who traveled all over Ireland to rescue old recipes and bring them back to use.

Beecher, Catherine, and Harriet Beecher Stowe. *The New Housekeeper's Manual: Embracing a New Revised Edition of The American Woman's Home, or, Principles of Domestic Science.* New York: J. B. Ford, 1873. Though her more famous sister shares the title page, Catherine Beecher wrote most of this high-minded domestic handbook whose premise is that a well-run home is a woman's Christian duty. Beecher tried here to professionalize domesticity and elevate household chores to the level of sanctified moral obligations. In passing, she praises the courage and industry of Irish immigrant servants.

Beecher, Eunice. *The Law of a Household.* Boston: Small, Maynard, 1912. The author was the wife of the New England minister Henry Ward Beecher, but unlike her sisters-in-law Catherine Beecher and Harriet Beecher Stowe, this stern and demanding homemaker had a low opinion of Irish servants. Here she sets out the duties and responsibilities of her large household staff as a blueprint for other privileged matrons to follow in managing their domestic help.

Dudden, Faye E. *Serving Women: Household Service in Nineteenth-Century America.* Middletown, CT: Wesleyan, 1983. This study of domestic service draws on letters, diaries, memoirs, and contemporary magazines and literature to explore the life of nineteenth-century female servants in America. Especially useful is information on Irish household servants and the prejudices and derisive jokes they endured.

Miller, Kerby A. *Emigrants and Exiles: Ireland and the Irish Exodus to North America*. New York: Oxford, 1985. This classic work on Irish immigrants surveys the early history of Irish immigration and not just the post-famine experience.

Nicholson, Asenath. *Nature's Own Book*. New York: Wilbur & Whipple, 1835. The book is largely given over to the vegetarian doctrines of Sylvester Graham, whom the author quotes liberally when she is not offering personal testimonials to the efficacy of his beliefs about natural foods and health. A limited number of recipes suggest the author's allegiance to such staples as bread, rice, potatoes, and puddings.

———. *Ireland's Welcome to the Stranger; or, An Excursion Through Ireland in 1844 and 1845 for the Purpose of Personally Investigating the Conditions of the Poor*. London: Gilpin, 1847. A valuable record of what Ireland was like on the eve of the famine, the book traces the eccentric American woman's travels throughout the country and explains her reformist motives in learning about the Irish and bringing them Bibles.

———. *Annals of the Famine in Ireland*. Edited by Maureen Murphy. Dublin: Lilliput, 1998. First published in 1851, this vivid eyewitness account of the Great Hunger shows the author as a resourceful American activist who used her knowledge of vegetarian cooking to help relieve the starvation she found throughout Ireland.

Nolan, Janet A. *Ourselves Alone: Women's Emigration from Ireland 1885–1920*. Lexington: University Press of Kentucky, 1989. Using a wide range of sources including personal reminiscences, oral histories, interviews, letters, and diaries in addition to emigration records, Nolan provides an account of the immigration experience of women who left Ireland at the end of the nineteenth century and the beginning of the twentieth.

Seely, Lida. *Mrs. Seely's Cook Book: A Manual of French and American Cookery*. New York: Grosset & Dunlap, 1902. Compiled by the owner of a New York employment agency that found work for domestic servants, this collection of recipes for foods served in the homes of the well-to-do also includes a detailed description of the daily responsibilities of the various types of servants she placed. Seely provides a clear picture of how hard the work was and how long the hours were of Irish immigrants who largely took these jobs in the late nineteenth and early twentieth centuries.

2. PRETTY MUCH OF A MUCHNESS:
Civil War Nurses and Diet Kitchens

Alcott, Louisa May. *Hospital Sketches*. Boston: Redpath, 1863. First appearing serially in the antislavery weekly *Commonwealth*, these sketches drew from the writer's brief nursing work in Georgetown's Union Hotel Hospital, where she aided the wounded from the battle of Fredericksburg. After contracting typhoid, Alcott returned home to Massachusetts, and began turning letters she had written to her family from the hospital into newspaper articles and then a book that delivered details of the war to eager readers. Many have commented on her artful ability to balance pathos and humor and avoid the cloying pieties found in other reminiscences of the war.

Chesnut, Mary Boykin. *Mary Chesnut's Civil War*. Edited by C. Vann Woodward. New Haven: Yale University Press, 1981. Considered a masterpiece of Civil War commentary, Chesnut's journals are a vivid account of civilian conditions in the Confederacy as seen by a privileged woman of the South. Woodward's Pulitzer Prize–winning edition of Chesnut's work restores passages that had been omitted from earlier editions.

Confederate Receipt Book: A Compilation of Over One Hundred Receipts Adapted to the Times. Athens: University of Georgia, 1960. Originally published in 1863 in Richmond, Virginia, this collection of recipes, gathered from contemporary newspapers, illustrates the severity of food shortages endured by Southerners during the Civil War. Emphasis is on substitutes (using green corn to make "artificial oysters") and on avoiding waste (making cottage cheese from milk turning sour).

Cumming, Kate. *Journal of Hospital Life in the Confederate Army of Tennessee from the Battle of Shiloh to the End of the War*. Baton Rouge: Louisiana State University, 1959. A full record of the actual workings of several Confederate hospitals, this journal has less literary appeal than the diaries of Phoebe Pember and Mary Boykin Chesnut, but it is valuable as the vivid account of a dedicated, hardworking nurse who faulted other Southern women who did not help the cause by attending sick and wounded soldiers.

Faust, Drew Gilpin. *Mothers of Invention: Women of the Slaveholding South in the American Civil War*. Chapel Hill: University of North Carolina, 1996. Drawing on diaries, letters, and other writings by privileged women from the South, Faust analyzes the impact of the Civil War on their protected and elite status. The women's stories dramatize how they tried to cope with the social and economic changes wrought by the war and Reconstruction.

Livermore, Mary. *My Story of the War*. New York: Arno, 1972 [c1887]. A tireless Civil War worker, Livermore devoted herself to the Northern cause by volunteering her services to the Sanitary Commission, on whose behalf she toured military hospitals and made recommendations for improvements in food and medical services. Her account of the legendary Union nurse named Mother Bickerdyke is a high point of this memoir.

Nightingale, Florence. *Notes on Nursing: What It Is and What It Is Not*. New York: Appleton-Century, 1946. First published in 1860, the book had an extraordinary impact on women who served as nurses in the Civil War in the North and the South. It is full of practical advice about the care and feeding of the sick and wounded, and became a model for many Union and Confederate hospital diet kitchens run by women volunteers.

Mrs. Winslow's Domestic Receipt Book for 1862. Boston: Rand & Avery, 1862. Throughout the 1860s and 1870s, Mrs. Winslow produced an annual 32-page pamphlet that was mainly a cookbook but also offered tips on such other domestic chores as laundry work and care of the sick. Like some of the others in the series, the pamphlet of this year also contained an inspirational story meant to uplift female readers.

Pember, Phoebe Yates. *A Southern Woman's Story: Life in Confederate Richmond, Including Unpublished Letters Written from the Chimborazo Hospital*. Wilmington, NC: Broadfoot, 1991. Along with Mary Chesnut, Phoebe Pember was one of the most articulate and intelligent women who described the Civil War experiences of privileged Southern women. Written sometime between 1865 and 1879, when it was first published, her memoir is an honest and often witty narrative of her volunteer work as a nurse at what was at the time the largest military hospital in the world.

Wittenmyer, Annie. *A Collection of Recipes for the Use of Special Diet Kitchens in Military Hospitals, Prepared and Published Under the Auspices of the U.S. Christian Commission*. St. Louis, 1864. In this rare little treatise on cooking for the sick and wounded of war, the author pays homage to Florence Nightingale, who first brought attention to deplorable conditions in military hospitals, and borrows Mrs. Winslow's recipes. Wittenmyer spells out procedures for managing diet kitchens and provides recipes for foods believed to be restorative. Broths and milk puddings are unsurprising offerings, but oyster fritters and fried mush are not what one expects to find on the sickroom tray.

Woolsey, Jane. *Hospital Days: Reminiscence of a Civil War Nurse*. Roseville, MN: Edinborough Press, 1996. (Published originally in 1868.)

From an abolitionist family, Woolsey was drawn into the war immediately after the attack on Fort Sumter and soon took on responsibilities as a Union nurse. Her book provides a clear description of the duties that defined the supporting role played by women, especially their assistance in the diet kitchens set up in most of the hospitals. Detailed, too, are the meals served to soldiers with different complaints.

3. THEY DIETED FOR OUR SINS:
America's Food Reformers

Carson, Gerald. *Cornflake Crusade*. New York: Rinehart, 1957. This is a popular history of health crazes that gripped America throughout the nineteenth century, giving special attention to Sylvester Graham, the Kellogg brothers, and C. W. Post.

Graham, Roy E. *Ellen G. White, Co-founder of the Seventh-day Adventist Church*. New York: Peter Lang, 1985. This published dissertation is both a full-scale biography of Ellen G. White and a denominational history of the Seventh Day Adventist Church that she cofounded and profoundly influenced during its early development.

Graham, Sylvester. *A Treatise on Bread and Bread-Making*. Boston: Light & Stearns, 1837. Graham considered homemade bread the linchpin of healthful nutrition. Here the minister offers his moralistic philosophy of diet, along with some general guidelines for producing loaves made of unbolted flour that he considered the ultimate health food.

———. *Lectures on the Science of Human Life*. Boston: Marsh, Capen, Lyon and Webb, 1839. This influential collection of the minister's opinions on health and nutrition is a mix of vegetarian advocacy and harrowing warnings about the sicknesses and debility Graham attributed to sexual indulgence.

Green, Harvey. *Fit for America: Health, Fitness, Sport and American Society*. New York: Pantheon, 1986. In this social history of the quest for fitness in America, Green surveys mainly nineteenth-century figures who started fads and led movements that stressed various diet and exercise regimens or used electrical and mechanical gadgets, all in pursuit of fitness and better health.

Kellogg, Ella E. *Science in the Kitchen*. Battle Creek, MI: Modern Medicine, 1892. This collection of vegetarian recipes is strong evidence that Ella Kellogg contributed mightily to her husband's success. Hidden away in a test kitchen at Dr. Kellogg's sanitarium, his wife helped develop recipes for the foods that were served there in the glory days of the "San" and later became the basis for the Kellogg breakfast-food empire.

Nissenbaum, Stephen. *Sex, Diet and Debility in Jacksonian America: Sylvester Graham and Health Reform.* Westport, CT: Greenwood, 1980. Nissenbaum's thesis in this study is that the repression we associate with America's Victorian Age had its roots in Sylvester Graham's attitude toward sex as the cause of much mental and physical illness.

Numbers, Ronald L. *Prophetess of Health: A Study of Ellen G. White.* New York: Harper & Row, 1976. As influential a religious leader in her time as Mary Baker Eddy, Ellen G. White connected her spiritual beliefs to contemporary health reform movements. In his book, Numbers focuses on this aspect of her leadership role in the Seventh Day Adventist Church.

Richards, Ellen H. "The Story of the New England Kitchen." In *Rumford Kitchen Leaflets, No. 17.* Boston: Richards, 1893. Written just a few years after the New England Kitchen closed, this account describes the idealist goals of its founders, including Richards and other reformers, who tried to introduce Yankee cooking to the working poor of Boston. These were mostly Irish, Italian, and Jewish immigrants, who preferred their own food and refused the bland offerings of the Kitchen, showing how relevant to food preferences are the cultural backgrounds of any group.

Taylor, Elizabeth. *Elizabeth Takes Off: On Weight Gain, Weight Loss, Self-Image and Self-Esteem.* New York: Putnam, 1987. After a period when her weight was at an all-time high and she was the target of derisive humor from comedians, Elizabeth Taylor struck back by trimming down to her former gorgeous self and telling the world how she did it. The book is far more interesting as a celebrity memoir than a reliable guide to diet and weight reduction.

Taylor, Renee. *My Life on a Diet: Confessions of a Hollywood Diet Junkie.* New York: Putnam, 1986. Written by a comedy writer and actress and sometimes referred to as a spoof of celebrity diet books, Taylor's book nevertheless rings true as a description of the agonies endured by the overweight in pursuit of ever elusive slimness. Taylor provides hilarious accounts of some of her bizarre attempts to lose weight quickly when she was under pressure to pursue her career on stage and in films and TV.

Whorton, James C. *Crusaders for Fitness: The History of American Health Reformers.* Princeton: Princeton University Press, 1982. This standard study of American health reformers explains why men like Sylvester

Graham and John Henry Kellogg who are now considered crackpots and faddists were incredibly influential in their day in determining American diet.

4. THE HARVEY GIRLS:
Good Women and Good Food Civilize the American West

Foster, George H., and Peter C. Weiglin. *The Harvey House Cookbook: Memories of Dining Along the Santa Fe Railroad.* Atlanta: Longstreet, 1992. More than 200 recipes gathered by the authors provide a good sense of the sophisticated food that Fred Harvey served to Santa Fe railroad passengers and Southwestern Americans who lived near the hotel restaurants that bore Harvey's name in the nineteenth and early twentieth centuries.

Mencken, August. *The Railroad Passenger Car: An Illustrated History of the First Hundred Years with Accounts by Contemporary Passengers.* Baltimore: Johns Hopkins, 1957. A pioneering work on railroad history, Mencken's book taps into such diverse sources as records from the U.S. Patent Office, old railroad journals, newspaper articles, and travelers' accounts to bring together the story of the early development of railroad transportation. Mencken's descriptions of the way in which passengers were fed during long train rides when railroading was new are especially noteworthy and often hilarious.

Poling-Kempes, Lesley. *The Harvey Girls: Women Who Opened the West.* New York: Paragon House, 1989. The book's oral history accounts of former Harvey Girls are especially valuable in establishing the importance of the Harvey Girls in the development of the American Southwest. Recollections of the former waitresses are seen in the context of Fred Harvey's career as a restaurateur, the early days of American rail transportation, and the decline of American railroads after World War II.

5. HOME COOKING IN THE FDR WHITE HOUSE:
The Indomitable Mrs. Nesbitt

Nesbitt, Victoria Henrietta. *The Presidential Cookbook: Feeding the Roosevelts and Their Guests.* Garden City, NY: Doubleday, 1951. Mrs. Nesbitt's cookbook proves once and for all that visitors to the FDR White House were right in criticizing the bland, uninspired food that was served by the Roosevelts' housekeeper. Her baked goods, however, are far more appealing, and she is far more spirited in her descriptions of cakes, pies and cookies.

———. *White House Diary*. Garden City, NY: Doubleday, 1948. In this memoir of the years she served as the White House housekeeper during the FDR administration, Henrietta Nesbitt defends herself against charges that she served bad food. She explains that the Depression, war shortages, a limited White House food budget, and concern for the health of the President were the main reasons her meals were simple but nourishing.

Parks, Lillian Rogers. *The Roosevelts, a Family in Turmoil*. Englewood Cliffs, NJ: Prentice-Hall, 1981. A backstairs, tell-all description of the domestic side of FDR's administration written by a White House maid. Parks is harsh on the subject of Henrietta Nesbitt, the White House housekeeper, who was unpopular with the staff.

6. COOKING BEHIND BARBED WIRE:
POWs During World War II

Crouter, Natalie. *Forbidden Diary: A Record of Wartime Internment, 1942–1945*. New York: B. Franklin, 1980. This diary, kept secretly by the author throughout her four-year internment in Japanese prison camps, provides a vivid account of the daily life of American civilian women trapped in the Philippines at the outbreak of World War II. Descriptions of how prisoners dealt with food scarcity are central to this book.

Danner, Dorothy Still. *What a Way to Spend a War: Navy Nurse POWs in the Philippines*. Annapolis: Naval Institute Press, 1995. A U.S. Navy nurse who was captured in the Philippines after the Japanese invasion, Danner wrote this recollection of her World War II imprisonment a half century later. After the liberation, she returned to California, where she married and had children, but her POW experience remained the defining moment of her life.

Hayes, Thomas. *Bilibid Diary: The Secret Notebooks of Commander Thomas Hayes, POW the Philippines, 1942–45*. Hamden, CT: Archon, 1987. This extraordinary document is all the more moving in that it survived its author, Commander Thomas Hayes, a navy surgeon, who was killed in the last days of the war when the Japanese were evacuating POWs from the Philippines to Japan. His descriptions of life in Bilibid, the infamous Manila prison camp, make clear that military POWs suffered far more deprivations than civilians interned in other Japanese camps.

Kaminski, Theresa. *Prisoners in Paradise: American Women in the Wartime South Pacific*. Lawrence: University Press of Kansas, 2000. This broad overview of World War II imprisonment draws on letters, diaries, and interviews for the survival stories of American women in the aftermath of Pearl Harbor. Included, too, are accounts of civilian women who avoided captivity by the Japanese by fleeing into the Philippine hills, where they waited out the war.

Monahan, Evelyn M., and Rosemary Neidel-Greenlee. *All This Hell: U.S. Nurses Imprisoned by the Japanese.* Lexington: University Press of Kentucky, 2000. In the continuing effort to uncover the wartime experiences of women who served in World War II, the authors, both veterans of the Vietnam War, interviewed U.S. military nurses and provided accounts of their experiences. The authors charge that the nurses were required to sign agreements not to discuss their experiences at the hands of the Japanese, which explains why this history was not offered earlier.

Norman, Elizabeth M. *We Band of Angels: The Untold Story of American Nurses Trapped on Bataan by the Japanese.* New York: Random House, 1999. This study of American military nurses caught in the Philippines at the start of the war derives from interviews with survivors as well as such traditional sources as unpublished diaries, journals, and letters. Oral-history testimonies are of particular value, since the nurses' stories might otherwise have never been recorded.

Recipes Out of Bilibid; collected by Colonel H. C. Fowler and compiled and tested by Dorothy Wagner. New York: G. W. Stewart, 1946. This prison camp cookbook is one of the most extraordinary artifacts to have come out of World War II in the Pacific. Recipes were collected by a captured American officer from fellow POWs who were interned in Bilibid, a notorious prison camp where many captives died of starvation and disease. The moving introduction by Dorothy Wagner, to whom the recipes were entrusted, makes it clear that discussing favorite foods and writing down recipes became a way for the prisoners to remember their homes and families.

Thompson, Dorothy Davis. *The Road Back: A Pacific POW's Liberation Story.* Lubbock: Texas Tech University Press, 1996. This is another of the recently published accounts of the experiences of women nurses and civilians imprisoned in Japanese prison camps in the Philippines during World War II. Thompson was interned in Santo Tomás, where she nursed other inmates until she herself fell seriously ill and was released before the end of the war in a prisoner exchange.

Vaughan, Elizabeth. *The Ordeal of Elizabeth Vaughan: A Wartime Diary of the Philippines.* Athens: University of Georgia, 1985. The author, a sociologist, provides a riveting and poignant account of how she and other civilian women coped as they tried to raise young children within the confines and deprivations of Japanese World War II prison camps in the Philippines.

7. SACHERTORTE IN HARVARD SQUARE:
Jewish Refugees Find Friends and Work

Unpublished records of the Window Shop at the Schlesinger Library, Radcliffe Institute for Advanced Study, Harvard University, Cambridge, Massachusetts.

8. FOOD KEEPS THE FAITH:
African-American Cooks and Their Heritage

Butler, Cleora. *Cleora's Kitchens: The Memoir of a Cook & Eight Decades of Great American Food*. Tulsa: Council Oak Books, 1985. This unique cookbook and memoir presents the recipes and life story of an African-American woman from the Southwest who, like other members of her family, earned her living by preparing food for others. Whether she worked in other people's homes, catered from her own home, or operated a restaurant, Butler was always enthusiastic about her work and conscious of the importance of good food in people's lives.

Chase, Leah. *The Dooky Chase Cookbook*. Gretna, LA: Pelican, 1990. Full of down-to earth recipes and illustrated with paintings by African-American artists, this cookbook describes Leah Chase's Louisiana Creole background and her career as a successful restaurateur at one of New Orleans's most popular eating places.

Darden, Norma Jean, and Carole Darden. *Spoonbread and Strawberry Wine: Recipes and Reminiscences of a Family*. Garden City, NY: Doubleday, 1978. Combining family history and regional recipes provided by the authors' relatives, this book describes the search of two African-American professional women from the Northeast for their roots in the South. Cooking becomes the key to unlocking their relatives' memories and discovering the lives of the authors' forebears.

Fox, Minnie C. *The Blue Grass Cook Book*. New York: Duffield & Co., 1904. Full of nostalgia for the Old South, the compiler gathered recipes from all over Kentucky without acknowledging that many of the dishes were the creation of African-American cooks. The book is illustrated with photographs of black cooks who are not identified.

Harris, Jessica B. *Iron Pots and Wooden Spoons: Africa's Gifts to New World Cooking*. New York: Atheneum, 1989. The author traces the ways in which African food came to the New World and influenced its food. Over 175 recipes are given, including Creole, Cajun, and Caribbean dishes that have their roots in West African and Central African cuisine.

———. *The Welcome Table: African-American Heritage Cooking*. New York: Simon & Schuster, 1995. This collection of African-American recipes was gathered from home and community meals all over the United States and includes many historical anecdotes and personal reminiscences and reflections.

———. *The Africa Cookbook: Tastes of a Continent*. New York: Simon & Schuster, 1998. The author provides a culinary tour of the continent and offers more than 200 recipes from home kitchens in Africa, showing the diversity of that continent's cooking.

Hess, Karen. *The Carolina Rice Kitchen: The African Connection*. Columbia, SC: University of South Carolina, 1992. The author traces the origins of the Carolina rice industry to slaves from rice-cultivating parts of Africa. She attributes the decline of the industry after Emancipation to the former slavemasters whose ancestors came from rice-eating countries but who lacked sufficient experience in growing rice.

Lewis, Edna. *The Edna Lewis Cookbook*. Indianapolis: Bobbs-Merrill, 1972. This first cookbook by a beloved author of books on country cooking grew out of her early experiences at a Manhattan restaurant serving continental food. While some homey recipes exist here, they are overshadowed by recipes for such French standbys as Crêpes Suzettes, Quiche Lorraine, and Coquilles St. Jacques.

———. *The Taste of Country Cooking*. New York: Knopf, 1976. This is the book that established Edna Lewis's reputation as a gifted cook. The book is organized around the seasons, and its format allowed her to demonstrate her deep knowledge of the connections between wholesome Southern foods, the land, and the customs of her Virginia family and neighbors.

———. *In Pursuit of Flavor*. New York: Knopf, 1988. The third and last to date of Lewis's cookbooks continues to emphasize down-to-earth foods, with sections on gardens and orchards, farmyards, lakes, streams, and oceans.

Smart-Grosvenor, Vertamae. *Vibration Cooking, Or, The Travel Notes of a Geechee Girl*. New York: Ballantine, 1970. Written by an African-American woman with a strong, distinctive voice, this cookbook mixes country and more cosmopolitan recipes with memories of the author's South Carolina background and her subsequent adventures in Paris and New York.

———. *Vertamae Cooks in The Americas' Family Kitchen*. San Francisco: KQED Books, 1996. This companion cookbook to Smart-Grosvenor's popular PBS cooking series offers African-American recipes from the author's native South Carolina and from other countries with food that bears the influence of Africa.

———. *Vertamae Cooks Again, More Recipes from The Americas' Family Kitchen*. San Francisco: Bay Books, 1999. Recipes from North, South, and Central America as well as from Haiti, the Bahamas, and Cuba are featured in this second PBS companion cookbook.

Woods, Sylvia. *Sylvia's Soul Food: Recipes from Harlem's World Famous Restaurant*. New York: Hearst, 1992. Fried chicken, collard greens, ham hocks, macaroni and cheese—all these foods are from a self-made woman who runs a successful family restaurant in Harlem that attracts visitors from everywhere.

———. *Sylvia's Family Soul Food Cookbook: From Hemingway, South Carolina, to Harlem*. New York: Morrow, 1999. Sylvia Woods's second collection of recipes, as much memoir and family history as cookbook, makes connections between her Southern, African-American food and the people who either gave her recipes or were an important part of her South Carolina background. Every dish is a reminder of a particular bond with the author's roots.

9. GROWING UP WITH *GOURMET*:
What Cookbooks Mean

Birmingham, Frederic. *The Complete Cookbook for Men*. New York: Harper & Brothers, 1961. This amusing book assumes that women in the kitchen are dull and uninspired while men have great flair and creativity. The perspective allows Birmingham to justify his status as a home cook at a time when few other men prepared family meals. His recipes demonstrate that behind his façade was a skilled home cook.

Child, Lydia Maria. *The Frugal Housewife: Dedicated to Those Who Are Not Ashamed of Economy*. Boston: Carter & Hendee, 1829. This enormously popular household manual was unique in its time for addressing the domestic concerns of women with limited means. Accustomed to scrimping because of the financial misadventures of her reformist husband, the author, who was young and childless, assumed the persona of a mature housewife with a large brood of children as she offered readers advice on home economy.

Conrad, Jessie. *A Handbook of Cookery for a Small House*. London: William Heinemann, 1923. This book features recipes for hearty food from the wife of famous novelist Joseph Conrad, whose stirring preface includes memorable praise for cookbooks in general and those who write them.

Davis, Myrna. *The Potato Book*. Bridgehampton, NY: Hampton Day School Press, 1972. Compiled to raise money for a Long Island school, this cookbook is memorable for its brief preface written by Truman Capote. In his typically witty style, Capote offers a baked potato recipe that leans heavily on caviar and must be accompanied by ice-cold vodka.

Fisher, M.F.K. *The Art of Eating: The Collected Gastronomical Works of M.F.K. Fisher*. Cleveland: World, 1954. In these five books, Fisher raised food writing to the level of a literary genre by deftly expressing her thoughts and feelings about her personal eating preferences and the sensual allure of food.

The Gourmet Cookbook. New York: Gourmet, 1950. This compilation of what was considered the best recipes from the first years of the magazine reflects the publication's early epicurean leanings, with much French fare and a long chapter on game.

Harland, Marion. *Common Sense in the Household: A Manual of Practical Housewifery*. New York: Scribners, 1871. In this enormously successful book, the author, whose real name was Mary Virginia Hawes Terhune, holds the literary equivalent of motherly chats with her readers before presenting recipes and rules to help them run their homes smoothly. True to her title, she gives no-nonsense advice in the certain knowledge that domestic responsibilities are complicated and women crave practical instruction.

Hellman, Lillian, and Peter Feibleman. *Eating Together: Recipes' Recollections*. Boston: Little, Brown, 1984. Written in the last years of Hellman's life and published after her death, this combined memoir and cookbook coauthored by the two writers is a touching reminder of the impact of food on love and friendship.

Owen, Catherine. *Ten Dollars Enough*. Boston: Houghton Mifflin, 1886. This is the first volume of a two-volume family saga that is actually a novelized cookbook. Here, the heroine, Molly Bishop, uses her expertise as a cook and homemaker to create harmony with her in-laws and make possible the purchase of a home, where Molly and her adoring husband settle down to raise a family.

———. *Molly Bishop's Family*. Boston: Houghton Mifflin, 1888. In this continuation of Molly Bishop's story, her happy marriage ends abruptly with the death of her husband, but her well-developed domestic skills allow her to open a popular boardinghouse that becomes known for its good food. Molly raises her three children in comfort and at the same time teaches them to be self-sufficient and prepared for whatever life may bring.

———. *Gentle Breadwinners: The Story of One of Them*. Boston: Houghton Mifflin, 1888. This cautionary tale blends narrative with recipes to convey Owen's constant message that all women, no matter how financially secure they may be, must prepare themselves to earn a living. Here the heroine falls on hard times after the death of her father, but becomes independent by refining her baking skills and creating a baked goods business.

Rawlings, Marjorie Kinnan. *Cross Creek Cookery*. New York: Scribners, 1942. Putting to work her considerable talents as a writer, the author of *The Yearling* produced this memorable account of her life in rural Cross Creek, Florida, and of the food she prepared and served there. Recipes include such country dishes as swamp cabbage salad, hushpuppies, and crackling bread.

Shay, Frank. *The Best Men Are Cooks*. New York: Coward-McCann, 1941. A representative example of a home-cooking handbook written by a man for other men. The author, a fine home cook, felt compelled to poke fun at women cooks and assume a macho role as he confronts the dangerous world of open-flame outdoor cooking.

Weaver, Louise Bennett, and Helen Cowles LeCron. *A Thousand Ways to Please a Husband with Bettina's Best Recipes* [or] *The Romance of Cookery and Housekeeping*. New York: Britton, 1917. The authors attempt to romanticize the daily chores of cooking through the fictional lives of newlyweds Bettina and Bob, whose various meals make up the plot of this unintentionally funny novelized cookbook. Always didactic but never nagging, Bettina instructs Bob and others on the proper way to cook various dishes and entertain.

INDEX